READINGS ON LATIN AMERICA AND ITS PEOPLE

Volume 2

Since 1800

Mark Wasserman
Rutgers University

Cheryl E. Martin
University of Texas, El Paso

Prentice Hall

Boston Columbus Indianapolis New York San Francisco Upper Saddle River
Amsterdam Cape Town Dubai London Madrid Milan Munich Paris Montréal Toronto
Delhi Mexico City São Paulo Sydney Hong Kong Seoul Singapore Taipei Tokyo

Editorial Director: Craig Campanella
Editorial Assistant: Lauren Aylward
Director of Marketing: Brandy Dawson
Senior Marketing Manager: Maureen Prado Roberts
Senior Managing Editor: Ann Marie McCarthy
Senior Production Project Manager: Lynn Savino Wendel
AV Project Manager: Mirella Signoretto
Operations Specialist: Christina Amato
Art Director, Creative Services: Jayne Conte
Cover Designer: Bruce Kenselaar
Cover Art: Bruno Barbey, Magnum Photos, Inc.
Manager, Visual Research: Beth Brenzel
Manager, Rights and Permissions: Zina Arabia
Image Permission Coordinator: Richard Rodrigues
Manager, Cover Visual Research and Permissions: Karen Sanatar
Image Cover Permission Coordinator: Cathy Mazzucca
Photo Researcher: Shelia Norman
Full-Service Project Management/Composition: Christian Holdener, S4Carlisle Publishing Services
Printer/Binder: Courier Companies, Inc.
Cover Printer: Courier Companies, Inc.

This book was set in 10/12 New Baskerville.

Library of Congress Cataloging-in-Publication Data

Readings on Latin America and its people / [edited by] Cheryl E. Martin, Mark Wasserman.
   p. cm.
   Includes bibliographical references.
   ISBN 978-0-321-35582-9 (v. 1)—ISBN 978-0-321-35581-2 (v. 2)
   1. Latin America—History—Sources. I. Martin, Cheryl English, 1945-
II. Wasserman, Mark, 1946-
F1410.R378 2009
980—dc22   2009039604

10 9 8 7 6 5 4 3 2 1

Prentice Hall
is an imprint of

ISBN 13: 978-0-321-35581-2
ISBN 10: 0-321-35581-4

CONTENTS

TOPICAL TABLE OF CONTENTS

ACKNOWLEDGMENTS

The idea for *Readings on Latin America and Its People* came from Janet Lanphier, whose cajoling led us to a worthwhile and enjoyable undertaking. Two former doctoral students at Rutgers, now accomplished scholars and teachers, Anne Rubenstein and Glen Kuecker, were particularly helpful in suggesting new and interesting materials. Thanks, too, to the reviewers for their thorough and thoughtful comments and suggestions: *Jordana Dym,* Skidmore College; *Kevin Gannon,* Grand View College; *José Morales,* New Jersey City University; *Jason L. Ward,* Lee University.

PREFACE

Readings on Latin America and Its People is meant, like *Latin America and Its People* to emphasize the texture of everyday life for men and women, young and old, rich and poor. It is not always a pretty picture. The brutality of the European conquest of indigenous peoples, of Latin America's nineteenth-century wars and the terror of the dictatorships during the 1970s were horrible and catastrophic. The lives and work of slaves in colonial and post-independence Brazil and Cuba were harsh and oppressive. Latin Americans always have been overwhelmingly poor. The countryside, since the beginnings of agriculture, has been a place of hardship and uncertainty. Country dwellers struggled daily against the elements to produce enough to feed their families. Men and women toiled from before dawn to well after dusk often with little to show other than half-starved children. On the large estates, known as haciendas and fazendas, workers tilled and weeded the soil, and harvested crops for scant wages. At the end of the year, they were likely to owe more to the landowners than the latter had paid them. The rich mines exploited by the Europeans were cruelly dangerous. Working underground was almost always a death sentence. Mine owners cast aside their injured or sick employees.

The ever-growing cities were hardly better. They were and remain noisy, smelly, and unhealthful. Since the Europeans arrived, the metropolises have never had sufficient water, sewers, housing, educational facilities, or medical care. Latin America, too, has always been a region of bitter contrasts, between wealthy and impoverished, between traditional and modern, between the physical beauty of the geography and architecture and the wretchedness of the slums, and between low technology and high technology. The dilemma for the authors has been (and remains) how to illustrate the various, often contradictory, aspects of Latin American life without descending into hopelessness.

Historians are like detectives reconstructing the everyday lives of men, women, and children in past times. They must diligently search out clues that reveal people at work, worship, and play; in courtrooms, schools, and markets; and coping with the commonplace demands of supporting their families and the extraordinary challenges of war, social unrest, and natural disasters. These clues can be found in what are known as primary sources, such as official documents, letters, diaries, images, and eyewitness testimonies that date from the time period they are studying. Remnants of the material culture of past societies give us further insights about the everyday lives of people—their dwellings, the tools they used, the religious symbols they revered. Historians also look to secondary sources—books and articles written by other scholars—for guidance in the interpretation of all of these primary sources, but at the same time they must be careful not to let preconceived notions close their minds to other possible interpretations.

Working with primary sources presents many challenges. Written documents have obvious biases, in that they most faithfully reflect the viewpoints of privileged groups—those able to read and write. Even when a source purports to represent the words of the illiterate, we must remember that those words were filtered through the person who wrote them down. Of course, we should also examine all written sources critically, keeping in mind that people do not always tell the truth. Images pose problems as well. We cannot be sure whether paintings and drawings depict reality or the artist's idealized version of that reality. Even the photographs available to historians studying the nineteenth and twentieth centuries require critical analysis. The photographer chooses which scenes to record, and we cannot know for certain whether a given image represents a staged or spontaneous event. People who appear in historical photographs may have tried to present themselves in ways that may or may not have conformed to the everyday reality of their lives.

Historians must also acknowledge the many factors that have influenced the range of primary sources that have survived down to the present. Those who study relatively recent times, since the invention of modern mass media, may be overwhelmed by the sheer volume of materials available. They have access to newspapers and magazines; the massive paper trail generated by governments, churches, educational systems, and corporations; photographs; audio and video resources; and digitized data bases. These sources are often well guarded and kept in climate-controlled archives and museums staffed by professional curators and preservationists. Historians of the recent past must remember, however, that some of the most interesting material may never have reached an official repository. They need to remain on the lookout for treasures hidden in someone's closet or attic. To obtain as complete a picture as possible, they need to seek out individuals able to share their living memories and then check these oral testimonies against other evidence. The challenge of sifting through all of these sources to identify what is truly significant can be daunting for the historian, even with all of the convenience offered by electronically searchable data bases and modern methods of cataloguing information.

The study of pre-twentieth-century history is much like working a jigsaw puzzle, except that many of the pieces are missing and there are no clearly marked borders to help in forming an initial framework for our findings. This is particularly true when we go about examining documents and artifacts that might convey information on the daily lives of "ordinary" people. Moreover, if we are careful not to begin our inquiry with set notions of what we expect to uncover when reading the past, we are working without a picture of the finished puzzle to guide us. Without the box cover, a puzzle solver can only determine if a blue piece is sky, water, or perhaps an article of clothing by seeing how it fits with other pieces, a process that usually involves considerable trial and error, even if all the pieces are there. The historian searching for evidence on the lives of people in past societies must carefully work with the available clues and accept the reality that the resulting picture must necessarily remain incomplete.

Our first intent, therefore, is to explore the detail of daily life through various prisms.

In Chapter One, "Mexican Independence," for example, we offer the remembrances of Lucas Alamán, Mexico's foremost conservative politician and intellectual, of the disturbing plunder and massacre of the wealthy whites of Guanajuato in 1810. The author's trauma is quite evident. His memories of the incident scarred his worldview for the rest of his life. In Chapter Three "War," we present firsthand accounts of the terror and disorder of battle from a British mercenary, Gustave Hippisley, who was apparently neutral in his sentiments and observations, juxtaposed with the obviously and passionately self-interested Mexican general, Antonio López de Santa Anna. The reminiscences of the participants bring the Paraguayan War, perhaps the most tragic in Latin American history, into vivid focus.

A second goal is to explore the mindset of everyday people. Explaining why people acted as they did is far and away the most difficult undertaking for an historian of any place or time. In Chapter Seven, we present documents that provide us with insight into the reasons that military officers were brought to the point of committing unspeakable atrocities against their fellow citizens whom they had sworn to protect. In Chapter Ten we attempt to understand how Mexican peasants, miners, and middle class made their decisions to rise up against the seemingly invincible regime of General Porfirio Díaz in 1910.

There are three notable omissions to the chapters in Volume II. First, since the preponderance of the materials illuminate daily life, the editors often have left aside many issues of politics. For example, there is no discussion of populism, so important in mid-twentieth century South America. In Chapter 7, "The Military," the emphasis is on the mindset of military officers and the conditions of rank and file soldiers, rather than the politics of the military. Second, the volume considers Cuba only as one country in Latin America—no more important or studied than any other. Consequently, the revolution of 1959 that we explore only in Chapter 8, "Everyday Life in the Countryside during the Twentieth Century," is one example of land reform (and not a very successful one). Finally, the reader will note the nearly complete absence of the United States from the book. It is our belief that for courses about Latin America, our students should learn about Latin America. Latin Americans lead their own lives, determine their own histories. The United States should not be central to the analysis, as it is in so many other books about Latin America. Latin Americans have their own histories. There is not nearly enough space in the volume to present all that is worthy to know about Latin America, so discussion of the United States is hardly appropriate.

The topics covered in these chapters, and the people whose lives are documented here, represent only a small fragment of the Latin American experience. The region's history is simply too rich to contain in any single volume. Many other stories can be found in our companion textbook, *Latin America and Its People*, and still others in the works of many historians who have researched this vibrant and diverse people. Still other stories remain untold, awaiting their historian. We invite our readers to sample the historian's craft in the readings in this volume, and hope that some of you will be inspired to search out these stories in the archives of Latin America. You will have to get your hands dirty and puzzle over the meaning of widely scattered bits of evidence, but it is an exciting adventure of discovery.

1　MEXICAN INDEPENDENCE

INTRODUCTION

After three centuries of Spanish colonial rule, New Spain and the many other neighboring political entities in Mesoamerica broke loose from the metropolis and proclaimed independence as Mexico in 1821. More than a decade of often brutal war had preceded separation. The rebellion divided into two movements and into two stages. The first movement involved the upper classes, American-born Spaniards (known as creoles), typified by Father Miguel Hidalgo and his conspirators in 1810. They had calculated that colonial rule was no longer beneficial. They, too, chafed against the Spanish Crown having excluded them from important offices prior to 1808 and then reneging on promises for extensive self-government after the Napoleonic invasion and occupation of Iberia (1808–1814). The second movement was a broad-ranging revolt of the lower classes in the countryside. Country people protested government meddling in their villages, over-taxation, landlessness, and severe food shortages. The first stage began in 1810 and lasted until 1815 with the defeat of both Hidalgo and his successor, Father José María Morelos. The second stage, a guerrilla war led by Vicente Guerrero and Guadalupe Victoria and comprised predominantly of the lower classes, ended only when the rebels negotiated a deal with rogue royalist general Agustín de Iturbide in 1821. The Treaty of the Three Guarantees, September 27, 1821, engendered independent Mexico.

Father Miguel Hidalgo issued the Grito de Dolores (the Cry of Dolores)—the Mexican Cry for Independence—on September 10, 1816. His small group of creoles had plotted their rebellion for months. When the time came to rise up, they hoped that disgruntled fellow creoles, many of whom the colonial government had trained as militia officers, and the lower classes would join them. They succeeded far beyond any outcome they could have imagined. Almost overnight, sixty thousand angry, landless, hungry, country people swelled the ranks of the rebel army. The army of the masses, consisting of Indians and mestizos and led by a small group of creoles, struck terror in the hearts of the upper class. Most creoles side with the Spanish Crown. There followed a number of rebel victories, including the slaughter of Spaniards hiding in the granary in the city of Guanajuato. The rebel army may have reached 100,000. With the banner of the Virgin of Guadalupe—the patron saint of New Spain—protecting it, shouting epithets against Spaniards, the rebel army marched to the outskirts of Mexico City, but its leaders, unable to fully control their soldiers, turned away. A reinforced Spanish army then inflicted a series of defeats on the rebels. The royalists captured Father Hidalgo in Chihuahua and executed him in May 1811.

The rebellion continued in south-central Mexico, led by another priest, Father José María Morelos. Morelos, like Hidalgo, had become disaffected with Spanish rule. A mixed blood from the hot lands of Guerrero, the church had never permitted him other than a desperately poor parish; he thought himself worthy of more. He also believed that more influential relatives had cheated him of an inheritance. Father Morelos proved a brilliant military leader, ruling over a vast territory that included present-day Morelos, parts of Puebla, and Guerrero. The Spanish army, however, eventually defeated him as well. In late 1815, the Spaniards captured and executed him.

Vicente Guerrero, one of Morelos's lieutenants, carried on the fight, harassing the ostensibly victorious Spanish army for the next six years. Finally, in the fall of 1821, the leading royalist General Agustín de Iturbide worked out an arrangement that brought about independence with the creoles in charge. The Plan de Iguala, February 24, 1821, provided "Three Guarantees": independence; the equality of creoles and Spaniards; and continuation of the preeminent role of the Roman Catholic Church.

WHY DID PEOPLE REBEL?

It is, of course, quite difficult for historians to determine why individuals chose to rebel. The long war of independence with its high casualties (perhaps a million people died) and destruction did not leave an extensive paper trail. Historian Eric Van Young discovered a revealing letter composed by Chito Villagrán, a guerrilla leader, written in 1812 setting out why he and other country people rose up against Spanish rule. Van Young traced Villagrán's life through his evolution from delinquent to criminal to rebel (not an unusual route for large-scale social movements). Although it is not certain that he himself actually wrote this letter to Father Diego Antonio Rodríguez, a local curate, it was likely that he dictated the sentiments.

LETTER OF CHITO VILLAGRÁN TO DR. DIEGO ANTONIO RODRÍGUEZ, JUNE 8, 1812

Supposing [it were true] that our insurrection were against our legitimate King and beloved monarch the Lord Don Ferdinand VII, and that we intended to throw off the yoke of his domination; and supposing that the Lord Pope Alexander VII [sic] and his successors had authority over the distribution of the Kingdoms of the earth as is argued, since his Kingdom is purely spiritual according to the teachings of Jesus Christ in the Gospels, and that the Bull were not fraudulent in which His Holiness orders that two mental lines be formed so that what is conquered on one side belongs to the King of Spain, and that conquered on the other side belongs to the King of Portugal, as is treated at length by Joseph Torrubia in his work on general history, where he includes the complete Bull of Alexander VII [sic] that you cite in your letter; and supposing that Cortés had not been sent by the ambition of [Diego] Velásquez, as Solís says, to the conquest of this Kingdom, but by Charles V, and that the embassy to Moctezuma had been genuine, and not invited in his [Cortés] head; and supposing that it were legitimate for a Christian King to despoil of his dominions a gentile King so that his vassals embrace the Catholic religion, since Moctezuma was as much natural lord of these kingdoms as Charles V was of his (Solorzano treats of this at length—James the Apostle brought religion to Spain, but

Edicto Bula papas?

did not because of that despoil its Kings of their Crown); and supposing that this were not the time determined by God for the Europeans to pay for the iniquities, robberies, cruelties, and deaths that with such impiety they committed in the Conquest of these Kingdoms, as noted in the representations of Bishop Las Casas, of Garcilaso de la Vega, of the cited Solís, and of many other authors; and supposing, finally, that all this were true, and that the entire American Nation had risen in mass as they have, asking a new government that will not overturn or suppress the edicts and laws of the Sovereign, or asking a King of the nation itself, and not a foreigner (or de fee), according to the expression of Padre Vieira in favor of the Americans of Brazil; I ask you, according to what has been said, upon what basis rest the censures fulminated against Senor Hidalgo and those who follow his party by the Holy Tribunal and the so-called Bishop of Valladolid?

If the Church does not hurl anathemas against the infamous Napoleon because, being a Corsican, he takes control of the Kingdom of France, nor against his brother Joseph who was crowned in Spain, nor against the Dutch who, renouncing their National Government, acknowledge [as monarch] the intruder Louis Bonaparte, why does it hurl anathemas against a nation that, to maintain pristine the Catholic Religion it professes, takes up arms to demand and acquire the rights usurped from it so long ago, to throw off a tyrannical government, and to take unto itself the sovereignty of its King, don Ferdinand, whom Napoleon and his emissaries (most of the Europeans [in New Spain]), after persecuting and almost decapitating, are trying to despoil of his rights? I cannot persuade myself, Senor Priest, that the anathemas fulminated by the Church fall on the defense we are making of Religion, and liberty, and thus I believe firmly that we are not comprehended in their penalties. I assume that you are informed that the Edict of the Holy Tribunal of the Faith, and the proclamation of the late Archbishop, tell us that Napoleon has despoiled our Ferdinand of his Kingdom; that his brother Joseph is King of Spain and proclaims himself also King of the Indies; that there are five hundred Spanish emissaries in our Kingdom, sent to seduce us; and finally that we should prepare to defend ourselves because all this threatened total ruin to our Religion.

According to what I have said, which you cannot deny, tell me, Señor Priest, should we permit our Religion and our liberty to perish, or should we not take up arms to defend both? If from fear of censure we had followed our generals, what would our fate have been by now? You, with your fervor, can infer the results. God's Law commands us not to take the life of our neighbors, and that we are forbidden to take what is not ours, and he who denies this is a heretic because he denies the precepts of the Decalogue. Furthermore, it is the case that the Europeans are our neighbors, as are all the sons of Adam be they of any nation or religion—this is true. But tell me, Señor Priest: a Jew, an Aterite, a Calomite, or a Lutheran—are they our neighbors? There is no doubt that they are. And would you fail to hand over one of these people, if you saw him, to the Holy Tribunal of the Faith, or inform it of his presence, so that he be killed, burned, punished, and all his possessions confiscated? There is no doubt. But is not this man your neighbor? Does not the Devine Law command that you see him as yourself? This means that for them there is no law, nor are they protected by the laws of charity. And why? So that their false doctrines not contaminate others. And shouldn't these principles operate against the Europeans, and shouldn't they be destroyed, whose unjust possession of the government not only deprives our

King of his rights, and tyrannizes us, but also threatens the loss of our Religion, and that we remain slaves forever—should they only be seen as our neighbors? Ah, Father Priest, how little you know of this matter of the Catholic, Christian American Nation of today! I assure you that if you scruple to discuss and communicate with the Americans for fear of anathemas, how much more scruple should we have in discussing with the Europeans, and with those of their party. Because it is doubtful if we are included in the anathemas, which are inspired by the passion of partisanship and the defense of material interests which the Europeans did not bring with them from their own land; but the Europeans and their allies are included in the anathemas of sacred canons and councils of the Church, hurled against those who burn homes, lay waste fields, profane churches, etc. Assume that not Saint Thomas the Apostle but the Europeans brought the faith to these regions, but seeing that they intend to destroy that which they have built, it is necessary to persecute them and drive them out. The Jews were the people beloved of God, those entrusted with the Religion, and from whom the Messiah came, but not because of that do we forbear to burn them when we see them. I could say much to you in answer to your letters. . . .

• • •

Another similar view comes from El Despertador Americano of January 1811. Published from December 20, 1810, for seven issues, it served as the voice of the rebellion led by father Hidalgo. This issue protests the indignities creoles suffered at the hands of the Spaniards, disdainfully called gachupines.

EL DESPERTADOR AMERICANO, JANUARY 1881

Why do you fight on the side of the Europeans? Are you moved, perchance, by the defense of religion, the defense of our most holy faith? But this is precisely our cause. In this respect our viewpoint is the same as yours. . . . By prolonging this senseless and unjust war you leave all of us open to attack by the vassals of José Napoleon, who would destroy Christianity among us, as they have already done in Spain. . . . Are you moved by the excommunication that the European Inquisitors have pronounced against our leader? . . . How simple-minded and naïve! The entire Nation . . . recognized from the beginning that this edict, expedited in a moment of disgrace, . . . was nothing more than a cunning trick of the Gachupines. As soon as they learned of the outbreak of our revolution, they were paralyzed by fear. They saw that they were a handful against millions, they saw that it was impossible for them to receive help from Frenchified Spain, they saw that the maritime powers of the entire world would support our independence so that they could trade directly with us without having to pay large sums to the Gachupin middlemen. . . . [The Gachupines] approached the Inquisitors, who to our disfortune are all Gachupines themselves and concerned with the fate of their European compatriots . . . issued with a haste unworthy of such an important matter,

the deadly edict with which they believe they will ruin Hidalgo and his followers, that
is to say, all Creoles. They filled the edict with the most (filthy) and indecent expressions, *sucias*
more likely to scandalize than to edify; they crafted it with such blindness that they did
not see its enormous contradictions that even a child could perceive. . . . The edict is
circulated not by proper ecclesiastical authorities but by merchants and subdelegados,
without the customary seal of the Inquisition and signatures of the Inquisitors. . . . Suppose for an instant (although it is not so) that our Liberating Hero had fallen into
some error contrary to the faith. Would this in any way undetermine the justice of our
aspirations for independence, our wish to free ourselves from a Spain dominated by a
drunken king and flooded with the horrors of impiety? . . . The sole crime of this new
Washington lies in his having raised his voice for the liberty of our fatherland in having
uncovered the Gachupins' plots to surrender us to Jose, and having opposed the
carrying out of such a criminal and detestable design. . . . The Holy Office of the
Inquisition established in Mexico, that respectable tribunal which according to its
stated purpose should only watch over the preservation of the Catholic Faith, has
openly degenerated of late, converting itself into a police force, a bloody organization
that has involved itself in matters that are purely political. . . .

Do you fight, our dear brothers, for the legitimate Spanish King, the unfortunate
captive Fernando? But don't you notice that Gachupines now don't even remember *desfortunado*
that (hapless) monarch? Don't you see that Spain has recognized an intruder as king. . . .
"Joe Bottles," that king of cups? . . . Do you fight for your fatherland? But, oh, your fatherland, America, the legitimate mother who conceived you in her breast . . . now
looks upon you as expatriate and rebellious children who have taken up arms against
her. Have you not allied yourselves with the tyrants who for three hundred years have
sacked, devastated, and crushed America? . . . Look at this vast continent, at the opulent region where you were born. . . . Who are the owners of the richest mines? . . . Who
own the biggest haciendas? . . . Who marry the most beautiful American women with
the best dowries? Who hold the prime posts in the judiciary, the viceroyalties, the in-
tendancies . . . the most eminent honors, the most abundant stipends in our churches?
The Gachupines! If once in a while, guided by their maquiavellianism, they entrust
some high position to someone who is native-born, it is only the kind of position that
requires hard work, and they choose old Creoles who can barely do the job because of
their advanced age, or better yet, they prefer the most inept and ignorant, so that later
on they can discredit the capabilities of the entire nation.

In whose hands does our commerce lie? Who has confined it to a single port and
burdened it with onerous taxes? . . . Who has impeded all sorts of American manufac-
tures with the false pretext of not hurting industries in Spain, as if nobody knew that
almost everything they resell to us comes from foreign factories? Who has established
monopolies on salt, tobacco, mercury, . . . mescal, gunpowder . . . leaving no job for
the honorable Creole? . . . Adding insult to injury, they throw up our supposed laziness *vagabundos*
in our faces and treat us like (vagrants? Who collects an annual twenty million pesos
from this America? . . . Meanwhile, the poor Creole redoubles his efforts. . . . The
Gachupines have followed their ancient maxim of destroying in order to dominate, of
keeping us in misery so that we lack the strength to rise up against their tyranny. . . .

Finally, are you fighting because you are terrified of Spanish power? Don't you
realize that this power that was once so formidable has been destroyed to its very roots
by the French and is now, by the just disposition of Providence, nothing more than a

scarecrow, an insubstantial ghost? Don't you see that your arms are the last resort they have been able to summon in order to prolong the convulsions of their moribund despotism? How can you be scared of this despicable gang of Europeans who watch over you from the rear, never exposing themselves to our fire? Americans, such fear has no place in manly chests, it is suited only to the lowly and worthless slaves. Remember that you are Americans, turn your bayonets against these treacherous ones and return to our camps. If your souls are prone to fear, know that there is less risk to your lives if you choose this easy and honorable alternative, given that you are 10,000 against 800,000, than if you choose otherwise and expose yourselves to our just wrath. It is irrational and foolish to go against the impetus of an entire Nation that has risen up for its independence. It is not possible to upset the plans of our Father and Liberator. . . . All of our enemies shall be ground to dust by the intrepid Allende.

El Despertador Americano, January 1811. Translated by Cheryl E. Martin.

THE WAR OF HATE

From the beginning, the creoles counted on the lower classes to fight the war of independence. The multitudes who joined Hidalgo's army surprised and frightened the creole leadership. Their concerns manifested themselves when the rebel army killed the Spaniards who had sought protection in the granary in Guanajuato, a mining town north of Mexico City. Historian and politician Lucas Alamán's description of this event indicates just how shocking it was to the creoles. Creole mistrust of the lower classes was to underlie all of the political development of the nineteenth century.

EXCERPT, LUCAS ALAMÁN, THE ALHÓNDIGA

The city of Guanajuato is situated at the base of a deep, narrow valley which is dominated on all sides by high rugged mountains. . . . The town had perhaps seventy thousand inhabitants including those of the mining camps. Of these, the Valenciana mines, which had been for many years enjoying uninterrupted prosperity, had something like twenty thousand people. The region enjoyed great abundance: the huge sums that were distributed each week among the people as wages for their work in the mines and related haciendas sparked commercial activity; the great consumption of foodstuffs by the people, and the pasturing of the many horses and mules used in the mining operations, had caused agriculture to flourish for many leagues around. In the city there were many rich homes, and many more which enjoyed a comfortable middle-class existence: commerce was almost exclusively in the hands of the Europeans, but many Creole families supported themselves easily from mining-related activities, and they were all respectable in the orderliness of their dress and in the decorum they observed. The people, occupied in the hard and risky labor of the mines, were lively, happy, prodigal, and brave.

So populous a city, situated amid the craggy hills which have been aptly compared to a sheet of crumpled paper, could not defend itself unless the mass of its inhabitants were united; so it was essential that its defense have the support of the common people. This was made fully clear when the intendant sounded the general alarm on September 18: a large number of people came armed with rocks, and they occupied the hills, streets, plazas, and rooftops in the early morning of the 20th, when the advance guard at Marfil believed Hidalgo was drawing near, which is why the alarm was sounded, and the intendant with his troops and armed peasants rode down the glen to meet him.

The intendant, however, believed from that moment that the people were changing their minds, and he feared that the lower classes of the city would join Hidalgo when he arrived; thus, he changed his plan, deciding instead to take cover at a strong, defensible point while awaiting aid from the Viceroy or from the troops which [General Félix] Calleja [commander-in-chief of the royalist forces] was supposed to recruit from San Luis Potosí.

In order to ensure the provision of corn, a food of primary necessity for the people and for the many of beasts employed in the mines, the intendant had built a spacious public granary, or *alhóndiga*, in which a quantity sufficient for a year's consumption could be stored, thus avoiding the inconvenience of frequent fluctuations in the price of this grain, which was caused especially by the difficulty of travelling the roads during the rainy season.

The Alhóndiga de Granaditas, which acquired so much and such lamentable celebrity on this occasion, was very sturdily built and it dominated the principal entrance to the city, but it was itself dominated by El Cuarto Hill . . . and by San Miguel Hill, which was a greater distance off to the south. This was the point where the intendant resolved to make a stand, and on the night of the 24th, without anyone realizing it, he moved his troops and armed peasants, as well as the entire royal treasury, the treasuries of the municipalities, and all of the archives of the government and the city council [to the Alhóndiga]. . . .

At dawn on the 25th, the town was surprised to see the moats closed off and the trenches demolished, and [immediately] they knew everything that had happened the preceding night. There was general consternation at seeing the city abandoned, for nearly all of the Europeans with their treasures, as well as many creoles, had gone to the Alhóndiga and shut themselves in. As near as can be determined, the sum gathered there in silver ingots, cash, mercury from the royal treasury, and valuable objects was worth no less than three million pesos. So great was the wealth of the country back then that such a large sum was gathered in a few moments in one provincial city!

Hidalgo . . . returned from Celaya toward Guanajuato, at every step augmenting the crowd that followed him. Riaño knew well the difficulty of his position. . . . "The people," he told Calleja on the 26th, "voluntarily surrender themselves to the insurgents. They already did so in Dolores, San Miguel, Celaya, Salamanca, Irapuato; the same shall soon happen at Sialo. The seduction spreads here, there was no security or confidence. I have fortified myself in the most suitable place in the city, and I will fight to the death, if the five hundred men I have at my side do not forsake me. I have very little gunpowder, because there absolutely is none, and the cavalry is poorly mounted and armed, with no weapons but their glass swords, and the infantry their mended rifles, and it is not impossible that these troops might be seduced [by the rebels]. The insurgents are bearing down on me, supplies are impeded, mail is intercepted."

A little before twelve o'clock, in the avenue of Our Lady of Guanajuato, which is the entrance to the city from the plains of Marfil, there appeared a huge crowd of Indians with few rifles; most were carrying lances, sticks, slings, and arrows. The first of this group passed the bridge . . . and arrived in front of the adjoining trench, at the foot of Mendizabal Hill. Gilberto de Riaño—to whom his father had entrusted the command of that point, which he deemed the most hazardous—ordered them to stop in the name of the king, and since the crowd continued to advance, he gave the order to open fire, whereupon some Indians fell dead and the rest retreated hurriedly. In the avenue, a man from Guanajuato said they should go to El Cuarto Hill, and he showed them the way. The remaining groups of Hidalgo's footsoldiers, perhaps 20,000 Indians, joined by the people from the mines and the lower classes of Guanajuato, were occupying the heights and all the mines and all of the houses around [the Alhóndiga de] Granaditas, in which they placed soldiers from Celaya armed with rifles; meanwhile a corps of around two thousand cavalry-men, composed of country people with lances, mixed in among the ranks of the dragoons of the Queen's regiment led by Hidalgo, climbed along the road called Yerbabuena and arrived at [the top of San Miguel Hill], and from there went down to the city. Hidalgo went to the headquarters of the Prince's cavalry regiment, where he remained throughout the action. The column continued crossing through the town in order to station itself at Belen Street, and as they passed by they sacked a store that sold sweets, and they freed all the prisoners of both sexes who were locked up in the jail—no fewer than three or four hundred persons, among them serious criminals. They made the male prisoners march on the Alhóndiga.

The intendant's death introduced division and discord among the defenders of the Alhóndiga, at the moment when it was most necessary that they act in unison and with firm resolution. The counselor of the intendancy, Manuel Pérez Valdés, citing the fact that in the ordinance of the intendancy leadership falls to the counselor when the [intendant] is accidently removed, claimed that since he was now the superior authority of the provinces, nothing should be done except by his command. He was inclined to surrender.

Once the trenches were abandoned and the troops who defended the roof withdrawn, that wild mob rushed to the base of the building: those in front were pushed by those who followed, unable to turn around, as in an ocean storm when some waves are impelled by others till they dash against the rocks. The brave man could not show his mettle, nor could the coward find a way to flee. The cavalry was completely routed, unable to use its weapons and horses. Captain Castilla died, some soldiers perished; the rest joined the conquerors. The valiant José Francisco Valenzuela, turning his horse about, rode up the hill three times, opening a path with his sword; he was dragged from his saddle and suspended on the points of the lances of those who surrounded him in a large numbers; even so, he killed some of those closest to him before receiving his death blow, shouting "Long live Spain!" until he gave up his final breath.

No more than a few isolated shots were heard from some who still held out, such as the Spaniard Raymayor, who did not let the Indians come near till all of his cartridges were spent. The Europeans at the Hacienda of Dolores tried to save themselves through a back door that opened upon the log bridge over the Cata River, but they found that the assailants had already taken that bridge. They then retired to the well, where—since it was a high, strong spot—they defended themselves until the last of their ammunition ran out, causing much carnage among the insurgents. . . . The few Europeans who remained alive at the end fell or were thrown into the well, and they drowned.

The taking of the Alhóndiga de Granaditas was entirely the work of the common people of Guanajuato, together with numerous bands of Indians led by Hidalgo. As for Hidalgo and his fellow leaders, there was not, nor could there have been, any disposition other than to lead the people to the hills and begin the attack. But once it begun, it was impossible to maintain any order at all: there was no one to receive or follow orders, for there was no organization at all in that riotous crowd, nor were there lesser chiefs to lead the people. They rushed with extraordinary valor to take part in the first action of the war, once committed to combat, Indians and people of villages could not turn back, for the crowd surged forward upon those who went first, obliging them to win land and to instantaneously occupy any space left by those who died. The resistance of the besieged defenders, though intrepid, was without order or plan, since the intendant died before anyone else, and it is to this we may attribute the quick termination of the action, for by five in the afternoon it was all over.

The insurgents, after taking over the Alhóndiga, gave free reign to their vengefulness. Those who had surrendered begged their conquerors in vain for clemency; on their knees, they prayed that their lives be spared. Many of the soldiers of the battalion were dead; others escaped by taking off their uniforms and mixing with the crowd. Of the officers, many young men of the city's most distinguished families perished, and others were gravely wounded, among them Gilberto Riaño who died a few days later, and José María and Benigno Bustamante. Of the Spaniards, many of the richest and most important citizens died. . . . Some managed to hide in granary number 21, where the corpses of the intendant and several others lay, but they were discovered and killed without mercy. All were despoiled of their clothes. When the rebels stripped the corpse of José Miguel Carrica, they found he was covered with haircloth, which gave rise to the rumor that a *gachupín* saint had been found. Those who remained alive—naked, covered with wounds, tied up with rope—were taken to the public jail, which had been empty since the prisoners were freed. To get there, they had to cross the long expanse from the Alhóndiga while the unruly crowd threatened them with death at each step. It is said that, in order to avoid this menace, Captain José Joaquín Peláze managed to persuade his captors that Hidalgo had offered a cash reward if he were brought in alive, and thus he was guarded with greater care in that treacherous transit.

The people devoted themselves to pillaging everything that had been gathered at the Alhóndiga, and it all disappeared within a few moments. Hidalgo wanted to reserve the ingots of silver and money for himself, but he could not prevent the people from taking them. Later some of the ingots were found and taken back, for they belonged to the army's treasury and so could not be included in the general looting. The Alhóndiga presented the most dreadful spectacle: the food that had been stored there was scattered all around; naked corpses were found half-buried in corn and money, all of it stained with blood. The looters killed one another fighting among themselves for booty. A rumor spread that granaries holding the stores of gunpowder had been burned, and that the castle—which is what the people called Alhóndiga—was about to blow up; the Indians fled, and the people on horseback sped through the streets to escape. With that, the common people of Guanajuato, who may have been the ones who spread rumor, remained sole owner of the prize—at least until the rest, their fear having evaporated, came back to take their share.

The people who had stayed on the hilltops awaiting the results now came down to take part in the despoliation, even though they had not been involved in the combat. Together with the rest of the townspeople and the Indians who had come with Hidalgo, they began the general looting of the stores and homes of the Europeans of the city, which began that same afternoon and continued all through the night and all the next day. They ransacked more pitilessly than any foreign army could have done.

The looters grabbed the most valuable things from one another. The astute and clever people of Guanajuato took advantage of this ignorance of the Indians to take their loot away from them, or to buy it at a low price. They persuaded the Indians that ounces of gold were not coins, but copper medallions, and they bought them for two or three reales; they did the same with the jewelry, the value of which they themselves did not know. On the 29th, Hidalgo's birthday, Guanajuato presented the most lamentable aspect of disorder, ruin, and desolation. The plaza and the streets were full of fragments of furniture, the remains of the goods looted from the stores, and liquor that had been spilled once the people had drunk their fill. The people abandoned themselves to all manner of excess. Hidalgo's Indians made the strangest figures of all, for on top of their own clothing they wore the clothes they had taken from the homes of the Europeans, including the uniforms of magistrates, so that the Indians adorned themselves with embroidered dresscoats and gilded hats while barefoot and in the most complete state of inebriation.

The pillage was not limited to the homes and stores of the Europeans of the city; the same thing was done in the mines, and the looting became extensive at the metal-refining haciendas. The commoners of Guanajuato, having already killed in the Alhóndiga the industrious men of these establishments—the men who had enabled them to earn their keep by paying them considerable wages—now ruined the establishments themselves, dealing the death blow to the branch of mining that had been the source of the wealth not just of the city of Guanajuato, but of the whole province. Mexicans, too, were affected by all this devastation by virtue of the business relations they had with the Spaniards, especially in the field of metal refining. Some banking houses owned by Mexicans would advance the Spaniards funds at a discount on the value of the silver that they received in payment, according to the rules established in the mining ordinance for advances on the price of silver.

Hidalgo wanted to put a stop to this disorder, so he published a proclamation on Sunday, September 30. Not only was this proclamation not obeyed, but inasmuch as there was nothing left to loot in the houses and stores, the commoners began to drag the iron trellises down from the balconies, and they broke into the homes of Mexicans whom they suspected of hiding goods belonging to Spaniards. Among the homes so threatened was that of my own family, which was located atop a store that had belonged to a Spaniard. . . .

Hidalgo came on horseback to the plaza where my house was located, accompanied by his generals. At the head of the group was the painting of the image of Guadalupe, and an Indian on foot banging a drum. Some country people followed on horseback, along with some of the Queen's dragoons in two ranks. The priest and his generals presided over this procession-of-sorts, dressed in jackets like those worn by small town militia officers; in place of the insignia of the Queen's regiment, they had hung silver cords and tassels from their epaulets, which no doubt they had seen in some picture of the French generals' aides-de-camp; they all wore the images of the Virgin of Guadalupe on their hats. When Hidalgo's retinue arrived in front of the Posadas store where the largest mob was gathered, they ordered the mob to withdraw. When the people did not obey, [one of the officers] tried to keep them away from the doors of the store by forcing his way into the midst of the crowd. Nearby, the flagstones formed a sharp slope, and at the moment they were covered with all sorts of filth and were very slippery. [The officer] fell off his horse, and while trying to get up, he angrily drew his sword and began to wield it at the crowd; people fled in terror, leaving one man gravely wounded. Hidalgo continued circling the plaza, ordering that the men who were dragging the balconies off the houses be fired upon. With that the crowd began to disperse, though for some time large groups remained selling the objects they had ransacked for outrageous prices.

Lucas Alamán, *Historia de Mejico*, vol. I Mexico City: Imprenta de J. M. Lara, 1849, pp. 351–354, 379–382, 408–414, 416–444. Translation by Timothy Henderson in Gilbert M. Joseph and Timothy J. Henderson, eds. *The Mexico Reader*. Durham: Duke University Press, 2002. Reprinted by permission of Timothy J. Henderson.

. . .

THE RESOLUTION FOR INDEPENDENCE

The final agreement for independence after all the years of fighting was a backroom deal. Agustín de Iturbide, a royalist general, betrayed the Crown and negotiated with the rebels. The creoles were certain they would triumph and rule.

AGUSTÍN DE ITURBIDE, PLAN DE IGUALA
24 FEBRUARY 1821

AMERICANS

When I speak of Americans, I speak not only of those persons born in America, but of the Europeans, and Asians who reside here. May they all have the good grace to hear me!

The largest nations of the Earth have been dominated by other Nations, and so long they were not permitted to form their own opinions, they were not free. The European countries, although they achieved great heights in education and politics, were once slaves to the Roman Empire. That Empire, the most renowned in history, was like a father who, in his dotage, watched as his children and grandchildren left home, for they were of an age to start homes of their own and to fend for themselves, though they maintained all the respect, veneration and love due their father.

For three hundred years, North America was under the tutelage of Spain, the Most Catholic and pious, heroic and magnanimous of nations. Spain educated and aggrandized it, forming its opulent cities, its beautiful villages, its remote provinces and kingdoms, increasing its population and splendors, knowing every aspect of the natural opulence of its soil, its rich minerals, the advantages of its geographical situation. We have seen the damage caused by our great distance from the center of the Empire, and we know that the branch is now the equal of the trunk: public and general opinion declare that we should be absolutely independent from Spain and from all other Nations. Europeans and Americans from all regions likewise believe this to be so.

That the same voice which sounded in the village of Dolores in 1810, and which caused the people so much hardship due to the disorder, abandonment, and a multitude of vices, also convinced the people that a general union between Europeans, Americans, and Indians, is the only solid basis upon which our common happiness can rest. After the horrible experience of so many disasters, is there anyone who is now unwilling to support that union through which so much good can be achieved? European Spaniards: your fatherland is America, because you live here; here you shall have commerce and possessions! Americans: Who among you can say that you are not descended from Spaniards? We are held together by a dulcet chain formed by links of friendship, common interests, education and language, and a unity of sentiments. You shall see that these are close and powerful links, and that the happiness of the Kingdom depends on everyone uniting in a single opinion and speaking with a single voice.

The time has come to manifest the uniformity of your sentiments, so that our union can be the powerful hand that emancipates America without the need of foreign help. At the head of a valiant and resolved army, I have proclaimed the Independence of North America! It is now free, it is now its own Master, it no longer recognizes or depends upon Spain or any other Nation. All shall greet it as an Independent Nation, and with gallant hearts, we shall raise our voices, together with those of the troops that have resolved to die before abandoning this heroic enterprise. The Army is not animated by any desire other than to keep pure the Holy Religion we profess, and to preserve the general happiness. Listen, here is the firm basis upon which we found our resolution:

ART. 1. The Roman, Catholic, Apostolic Religion, without tolerance of any other.
ART. 2. The absolute Independence of this Kingdom.
ART. 3. Monarchial Government, limited by a Constitution suitable for the country.
ART. 4. Ferdinand VII or someone of his dynasty, or some other prince, shall become Emperor. We shall have an established monarchy so as to prevent acts of ambition.
ART. 5. There shall be an interim committee [*junta*] which shall convoke a Congress [Cortes] to enact this Plan.
ART. 6. This committee shall name a Governing body, and it will be composed of the representatives already proposed to the Viceroy.
ART. 7. It shall govern in accordance with the oath already made to the King, until the King shall come to Mexico, whereupon all previous orders shall be suspended.
ART. 8. If Ferdinand VII decides not to come to Mexico, the Committee of the Regency shall govern in the name of the Nation until the matter of who shall be crowned king is resolved.
ART. 9. This Government shall be sustained by the Army of the Three Guarantees.

ART. 10. The Congress shall decide if the Committee should continue or be replaced by a Regency until the arrival of the Emperor.

ART. 11. As soon as it is completed, the Constitution of the Mexican Empire shall enter into force.

ART. 12. All of the inhabitants of that Empire, with no considerations except those of merit and virtue, are citizens qualified to accept any employment.

ART. 13. All persons and properties shall be respected and protected.

ART. 14. The Regular and Secular Clergy shall retain all of their properties and privileges.

ART. 15. All Government officers and public employees shall remain in office, and shall be removed only if they oppose this plan. Those opposed to the plan shall be replaced by those who distinguish themselves by their adhesion to the plan, as well as by their virtue and merit.

ART. 16. A protecting Army shall be formed, which shall be called the Army of the Three Guarantees. Any of its members, from the highest to the lowest ranks, shall be executed if they violate any one of the Three Guarantees.

ART. 17. This Army shall observe their Orders to the letter, and its Chiefs and officers shall continue on the same footing as before.

ART. 18. The troops that compose the Army shall be considered as troops of the line, as shall all who come to embrace this Plan: all other citizens shall be considered a National Militia, and the rules for this and the form it shall take shall be decided by Congress.

ART. 19. Military ranks shall be determined by reports from the respective Chiefs, and shall be granted provisionally in the name of the Nation.

ART. 20. The interim Congress shall meet and proceed against crimes in complete accordance with the Spanish Constitution.

ART. 21. Those who conspire against Independence shall be consigned to prison; no further measures shall be taken against them until Congress dictates the punishment corresponding to the most serious crimes, including treason against His Devine Majesty.

ART. 22. Those who try to spread division and who are reputed to be conspirators against Independence shall be subject to close vigilance.

ART. 23. Inasmuch as the Congress which has been formed is a constituent Congress, Deputies must be elected with this understanding. The committee will decide on the rules and the time necessary for the task [of writing a Constitution].

AMERICANS

Herewith, the establishment and the creation of a new Empire. Herewith, the oath of the army of the Three Guarantees, whose voice is that of he who has the honor of leading it. Herewith, the object for which I ask your cooperation. I ask of you no more than what you yourselves have wished and longed for: union, fraternity, order, interior calm, vigilance, and horror toward any turbulent movement. These warriors want nothing more than the common happiness. Join us to bravely advance an enterprise that in all aspects (excepting, perhaps, the small role I have played in it) must be called heroic. Having no enemies to combat, we trust in the God of the

Armies, who is also the God of Peace, that those who make up this armed force, which brings together Europeans and Americans, dissidents and royalists, will be mere protectors, simple spectators to the great task that I have (outlined) today, which the fathers of the Nation shall retouch and perfect.

May the great nations of Europe marvel at seeing how North America frees itself without (shedding) a single drop of blood. In your joyful celebrations, say: Long live the Holy Religion we profess! Long live Independent North America, among all the Nations of the Earth! Long live the union that brings our happiness!

Agustín de Iturbide

"Plan of Iguala." Ernesto de la Torre Villar, et al, eds. *Historia documental de México,* vol. 2, Mexico City: UNAM, 1964, pp. 145–148. Translated by Timothy Henderson in Gilbert M. Joseph and Timothy J. Henderson, eds. *The Mexico Reader.* Durham: Duke University Press, 2002. Reprinted by permission of Timothy J. Henderson.

• • •

QUESTIONS

1. Did Chito Villagrán write the letter to his parish priest?
2. Why did Villagrán rebel against Spanish authority?
3. From EL DESPERTADOR's point of view, what was the cause of the wars of independence?
4. Can you detect any bias in the story historian Lucas Alamán relates about the destruction of the granary in Guanajuato? Why do you think he was biased against the lower classes?
5. Why did Iturbide have to issue Three Guarantees?
6. Who won the wars of independence in Mexico?

2 THE PRACTICE OF POLITICS: POPULAR PARTICIPATION IN THE NINETEENTH CENTURY

INTRODUCTION

In the aftermath of the Wars of Independence, popular participation in politics on all levels increased. Involvement by the middle and lower classes included voting in elections, mostly local, but, when permitted by the new constitutions, on the national level as well, engaging in public demonstrations, such as riots (see the description of the Parián riot later), or joining locally based, informal armed forces to bolster one elite political faction or another. Most people who lived in the countryside concerned themselves with the issue of local autonomy. They wanted to be left alone to follow their traditions and customs and to govern their own everyday lives. Controlling their localities meant that they would impose taxes, if needed; regulate access to land; and enforce traditional values. Country people fought against the intrusions of centralized governments and the reforms of Liberal politicians who sought to end collective landholding.

The distrust among social classes permeated the politics of modern Latin America. Wealthy residents, mostly merchants and large landowners, had every expectation of ruling the former Iberian colonies as independent nations. However, the long wars that won independence undermined their situation. The violent disagreements among themselves about the form and substance of government created opportunities for the lower classes, which comprised the vast majority of the population, and for the much smaller middle class to participate in the discourses and practices of politics. We might even call the first half century after independence a "golden age" for the subaltern classes in politics. Elites had to admit the lower classes into politics, because they needed the lower classes to fight in their armies. The lower classes, particularly in the countryside, exacted a steep price from their elite allies: local autonomy.

The last decades of the nineteenth century brought about an enormous transformation in political relationships. Latin American states, bolstered by professional armies, vastly improved transportation and communications, and booming export economies, usually under the guidance of strong dictatorships, consolidated their powers. Strengthened elites pushed the lower classes out of politics mostly through coercion. The subalterns would regain their role only after 1900 when they joined labor unions and political parties.

POPULAR CLASS PARTICIPATION

amohiaise *In urban areas, rioting had been an important method of communicating the disaffection of the poor with their plight since colonial times. These most often occurred in times of food shortages, generally the result of long periods of drought and accompanying harvest failures. Accusations of hoarding leveled against local merchants were the likely triggers for such demonstrations. Perhaps the most famous riot of the nineteenth century in Mexico took place in 1828 in the context of a revolt against President Guadalupe Victoria. On December 4, 1828, a mob of 5,000 stormed and looted fancy shops in the Parián Building on the Zocalo (the main square) in Mexico City. Historian Silvia Arrom, an expert on the Mexican urban poor during the nineteenth century, presents three views of the riot. The first is from Governor José María Tornel y Mendivil, who had to quell the upheaval.*

PARIAN RIOT 1829, DESCRIPTIONS

Numerous groups of insolent plebes forced the doors of the Parian, . . . [and] then began sacking the building, or Bazaar, which for more than a century was the emporium of commerce, . . . [and] contained cash and goods worth the enormous sum of two and-a-half million pesos. . . . Throughout that disgraceful day and all of the night, they stole without intermission and committed abominable crimes, including murders in cold blood to dispute both valuable articles and trinkets that passed from the hands of one thief to another. The devastation of the Parian was like that of a voracious fire: all the doors were unhinged and broken; some roofs burned, and not one display case was spared, nor a single shop.

· · ·

The second is from Lorenzo de Zavala, one of the leaders of the revolt against Victoria, who actually witnessed the riot.

PARIAN RIOT 1829, DESCRIPTIONS

The [national] palace was without any guards but those Zavala [sic] had ordered; the city was frightfully silent. The pillaging . . . had ceased by nightfall; a sepulchral silence reigned over the vast capital of Mexico; in the palace there was no one but Victoria, abandoned even by his servants. Many shops were open, their merchandise on the streets, in the plazas; their doors fractured. Not a voice could be heard; only the sound of the hours, announcing the passage of time, interrupted the profound dream that enveloped all mortals. What a night! What a terrible night!

The third was from José Maria Luis Mora, a liberal essayist ad politician, who sought to put the demonstration in a more positive light.

3 PARIAN RIOT 1829, DESCRIPTIONS

The riot of the Acordada, the most atrocious which Mexico has known, is in no way comparable to the insurrections and popular movements that have existed in France and England even in their present stage of civilization, for neither were buildings destroyed nor was there loss of life (with the sole exception of two murders, and an unsuccessful murder attempt); the looting was restricted to a few, fixed points, and it was easily contained once we put our minds to it. Compare this with the Lord Gordon riots in London, or the French Revolution in its early period.

Translated by Silvia Arrom and reprinted by permission from: José Maria Tornel y Mendivil. *Breve reseña histórica de los acontecimientos más notables de la nación Mexicana, desde el año do 1821 hasta nuestras dias* (Mexico City, 1852), 393–394; Lorenzo de Zavala, *Ensayo histico de las revoluciones de México desde 1808 hasta 1830* (Mexico City, 1845), II; José Maria Luis Mora, *México y sus revoluciones*, 3 vols. (1836), I, 80–81.

• • •

MOTIVATIONS FOR THE POPULAR CLASSES

An uprising took place in the province of Huantla in the department of Ayacucho from 1825 to 1828 against the newly independent government of Peru. Historian Cecelia Méndez has explored the motivations of the participants. She finds that indigenous peoples were fully engaged in the politics of the era. Two documents from the national archives in Peru testify to the participation and motivations of country people in nineteenth-century politics. Villagers did not sell their cooperation with elite political factions cheaply, demanding local autonomy or support in land disputes in return.

1 HUANTLA DOCUMENT

Attentive to the summons made to us in the past year of 1827, calling on us to take up arms against the rebels of Yquicha, we generally lent ourselves to this important service. . . . The enthusiasm, bravery and daring with which we, bearing all sorts of dangers, waged war on the Yquichanos, who were proud of the repeated victories which they had attained over the veteran troops, are only too well known. . . . In spite of this we were continually suspected of joining with the Yquicha dissidents solely because of our proximity to them; but also because of their seductive promises, with which they wanted to attract towns to their band of not having to pay either contribuciones or duties or the slightest tax. *Hence General Domingo Tristán, then Prefect of the Department, repeatedly promised us through the military commander of Tambo, don José de Quintanilla, that we would be exempted from the tax in reward for our sacrifices.*

• • •

2 HUANTLA DOCUMENT

The rebels of Yquicha who stirred up the towns, upset order, broke the dikes of obedience, and caused immense damage to the nation, were excused from paying the contribución because of an excess of compassion from the government, and they have enjoyed this grace in full; and although their crimes were the cause of the harm which they have suffered, the *Madre patria,* though ruined by these perverse sons, has shown them consideration, extending its tender and beneficent hand to them to wipe away their tears. And we who with robust arm and dauntless heart stood up to the revolution, and broke the hard neck of this hydra, *we who did more than we had to (it must be said), serving at our own expense,* and having rid the nation of this source of scandal, have brought the rebels under control and back to their duties, shall we remain in a worse condition so that the favor which was promised us remain void and without effect?

Being victims of seduction by the leaders [*corifeos*] of the Yquichano party which had expanded in those places, we have suffered the damages resulting from a destructive war. The pastures of those barren lands are not insulted [*sic*] by any domestic livestock, since the soldiers be they friends or enemies, did away with all of it. The *chacras* [farmed lands] have become forests, for we have only recently taken up agriculture. On the other hand, we had no other choice for our subsistence than to raise some livestock or other, and to cultivate the lands of said town, which, as they are situated in the Punas, yield no more than barely, potatoes, broad beans, and quinoa, provisions which are not all desirable.

Pp. 222, 224, "Huantla documents" from *The Plebian Republic: The Huantla Rebellion and the Making of the Peruvian State* by Cecilia Méndez. Copyright © 2005 by Duke University Press. All rights reserved. Used by permission of the publisher.

• • •

UPPER CLASS VIEW OF THE POOR

In the excerpt that follows, U.S. Minister John G. A. Williamson relates the story of an unsuccessful coup by disgruntled military officers, perhaps in conjunction with former supporters of the deceased hero of the Wars of Independence Simón Bolívar. Williamson observed the dilemma of the upper classes of the era: they needed the support of the middle and lower classes, but at the same time feared and despised them. Interestingly, the U.S. diplomat mistook the inaction of the mass of civilians in the city for indifference or cowardice, when it was more likely that the general population was actually quite clear in its preference for the ousted government backed by José Antonio Páez, who had served as president the previous five years.

1830 IN VENEZUELA, WILLIAMSON, *CARACAS DIARY*

9TH JULY 1835

The Government House taken possession of yesterday was to day crowded with the malcontents a great proportion of whom were the mere offscourings of the City and those in some Shape or way connected with the leaders and the family of Bolivar—However these are and have been very political in all the various movements & political changes. . . . Some have hazarded all, but the most of them who have had any thing, had previously conveyed it away— The scene exhibited in the Streets was singular indeed, at every corner near the Government House or the Presidents, crowds of the Citizens assembled merely to look on, without a sufficient energy to resist two hundred & fifty armed men—every one shrugging up his shoulders reconciling his patriotism & love of country to the circumstances of being non combatants.

. . . a military move and that as there was no person of the civil character but himself (General P.B. Méndez) he had consented to serve them in all things connected with the civil department, denying as it were any actual interference in the State of things only a subordinate to General Diego Ibarra, to whom he referred me as possessing all power until the arrival of General Mariño, who was daily & hourly expected from Maracay—assuring me at the same time that foreign citizens and property would not be molested when they remained entirely neuter in the revolution—and that no doubt General Ibarra would grant every thing necessary to the end. He insinuated at the same time that the black population were much to be feared, and in that case he would give me timely information as he stood as much in fear of such an event as I could on any foreigner—

JULY 10TH

The population exhibited a great deal of uneasiness and uncertainty, the President & Vice President removed as prisoners to the Government House—I had asked of General Méndez on yesterday to allow the privilege of communicating with the President, he said he could not grant it but that General Ibarra could, and that he would endeavor to obtain the permission and inform me—but never heard from him on this subject.

The president the night of the 9th at eleven o'clock was taken with the Vice President from the Government House and sent to La Guayra under an escort of 50 soldiers under General Justo Briceño, and two or three friends—

This Justo Briceño is another of those thirteen whose names I now record here, that sent the note through Carujo to the President on the morning of the 8th requesting his resignation.

JULY 11TH

The same excitement prevailing, without one act that would indicate resistance peaceably bowing their heads to the yoke of Military despotism, for on this day General Mariño had *issued his* gag Law, not permitting conversations upon the state of things on the Streets, or meetings in Public—The greatest humbling in this whole affair at an attempt at Government and to forestall public opinion in aid of their views, was a call upon the citizens to meet at the Theater under the protection of the *Patriotic Military*, and vote upon the subject of reforms & *of course* their decision *would* have been final, that is final in voting because if they had gone for that purpose they certainly would have voted them *all back again* to their silent & powerless insignificance.

They soon became sensible of this fact, that the time had gone by when a few military designing men could by an overt act of treason against the Laws & constitution of the Country uproot the same and then carry the head of families to thus publicly sanction such treasonable views against the best interests moral and social of the Country.

Finding this would not do, they soon changed their views upon the people and required them to vote at each magistrates or Alcaldes in their parish or square, which resulted in almost as perfect a (failure) as the former, not receiving more than some two or three Hundred, and the great body of them soldiers, in a city with a population of 25 thousand to thirty thousand—To get public opinion therefore to sanction their acts of the 8th, they had thus evidently lost public Confidence, and could not succeede in cajoling them to their personal ambition and the necessity of making *reforms* by subverting the Constitution and Laws; unless it was such reforms as struck at the root of all social Government—and placing themselves in the vacant seats of President Vice President & Secretaries. In addition to these facts they have some forebodings of the course that General Páez would take, the President and Council having on the morning of the 8th at about 2 o'clock, sent him his commission as commander in chief, with an order to raise ten thousand troops immediately in support of the Government—They still held out the belief that General Páez was with them and when there was no possibility of deception to their own treasonable views, they proclaimed him as *gefé* in chief—This did not take, the great body of the people were not to be deceived in this manner, they had dispatched a messenger to General Páez as well as the Government to inform him of events, and asking him to come to the protection of the Constitution & Laws.

JULY 12TH

This day passed by pretty much as the 10th—They are catching a number of vagabonds, are permitting them to join the army, by which means they have increased their number to near double the original body—

From this day up to the 27th the party in power were arranging or attempting to do so, every thing to organize a Government, but of what form, they had not by any one act exhibited sufficient light, to know what it should be, every thing was dark, suspicious, and without any actual Government existing, ruling only the Military who adhered to them, tho they had first by one mans decree and then by anothers filled all the vacant offices which they had made in the constitutional Government—still there was but an uproar "confusion worse confounded" in the Government House, one tangled yarn without an end, all officers and no officers, all Government and no Government this man to apply to and that one to apply. One did not know 'tother had not been informed—Briceño Méndez was factotum, and on applying to him it was Ibarra, applying to Ibarra, it was General Mariño—Such a real hotch potch of Government was never heard of or read of, but such I really did see—the Citizens stood with gaping mouths staring eyes & ears wide open to catch & see every thing, but the devil a bit did they or would raise an arm, or a hand to put down these plunderers of their nations honor and their countries glory—but in stupid amaze a population of able bodied Citizens to carry arms amounting at least to two thousand remained with arms foulded, and witnessed this farce of Military power take from his own house the President & Vice President & send them to La Guayra and then embark them for St. Thomas, without so much as the firing of a musket.

Indeed, they are only fit for the subjects of despotism, to say they are patriots, to say they love their Constitution or their Government is and must be hereafter a by word of reproach to them as a people.

One effort by two Hundred men would have undid the affair, the stones in the streets or the tiles from the houses afforded them ample means to crush at a blow the 250 men who had thus changed the Government or rather seized the power—

The arrival of General Mariño gives no security nor created any more enthusiasm in belief of their cause.

At length all the schemes if in reality they had any, failed the moment General Páez moved they fell one after another, first Valencia then Victoria, and on the night of the 27 was as near as Coquisas to the city of Caracas on the road to Valencia—Consternation seized them, they found out General Páez was not with them but against them, and they prepared about or from 7 to 9 o'clock at night of the 27 to leave Caracas—The whole day had been one of confusion and uncertainty—

The Government House was upside down and uncertainty depicted in the Countenance of every mothers son of them that you could meet—

The City looked lonely, deserted doors and windows closed, the very sound of your feet in the Street was solemn, dreadful, it echoed to the silence that prevailed around.

By ten o'clock after an exchange of a few shots about this hour which wounded some of their own men fired from their friends, the faction departed for the East, taking the road to the village of Petare at the end of the valley of Caracas; and without being harassed or molested escaped to Rio Chico & from there thence to Barcelona—General Páez entered next morning the 28th pursed *after the game was* fled as far as Petaré—understanding that he had made a halt at Savana Grande about 3 miles from Caracas I rode out at 10 o'clock to pay my respects to him, whom I found at General Olivarez House surrounded by a few of his friends & officers and some 5 hundred troops, after about fifteen minutes conversation he left me & persued with his remaining troops to Petaré—

He here remained for 24 hours and returned to Caracas—joined with the Council of Government & issued a request and appointed a commission to go off immediately for the President & Vice President.

The President returned about the 28th August, the Government is reestablished and an army raised & the faction persued to the East, by marching from various points an army of them—nothing but the ordinary movements in such cases takes place, some few prisoners made in a *private* way—

Jane Lucas de Grummond, ed. *Caracas Diary: The Journal of G. A. Williamson, First Diplomatic Representative of the United States to Venezuela.* Baton Rouge: Camelia Publishing Company, 1954.

• • •

The deep disdain that Mexican elites had for the lower classes, particularly in the countryside, comes through clearly in the reminiscences of Brantz Mayer who was a U.S. diplomat in Mexico in 1841 and 1842.

BRANTZ MAYER, *MEXICO AS IT WAS AND AS IT IS*

In the course of this afternoon we passed through several Indian villages, and saw numbers of people at work in the fields by the road side. Two things struck me: first, the miserable hovels in which the Indians are lodged, in comparison with which a decent dog-kennel at home is a comfortable household; and second, the fact that this, although the Sabbath, was no day of repose to these ever-working, but poor and thriftless people. Many of the wretched creatures were stowed away *under a roof of thatch, stuck on the bare ground, with a hole left at one end to crawl in!*

What can be the benefit of a Republican from of the government to masses of such a population? They have no ambition to improve their condition, or in so plenteous a country it would be improved; they are content to live and lie like the beasts of the field; they have no qualifications for self-government, and they can have no *hope*, when a life of such toil avails not to avoid such misery. Is it possible for such men to become Republicans? It appears to me that the life of a negro, under a good master, in our country, is far better than the beastly degradation of the Indian here. With us, he is at least a man; but in Mexico, even the instincts of his human nature are scarcely preserved.

It is true that these men are *free*, and have the unquestionable liberty, after raising their crop of fruits or vegetables, to trot with it fifty or sixty miles, on foot, to market; where the produce of their toil is, in a few hours spent, either at the gambling table or the pulque shop. After this they have the liberty, as soon as they get sober, to trot back again to their kennels in the mountains, if they are not previously *lassoed* by some recruiting sergeant, and forced to "volunteer" in the army. Yet what is the worth of such purposeless liberty or the worth of such purposeless life? There is not a single ingredient of a noble-spirited and highminded *mountain peasantry* in them. Mixed in their races, they have been enslaved and degraded by the conquest; ground into abject servility during the Colonial government; corrupted in spirit by the superstitious rites of an ignorant priesthood; and now, without hope, without education, without other interest in their welfare, than that of some good-hearted village curate, they drag out a miserable existence of beastiality and crime. Shall such men be expected to govern themselves?

Brantz Mayer, *Mexico As It Was and As It Is*. New York: J. Winchester, New World Press, 1844.

. . .

QUESTIONS

1. What did the villagers want as their reward for supporting the government against the rebels from Yquicha?
2. What was the price of rebellion to Yquichanos?
3. Could country people trust their local and national leaders?
4. How do you explain the contradiction between the rebels' "gag" order and their calling upon citizens to meet at the Theater and vote on proposed reforms?
5. Why did the rebel government fall so easily?
6. According to diplomat Williamson, what group in the general population did Venezuelan elites fear most?
7. Why did the attempted government takeover fail in Caracas?
8. Was Brantz Mayer prejudiced against indigenous people or against poor people? Why did he think country people were unqualified to be citizens?

3 WAR

INTRODUCTION

War dominated the politics and economics of Latin America from the era of independence (1808–1828) through to the early 1930s. The Wars of Independence were enormously destructive to people, infrastructure (buildings, roads, and bridges), commerce, and industry. The major international conflicts, such as the Mexican War with the United States (1846–1848), the War of the Triple Alliance or Paraguayan War (1864–1870), the War of the Pacific (1879–1884), and the Chaco War (1932–1934), caused catastrophic losses for Bolivia, Mexico, Paraguay, Peru, and Paraguay again, respectively. The wars profoundly affected the subsequent political and economic development of each of these nations.

The wars in and of themselves were horrendous experiences for their participants. Leaders and soldiers alike were poorly trained, badly equipped, and undersupplied. Blunders and betrayals predominated. Officers and soldiers profoundly distrusted each other. Courage frequently fell victim to ineptness and venality.

Few governments during the first decades after independence could afford to support ~~sizable~~ standing armies. Regimes sometimes expended considerable sums keeping officers on the payroll, so they would not rebel. There were few funds earmarked for the rank and file soldiers. Consequently, when governments required armies to defend their nations, such as in Mexico in 1846 and 1862 when the United States and then France invaded, they raised soldiers by an involuntary draft using coercion. They cleared the jails. Invariably soldiers were undisciplined, badly trained, if trained at all, dressed in rags, and sometimes shoeless. Armaments were usually obsolete European artillery and rifles bought at dear prices with borrowed funds. Governments rarely paid their soldiers. Medical care was virtually non-existent. Wounded soldiers were doomed. Officers treated their underlings with contempt and employed harsh punishments for even the most minor infractions. Not surprisingly, desertions were rampant. There were some volunteer soldiers, but they responded to local leadership and causes, and were less likely to leave their home territories to fight. Women served as the supply and medical corps of the armies. They accompanied their husbands and mates into battle, feeding them before and cleaning up the carnage afterwards.

Militaries began to professionalize in the 1860s, when governments contracted with Europeans to modernize their training and procedures. The focus was on a new officer corps with its own élan. To accomplish this, Latin American nations established military academies. It was in these schools that the insular, superior, impatient military originated. The officer corps was no longer comprised of the sons of the oligarchy, but rather selected members of the middle and upper classes. But well-trained officers were not enough. In the twentieth century, concerns turned toward transforming the non-commissioned officer ranks and the common soldiery. Modern mass armies required highly skilled soldiers to employ the new technologies. Conscripted "riff-raff" would not suffice. Therefore, governments adopted obligatory military service to provide the necessary standing armies.

WARS OF INDEPENDENCE

The Wars of Independence were enormously destructive with massive casualties, particularly in the war zones of central Mexico and Venezuela. Gustave Hippisley, a British mercenary soldier, joined the rebels in 1817 in Venezuela and observed The Liberator Simón Bolívar and his army close-up. He witnessed miserable conditions for the soldiers and a brutal war of hate.

prisando

WARS OF INDEPENDENCE, HIPPISLEY, A JOURNEY TO THE RIVERS ORINOCO…

Affairs all around appeared, indeed, like a flight where neither order nor regularity were preserved: every one seemed anxious for himself alone, some running one way, some another: all was confusion, terror, and dismay. The miserable hovels, under the   cesuchz
aparms name of houses, afforded scarcely any covering for man or beast: they were all open in front, and the old and almost worn-out inmates were wretchedly suffering under the
afliccion various evils of poverty, distress, and disease. So miserable a scene I had never before witnessed; and the horror I experienced on visiting the building set apart for an hospital, whither my poor countrymen must go if sick or wounded, was beyond expression. The unfortunate patriots who were inmates of this place sat or lay along the benches of flooring, waiting patiently the approach of the medical attendants. Some held up the stump of an arm, shattered by a ball, or lopped off with a sword; others lifted up a thigh, the leg belonging to which had suffered amputation by a similar process; others lay bleeding to death, with shots through several parts of their limbs and bodies: and my soul was sickened by beholding some, who, having lost the scalp or upper part of the skull, exposed the action of the bare brain to view. Yet hardly a groan escaped from the poor miserable sufferers, some of whom seemed to endure the agony they were undergoing with all the stoical indifference and resolution ascribed to their North
hermno American brethren, when put to the torture by their conquerors. The only cry that I heard was for water: their moans were so low and inaudible in other cases, that nothing could be distinguished. The hospital at this time contained about a hundred and fifty people. Colonel Wilson, in consequence of his arrival two days before me, was settled in quarters at the further extremity of the town; and to show me, I presume, that he wished to be on friendly terms, with me, he invited me to dine with him, which invitation I accepted, in order that no difference existing between us should appear to the native officer. At five o'clock we sat down to table, at which I also perceived five of my officers, who had been invited; it was a mess dinner, and some light claret and some rum were produced. Here we witnessed a guard taking some of the unfortunate prisoners to the spot for execution near the river, but my heart revolted at the idea of being a witness to the manner in which it was performed; some of the younger men of my regiment and some of the non-commissioned officers were there as spectators.

The native and black troops (freed slaves) can, and do, dash on with madness, which they call bravery, the result of revenge, hatred, and an abhorrence against the

odio

ascaramuzas

royalist party. The feelings of retaliation for their brethren and fellow soldiers taken prisoners in the various actions or skirmishes with the enemy keep alive all those passions of inhumanity, cruelty, and blood-thirstiness; and they are more savage in nature than the brutes that inhabit the woods and mountains of their country. Yet, under the name of courage, they will rush, without order, regularity, or discretion, upon the enemy, resolved at that moment to conquer or to die; and if in this onset they are beaten or repulsed, and find themselves able to "go about," and to retreat, "the devil take the hindermost" appears to be the general cry; for they all continue to run until they reach a place of safety: and it is allowed by the royalists troops themselves, that the patriotic army, with Bolivar at their head, was never beaten in this respect.

The final slaughter of the prisoners, after the battle, or during the retreat, is completely acquiesced in by Bolivar, who has himself condescended to witness this scene of butchery and infamy: yet it must be admitted that Morillo more than keeps pace in the sanguinary species of warfare, the example of which was first set by the royalist troops, and became to the latest moment a measure of retaliation, and, without doubt, will continue so, until mutual ideas of humanity invest the minds of the contending parties.

Bolivar has shewn, in some instances, a proneness to retaliation, refined beyond every species of cruelty attributed to the royalist chief. Witness the eight hundred men he put to death in the early part of his campaigns at Ocumare. Hence it was that the most noble the governor of Jamaica is said to have ordered him, when he touched there for a short period during his flight from the Main, to quit that island, in the following words: "Tell that butcher of human flesh to quit the island in three days from this notice." At the time Bolivar left Jamaica he prevailed on a very fine young man, then an officer in one of the West India regiment, to resign his commission in the British service, and to follow his fortunes in South America.

Gustave Hippisley. *A Narrative of the Expedition to the Rivers Orinoco and Apuré in South America.* London: John Murray, 1819.

· · ·

The independence wars exacted an enormous toll. The local leaders of a Peruvian village wrote to describe the wreckage in 1826.

Jamaludin

COST OF WAR, WARS OF INDEPENDENCE IN PERU

enado

The district finds itself exceedingly poor in resources, and still more backward because of the calamities that the *Yindigenas* from Yquicha and Caruhuran [*sic*] have perpetrated in the past year in the sowing and among the livestock; they have looted and burned almost all the district; most of their children have been killed and leaving blood-stained for the sake of the just cause of Independence the fields of [A]co and Carpampa, which have also distinguished themselves from the rest of the towns of the province by serving as Guerrillas in the pacification division under the command of Colonel Benavídez."

As cited in Cecilia Mendez Méndez, *The Plebian Republic: The Huantla Rebellion and the Making of the Peruvian State.* Durham: Duke University Press, 2005.

THE HORROR OF BATTLE

Perhaps, the most disastrous external war in terms of future economic development was the war between Mexico and the United States from 1846 to 1848. Antonio López de Santa Anna was the commanding general of Mexican forces. He told of the horror of battle and the narrow margin between victory and defeat. The fight to keep the U.S. invaders from the nation's capital, Mexico City, was perhaps the bloodiest series of battles.

WAR WITH THE UNITED STATES, SANTA ANNA AUTOBIOGRAPHY

We heard the sounds of cannons from the direction of Chapultepec. I knew then that the attack was exactly as I had previously planned for it. I immediately ordered all forces to move to the aid of that region, and I marched swiftly in the same direction. Although we marched as quickly as possible, we arrived just as the battle was ending. The brave generals, Antonio Leon and Francisco Perez, from their vantage point at Molino del Rey were able to check the enemy's advance to Chapultepec and force them to retreat, abandoning their dead.

If General Alvarez had followed orders and proceeded with division during the disorder in the enemy's ranks, the Mexican army's day would have been a glorious one. The entire fault lies in the lack of action by Alvarez.

Arriving at Moline del Rey, my sorrowful eyes fell on two stretchers bearing the brave General Leon and intrepid Colonel Balderas, both gravely wounded. Their two courageous battalions had lost two officers and eighty-six soldiers.

As you can tell, only Providence saved the enemy from complete disaster at our hands. It is only logical to assume that if a mere four thousand soldiers with only eight cannons could check and repulse him, he might have been completely routed if we had sent more than twelve thousand infantrymen and fifty-two cannons against him.

The defeat of the eighth of September weighed heavily on General Scott that he considered withdrawing to Puebla to recover his health (or so he said). He would have done just this if the Council of Generals he conferred with had not opposed this action. It is interesting to note what this same Council had to say about my military operations when they considered the suggestion of a retreat. I repeat these words—words which made them my praisers, although that was not their intention. I shall repeat only part of them, as modesty forbids my repeating them all. The last words of the famous General Smith are sufficient to show the high regard in which they held me. He said, "If we turn our backs on that man, we will never arrive in Puebla. I am not in favor of the retreat."

Scott, spurred on by his companions, struck again. He bombarded Chapultepec and took it four days later at the cost of many lives to our forces. The invaders, encouraged by this victory, attacked the sentry posts at Betlehen [Belen] and San Cosme. We resisted the attack, but treason aided them in obtaining a victory.

I was at the Betlehen sentry post, when an aide arrived from the forces at San Cosme. He implored me "My General, if you do not come to the aid of the sentry post at San Cosme, we will lose it. The enemy forces are large, and my commander is in urgent need of reinforcements."

I immediately ordered General Andres Terres to hold the entrenched lines under his command and set out for San Cosme with the reserve division and five howitzers. I succeeded in forcing back the enemy to such a point that they could not be seen. They left the battlefield scattered with their dead.

Our forces had scarcely caught their breaths when another aide arrived from the capital informing me that the Betlehen sentry post had been abandoned to the enemy. Although I doubted the seriousness of this message, I returned as quickly as possible. I was greatly surprised to see the enemy forces penetrating the Paseo Nuevo and attempting to enter the Citadel. A bloody battle to defend the Citadel began, and our greatest effort was needed to force the enemy back to the Betlehen sentry post. The enemy entrenched itself at the sentry post. I attacked twice but failed to dislodge the invaders.

I was anxious to learn how the enemy had taken the Betlehen sentry post and sent General Terres. Strangely enough, no one in the garrison had seen him. I reproached Lieutenant Colonel Castro, the head of the second active Battalion of Mexico, for abandoning the post. "General Terres," he replied, "commanded me to take up my position on the principal plaza. As nothing was happening there, I returned here on hearing the enemy's guns."

When I questioned Colonel Arguelles, commander of the advance guard, he replied, "General Terres ordered me to the Alameda. It was my duty to obey his orders." When I questioned Colonel Perdigon Garay, commander of another active battalion, he answered, "At the command of General Terres, I took up a position at the hermitage of La Piedad. When I saw that the enemy was entering the city, I hurried here."

The artillerymen verified the fact that General Terres had ordered them to transfer to the Citadel. All of these accusations verified the treason of General Terres.

General Terres soon presented himself before me. He was clothed in the uniform of the Mexican army and bedecked with the medals a generous Mexican nation had awarded him. I was angered and indignant at his arrogance. The blood pounded in my temples at the mere sight of him, and I threw myself at him, tearing the epaulets from his shoulders and striking him across the face with my horsewhip.

It was a mad, violent act, completely foreign to my natural inclinations. But I was completely overcome with fury at the ungrateful wretch who had betrayed my miserable country. I was disgusted by my actions, but, at least, I had spared the villain's life. Treason of this kind is usually punished by hanging. And, after all, Terres had not been born in the Republic.

Although we encountered so many difficulties, we managed to continue our defense of the capital without interruption. At eight that night I finally dismounted my horse to preside over a junta of war with the generals at the Citadel. The situation was very grave. Tired, hungry, and with my uniform tattered by the enemy's bullets, I discussed the grave situation with the junta of generals for three hours. During the entire session I was bowed down with pain. Each of the generals took the floor in turn. Each general bitterly deplored the lack of enthusiasm the people showed toward the war. The soldiers were the only ones fulfilling their duties, although they had not been paid for several days.

The generals felt that it was useless to continue to defend the city without people's support. They also felt that the people would be spared useless sacrifices if we surrendered. For these reasons and other insignificant ones, junta unanimously agreed to withdraw from the capital. They felt that the national honor had been upheld by our defense and that it was impossible to defend the capital after the surrender of the Betlehan sentry post. They also felt it the duty of the defenders of the capital not to involve the people in any unnecessary dangers. The junta ordered all forces with their artillery to march at daylight the following day to Guadalupe Hidalgo, leaving the capital under the command of the governor. It would be the governor's duty to protect the rights of the people and to obtain a guarantee of these rights from the enemy leader. Acting in accord with the junta's decisions, I issued the orders and they were carried out.

The invading army, considerably diminished in numbers, occupied the city. General Scott maintained troops in the principal plaza during the time I was in Guadalupe Hidalgo, arranging for the necessities of campaigning. Scott thought I intended some blow to him when I retreated from the city.

Excerpted from Chapter 3, "The Horror of Battle" in *The Eagle: The Autobiography of Santa Anna* ed. by Anna Fears Crawford. Copyright © 1988. Published by The State House Press. Reprinted by permission of Texas Frontier Heritage & Cultural Center, State House Press.

We get some idea of the condition of the Mexican army in this war from the invaders. Lieutenant William S. Henry reported poignantly on a young woman who died in battle.

TO MEXICO WITH TAYLOR AND SCOTT

Attracted by the sound of that everlasting *Mexican bugle* (whose first notes were given to us at the Colorado), I discovered the Mexican troops were marching out. I saw many of them pass. The infantry were miserably clad, brawny, thick-set fellows, chiefly shod with sandals; one regiment of Lancers were as fine looking men as I ever saw. Their horses were inferior animals; *one* of ours could ride over *three* of them. The streets were filled with the followers of the army, mounted on every thing, from a decent mustang to an humble, uncomplaining donkey. Some of the officers' wives, picturesquely wrapped in their gay-colored ponchos, were slowly riding after their chivalric husbands. The main Plaza is still occupied by the enemy, to which we have no access. General Ampudia left on the 25th, with two divisions of his army.

I visited Arista's Palace, which is directly under the hill on which the Bishop's Palace is situated. It is a long, low, white stone building, beautifully finished, claiming no particular order of architecture, with flat roof, thick walls, and stone floors. At the back of the house is a portico twenty feet in width, and a garden that reveals Oriental magnificence. Double walls of white masonry, about three feet high, filled in with earth, laid out in fanciful figures, with fountains in the center, roses, and numerous other plants, apparently growing out of the walls, and also in the enclosed space; vases, with choice exotics, arranged round them; a bold stream of water, running through a plaster raceway, leads to a marble bath, covered with trelliswork, over which the grape and other vines clamber. In the rear of this are beautiful groves of orange-trees and pomegranates, and a fine vegetable garden. Imagine the whole tastefully laid out and kept in the neatest order, and you can form some idea of one of the retreats of this Mexican nabob. It has been turned into a hospital, in which the wounded of Worth's division are lying. The oranges in the garden were kept for the wounded; but immediately outside there was a wilderness of them, where everyone picked what they pleased. Some of the houses occupied by the officers are very neatly, but simply furnished; many of the walls are hung with mirrors and choice paintings.

After riding over the city and examining minutely its defenses, my only astonishment is how they could yield it. It is a perfect Gibraltar. At the eastern extremity, where so many of our brave fellows fell, my wonder is that *any escaped.* There is a system of batteries, the only defending the other. General Worth conducted his movements with judgment and skill. His motto on starting was, *"A grade or a grave."* He escaped the latter, and it is to be hoped he will obtain the former. . . .

Grady McWhiney and Sue McWhiney, eds. *To Mexico with Taylor and Scott 1845–1847.* Waltham: Blaisdell Publishing, 1969 from Lieutenant William S. Henry, *Campaign Sketches of the War with Mexico.* New York: Harper & Brothers, 1847.

The Paraguayan War (1865–1870), which pitted Paraguay against the Triple Alliance of Brazil, Argentina, and Uruguay, was the most destructive in terms of civilian casualties with some estimates putting the death toll for Paraguayan males as high as seventy percent.

पावर्जन

PARAGUAYAN WAR DOCUMENTS

If to be an officer one chooses an existence riddled with privations and sacrifices to form part of the corps on the line, it is one of the most grave and unsupportable punishments of being a citizen. With the exception of some few volunteers encouraged by love to make a military career with a hard existence stationed on the frontiers, most soldiers had been rounded up by local judges or military commanders in unjust levies. . . .

According to one deputy in the national congress:

> It is true, Mr. President, that the soldiers of our army are not criminals and bandits, but are victims of force. They are citizens snatched from their homes by violence, sometimes in the name of necessity, and others of convenience, but always in the name of arbitrariness. These citizens, whom the law has violated, did not know of the prerogatives of the Constitution to which they were entitled, . . . The Argentine army . . . is a fantastic myth that is representing the torture of Prometheus in that the chiefs are vultures and the soldiers the victims.
>
> (*Prometheus is the figure in Greek mythology who had angered the gods and was punished by having his liver eaten by vultures every day only to have it restored at night and the ordeal repeated the next day.)

It is known . . . how they become soldiers. They snatch them from the homes of poor peasants, whose crime is to have been born in the humble condition of a *gaucho* to be a servant without salary, naked, and without basic foods and when they escape from jail, because for them the military camp is a prison, they are caught and they suffer the whip for the few hours of freedom they had won. . . .

THE AMBUSH

centinelas

In Tuyutí major Lucio V. Mansilla deployed his sentries in such a way so as to hear the regiment's noise as he sat mounted on a small horse. It was a cold night with a grand sky.

Being recognized I passed with incident by the first sentry and then by successive sentries until I reached the last. I spoke with him kiddingly, as was my style; I gave him a good swig of drink, returning tracing my previous path, I did the same with each sentry and continued to spur my horse, who moved slowly. I did not carry a whip or sword, or any arm at all. When I felt comfortable at the half way point between one sentry and another, suddenly I heard a gun shot and yelled "The Paraguayans!"

The darkness was almost complete; a dense fog had arisen. I shot here and there, but I could see nothing and all passed like a flash.

A moment later some sentries surrounded my horse. . . .

I spoke with the sentries as I gathered some dry pasture to use as a torch for lighting the horizon. He removed my doubts.

The Paraguayans had come by the stream in the water up to their noses like amphibians; they had stayed in front of my men, then without warning an instant after I passed in front of the sentry and given him a drink they had robbed him and fled to the other side of the stream.

TREATMENT OF SICKNESS

Doctor Lucilo del Castillo: The sickness spread with astonishing intensity, attacking a great number of people, principally those who were in the hospitals sick with other infections. The commanding general ordered that the sanitary corps take severe measures to effect hygiene in order to do all that was possible to prevent the spread to the troops. The army prohibited soldiers from the marshlands. . . . The army also permitted the *pantanales* troops distractions that would permit them to forget the bad situation and increase morale. The general suspended training exercises and allowed soldiers not on duty to leave the base during the day. The army also tried to improve the diet of the troops. . . . Soldiers were given a ration of coffee and sugar. Alcoholic beverages were forbidden.

Translated by Mark Wasserman from Miguel Angel del Marco, *La Guerra del Paragua*, Editorial Planeta, 1995.

The vivid prints on the next page were created as illustrations for the Asunción periodical Centinela during the Paraguayan War of 1864–70.

WOODCUTS FROM THE PARAGUAYAN WAR, 1867*

If all the trees gave the same fruit, how happy we would be.

Soldier in a coffin waiting to be taken to a better place.

The Emperor of Brazil receiving news of a bitter defeat in battle.

Marshall Francisco Solano López, President of Paraguay during the war.

Making faces at the enemy.

Satire poking fun at the Triple Alliance (Argentina, Brazil, Uruguay)

*Patrick Frank

CHACO WAR, ESTIGARRIBIA MEMOIRS

Information from all sources made known to us important assemblies of enemy troops in Camacho, Platamllos, Saavedra, and Nanawa. But in view of the dire scarcity of means of transport (the permanent plight of the Paraguayan army in the course of all the war) and the continual rains, we had to authorize the Army Corps commanders to reduce to a minimum the garrisons of their advanced posts. The troops in general could not receive more than half of the daily ration. In Nanawa, in which region the roads were utterly impassable, they could not receive but some meat after December 1st. The problem of providing officers for the Second Army Corps persisted largely. In order to remedy this deficiency I requested Asunción to send naval officers who were fired with the patriotic desire of taking part at the front of operations; and they came full of alacrity and quickly adapted themselves to the new environment of combat which was offered to them.

As a consequence of the diminution of effectives ordered in the advanced posts there remained in Corrales some 300 men. On January 1, 1933, this *fortín* was attacked by several enemy regiments and, after an heroic defense lasting throughout the day, the *fortín* was abandoned and left in the power of the enemy at 6 P.M. The brave defenders of Corrales, when they received the order to retire, were totally surrounded and they had to open a passage through the enemy at the point of the bayonet to their bases, saving all their equipment.

It was evident that the late copious rains had made the enemy movements very difficult; in fact the enemy had accomplished no operation of importance since the Paraguayans had taken the defensive now sometime ago, and despite the better facilities they possessed for their supplies, as we shall see later.

At last, on January 7th, the Bolivians pressed with troops of real weight upon the Paraguayan advanced troops of Herrera obliging them to retire somewhat to the rear. On the following day they attacked with numerous troops our post Mariscal López and took it after its defenders had expended their munitions. Nevertheless, our troops retired in good order upon Nanawa. The defenders of Mariscal López were armed with rifles of caliber 7, different from the rest of the armament of our army, and they had at their disposal only a scant quantity of ammunitions which could not be replaced.

Immediately I gave the order to retake that post but I had to cancel it the following day in view of the movement of some Bolivian units on the side of Samaklay, a movement which was in accordance with the information that Nanawa would be attacked with strong forces.

Fully informed, above all by the declaration of prisoners, of the preparations on the part of the enemy of a serious attack upon Nanawa in the near future, I ordered, beginning January 11th, that some regiments be sent as reinforcements for the garrison of this *fortín*, and I further ordered the transportation of the necessary replacements for the existing units in that place. Prisoners captured in those days in the Corrales sector stated that in that sector few troops were left, since the greater part had been sent to the south. As a typical example of the form in which the Paraguayan Command was restrained from taking advantage of the favorable moments which presented themselves I record here an episode. Since January 10th we had assembled in Toledo a mass of five thousand men who absolutely became unmovable because of the lack of means of transport. If we had had at our disposal means in sufficient quantities, we should have been able to operate with incalculable results. The enemy did not have sufficient troops to check us, because, as we have seen, all their forces were concentrated towards the south for the attack upon Nanawa. Unfortunately we had knowingly to miss that precious opportunity, as well as others, always for the same cause—the meagerness of means of transport.

Asunción, March 18, 1933

Strictly Confidential

My dear Colonel:

I desire to make you acquainted with the financial and diplomatic situation. Despite the efforts displayed, the negotiations of the neighbors, ABCP [Argentina, Brazil, Chile, and Perú] have practically failed. Bolivia opposes any agreement because she is confident of the success of her offensive and that ultimately she will dominate the Chaco. For my part I do not believe that we can obtain peace by these means unless some military disaster should overcome her or some internal disturbance should shake her. All this is improbable. Consequently, we must count upon the continuation of the war.

The resources of the Government are very limited. The gold reserves are already spent. There remains a small balance which we must preserve in order to provide munitions, means of transport, and the things which are absolutely indispensable. Already we are not in any position to acquire rifles, airplanes, artillery, and machine guns.

The plan of the Command must be, therefore, subordinated to those circumstances because they are irremediable. Some *inland financiers* dream of methods of which the least we can say is that they are ridiculous. Paraguay is poor, deprived of metals and of assets which might be transformed at once into metals. Against this there is no available expedient.

I understand that you cannot maintain your present positions without further contingents and more equipment. It is then a case of combining upon a strictly defensive plan whereby we have full security for detaining the enemy for some months and causing him considerable losses. Bolivia will lave to attack continually and waste her forces more rapidly and in a greater proportion than ourselves. According to calculations, Bolivia may resist economically for three months more, at the most. As a consequence we must be prepared to resist for that time *with the means at present at our disposal.* Munitions must be economized, arms preserved with extreme care and employed only in cases of real necessity. Our planes must be entrusted only with missions which are without danger. The loss of one airplane would cause a terrible impression on this nervous population, which is already sensitive to panic.

In order to develop the new plan we shall have to take into account, above all, the lines of transport which we shall have to serve. I hope that you will give the necessary instructions, accordingly.

I have the belief that a line strongly defensible where there can be no possible surprises such as that of Alihuatá would impress the enemy more than our present lines, which are exposed, as we have just seen, to *coups the main.*

Between Bolivia and Paraguay there is an essential difference. In Bolivia there does not exist any public opinion; their disasters are not known; there prevails a system of terror that prevents comment and the Bolivians absolutely do not know what passes in the Chaco. Thus it is that the terrific losses which they have suffered have not caused any discomfort to the Government. Further, the iron hand of Salamanca has silenced all those who would comment upon our successes.

On the other hand, among us, liberty reigns, and the people pass from enthusiasm to depression according to the information from the front. The generals criticize, despite my warning, the Command. I have just received a letter from General Escobar which I am going to answer, and afterwards I shall send to you a copy in order that you may see the bad spirit of those gentlemen. What can be done against such action? As a matter of fact anything that we may do is likely to impair things. In any case you can be assured that my personal and official authority will be on your side in good and, above all, in bad conditions. Not for a single moment have I believed in any intrigue to displace you, and notwithstanding my firm and resolute attitude, they are always furtively watching for some mishap to attain their ends. Therefore our tactics must be such as to evade any fortuitous operation and to be always sure even if we advance little or not at all. With the expressions of, &c, &c.,

Eusebio Ayala.

My reply to the foregoing letter follows:

P.C., March 20, 1933.

Dr. Eusebio Ayala,
President of the Republic.

My dear Mr. President:

I have received your interesting letter of the 18th inst., sent to me by hydroplane, and I have carefully made myself acquainted with its contents.

I think I can deduce from its contents that the impression in the Capital arising from the enemy incursion upon Alihuatá has been very strong, without there being sufficient reason for it. That event was nothing more than a fluctuation entirely normal in war and, happily, without any great importance, since it did not cost the life of a single man, the loss of a single rifle nor of any equipment, apart from ceding to the enemy a narrow stretch of territory in the desert.

Reflecting calmly and knowing that the final aim of a war is the destruction of the enemy forces and not geographical objectives, no matter how important they may be, and in view of the fact that the enemy did not succeed in capturing or killing a single Paraguayan soldier, the enemy plan, it can be affirmed, has failed in its essential part, and he has suffered, on the other hand, considerable losses in men and even in arms.

From the day that, in the middle of January, you were kind enough to grant me the interview at Kilometer 145 I have endeavored to adapt the operations of our troops to the true situation of the country which you have just confirmed in your letter. Thus, we have adopted a defensive attitude which certainly has given us resounding successes over the enemy troops. In Nanawa we have killed at least one thousand enemy soldiers; in Saavedra no fewer than five hundred; the same in Herrera, and finally, in Toledo, another thousand. The enemy wounded can be counted in thousands. All this at a cost to us of nothing more than one of our unimportant posts and some three hundred casualties, including dead, wounded, and missing.

We cannot assert that it is impossible to maintain our present positions. All will depend upon the proportion of the enemy effort. By now we have made ourselves strong in Toledo, Francia, and Nanawa, at which points we believe we can detain for a sufficient time the enemy advance despite the fact, as I expressed in one of my recent cyphered messages to the Ministry of. . . .

On the same day, the 14th, I personally inspected the Nanawa battlefield. I was a witness on that occasion of the most gruesome spectacle that I can recall in my life. In all that sector where the Bolivians had broken our lines and made their deepest penetration into our defensive system, fragments of legs and arms severed by the artillery were yet hanging from the trees. In one place there had fallen in an embrace a Paraguayan soldier and a Bolivian, and it could be seen that they had fought furiously hand to hand until the hand grenades which the Paraguayan had carried in his pocket, exploded, killing the two. This was evident from the fact that the thigh of the Paraguayan was splintered by the explosion on the side where he had the pocketful of explosives. What followed was even worse. As the field was littered with dead bodies, they had to be disposed of by incineration. Instead of placing wood among the corpses in order to feed the fire until their complete consumption was attained, they were simply piled and sprinkled with kerosene, thus setting fire to the whole. As long as there was kerosene the fire was maintained, but when this combustible was exhausted there remained a horrible heap of scorched human flesh which spread an unsupportable stench over the field. For months this atrocious sight remained in my eyes.

WOMEN AND WAR

Several excerpts show the roles women played in the wars, in this case the Mexican war with the United States.

SOLDADERAS, FROM JOHANNSEN

Some two or three hundred yards from the fort, I saw a Mexican female carrying water and food to the wounded men of both armies. I saw her lift the head of one poor fellow, give him water, and then take her handkerchief from her own head and bind up his wounds; attending one or two others in the same way, she went back for more food and water. As she was returning I heard the crack of one or two guns, and she, poor good creature fell; after a few struggles all was still—she was dead.

George Winston Smith and Charles Judah, *Chronicles of the Gringoes: The U.S. Army in the Mexican War, 1846–1848*, p. 90. Quotation from Robert W. Johannsen, *To the Halls of Montezuma: The Mexican War in the American Imagination*, p. 137.

. . .

SOLDADERAS, FROM SMITH AND JUDAH

The woman of sixty or more years—the mother with her infant wrapped in her rebosa—the wife . . . the youthful senorita frisking along with her lover's sombrero upon her head; even to the prattling girl who had followed padre and madre to the wars. . . . In addition to their bedding and wearing apparel, they pack upon their backs the food and the utensils to cook it in, and worn out as they are by the toils of the day, whilst their husbands or lover sleeps, they prepare his repast.

George Winston Smith and Charles Judah, *Chronicles of the Gringoes: The U.S. Army in the Mexican War, 1846–1848*, p. 90. Quotation from Robert W. Johannsen, *To the Halls of Montezuma: The Mexican War in the American Imagination*, p. 137.

SOLDADERAS, FROM GREGG, DIARY*

The night after his [Dr. Morton's] departure from Chihuahua, two Mexican girls, . . . who had been "in keeping" before, dressed themselves in men's clothing, shouldered muskets, and mounting horses, astride, they followed their paramours. One of these "beloved" men had sense of propriety and decency enough, to dispatch his Dulcinea back to Chihuahua, but the other continued with Dr. Morton to Saltillo, in whose tent I frequently saw her, living with him in the most public manner!

Maurice Garland Fulton, ed. *Diary and Letters of Josiah Gregg: Excursions in Mexico and California, 1847–1850*, p. 117.

"Soldiers and Proletarians"
Carl Sartorius, *Mexico about 1850*. (*Mexico*, 1858.) Reprint. *Stuttgart:*
FA Brockhaus Komm, 1961.

· · ·

CENTRAL AMERICA

Central America was the scene of almost constant warfare for four decades after independence from Spain as what eventually became five nations alternately fought each other and outsiders to determine national borders. William Walker led a filibuster of Americans against Nicaragua in the 1850s, at one point gaining control of the nation. A coalition of Central American nations defeated him in 1860. Costa Rican forces beat Walker in a battle at Rivas on April 11, 1856.

REPORT OF PRESIDENT DON JUAN RAFAEL MORA ON THE BATTLE OF RIVAS OF APRIL 11, 1856

General Headquarters, Rivas

Señor Minister of War:

April 15, 1856

I have already sent a report of the glorious day of the eleventh and I repeat it now in more detail, although it would never be possible to justly summarize the heroic actions of my valiant troops.

At seven in the morning, in response to the cunning maneuvers of the Filibuster Chief W. Walker, I sent a column of four hundred men under the command of Major Clodomiro Escalante in the direction of the little town of Potosí, where we had detected the enemy's presence.

The city of Rivas is open and surrounded by thick banana groves and peanut fields. Hardly a quarter of an hour had passed since the column left when Walker, doubtless hidden beforehand on the outskirts, invaded the city like a torrent from the side opposite to that taken by Major Escalante's men. Walker seized the plaza and came very close to the house occupied by my General Staff and the gunpowder depot across from it, which are both only two blocks from the plaza.

The first minutes were terrible. Our people and positions were outflanked, nearly encircled in a ring of fire and bullets. All of us gripped our weapons and went to the defense. Colonel Lorenzo Salazar backed up the General Staff with a handful of people and held off the enemy, giving the column that had left the city time to return and to occupy advantageous positions; until we could almost change the defense into an attack, forcing the enemy soldiers to hide in the houses.

We had stationed a small cannon with only four artillerymen near the plaza and the filibusters took it in their first charge. In an ill-considered effort to retake it, we lost some people. Three times our soldiers left the corner where our headquarters is located (the house of don José María Hurtado) and went running toward the cannon, two blocks away. And three times they suffered the murderous fire discharged by the enemy in the plaza, in the Town Hall and military building (where Walker was with his best people), in the church, in its belltower and the house of Señora Abarca, which our men called Doctor Cole's house.

At eleven o'clock the filibusters occupied the plaza and all the avenues around the church.

From the street in back of the war building, the city was ours toward the N.E.; we had the roads to La Virgen and San Juan.

The situation had improved, but we still had not won.

Strict, simultaneous orders went out from this headquarters: it was my wish to unite certain that were fighting in isolation. First, to organize, and then to surround the enemy, dislodge him, and throw him out of Rivas. A squad of dragoons was stationed in the door of the headquarters with the single purpose of passing written orders, and all officers were told to provide me with reports on the situation. I ordered that the ammunition stored in the other house be brought here, and I advised all officers to come and outfit themselves abundantly with munitions.

At nine o'clock I had requested reinforcements of one hundred men from La Virgen. Right away I sent orders for the troops stationed there and in San Juan to concentrate themselves in Rivas.

From this moment there began to be a progressive, decisive change in our favor.

Our men had set fire to one side of the war building and our fire was outflanking or closing in the enemy.

In mid-afternoon Commanders don Juan Alfaro Ruíz, and don Daniel Escalante arrived with the people from La Virgen: these troops occupied part of the war building, to the right of the church, and continued closing in the enemy until, in the night, they were able to seize Doctor Cole's house, the last one on this side of the plaza.

At night Colonel don Salvador Mora arrived with the people from San Juan del Sur.

Although the filibusters already had been surrounded, this force completed the security of our positions.

The firing had nearly ceased: the only things heard were occasional rounds from time to time which our people fired at the enemy troops who were fleeing and the joyous "vivas!" which our men yelled for the republic and its leaders.

Don Juan Alfaro Ruíz had surrounded the church and prepared to assault it at daybreak, at which time our soldiers invaded the plaza from all sides. Not finding any enemy troops other than those in the church, they entered and finished them off with bayonets.

Immediately I sent out pickets in all directions to pursue the fugitives.

This triumph has been great, due to the well-conceived surprise attack on the filibusters. Nevertheless, so much glory has been mixed with painful cries and sad mourning. We have lost the valiant officers General don José Manuel Quirós, Major don Juan Francisco Corral, Captains don Carlos Alvarado and, don Miguel Granados, Lieutenants don Florencio Quirós, don Pedro Dengo and don Juan Ureña, Second Lieutenants don Pablo Valverde and don Ramón Portugués, and Sergeant don Jerónimo Jiménez. The valiant Captain don Vicente Valverde also perished.

We counted 260 wounded, among them various notable leaders.

My first concern was to prepare the hospital, to bury the dead, and to organize the army again.

Walker's defeat is greater than I had thought. We have seized a large number of rifles, swords, pistols, more than fifty saddled horses, and many other things. It is not known what else the inhabitants may have hidden on the outskirts of the city.

Each moment prisoners arrive, both healthy and wounded. As of today we have shot seventeen.

In summary: our losses, counting the wounded who may die, will not exceed 110 men, including officers. The enemy's losses are not below 200, counting those we have executed. As at the battle of Santa Rosa [in northern Costa Rica on March 20], their wounded wander through the fields and many will die for lack of rest and care. Among the multitude of reports and dispatches I have received, the most certain is that Walker entered Granada the night before last with three hundred men, of whom twenty-five or thirty are wounded.

All the officers and soldiers of the army have distinguished themselves especially General don José María Cañas, Colonels don Lorenzo Salazar and don Manuel Argüello, Lieutenant don Juan Alfaro Ruíz, Captains don Santiago Millet and don Román Rivas.

According to careful examination of the various reports I have received Walker attacked with a force of between 1,200 and 1,300 men. I on this occasion, weakened by the dispersal of my people in the outposts at La Virgen, San Juan del Sur and elsewhere, had an equal or perhaps lesser number of soldiers.

I would have pursued the enemy without allowing him to rest, but we had all passed thirty hours without food and fourteen hours of massacre and fatigue.

It was my first duty to attend to the wounded, and now I am preparing to continue the campaign, flattering myself with the hope of being able to say to you very soon that *filibusterismo* no longer exists.

May God keep you,

Juan R. Mora

QUESTIONS

1. Hippisley depicts a truly horrifying battlefield. What accounts for the brutality of the wars of independence?
2. Who were apparently the greatest victims of the independence wars in Peru?
3. According to Antonio López de Santa Anna, what accounts for the margin between victory and defeat in battle?
4. What was Lieutenant Henry's assessment of Mexican troops?
5. What role did women play in the Mexican War with the United States?
6. Do the depictions of battle by the participants concur with the illustration from Sartorius?
7. How did the Battle of Rivas differ from the battles of the Mexico–United States war?
8. Why was the Paraguayan war the bloodiest of all the Latin American wars after 1825?
9. What were the conditions under which the Chaco War were fought?
10. Given the harsh realities of war presented in these excerpts, do you think war was a justifiable policy alternative?

4

EVERYDAY LIFE IN THE NINETEENTH CENTURY COUNTRYSIDE

INTRODUCTION

The juxtaposition of large estates with small holdings and villages defined much of nineteenth-century politics and economics in Latin America. The large estates were comprised of two general types: those that produced livestock and commercial crops, such as sugar, coffee, and cotton (known as plantations) for export, and those that produced primarily for domestic consumption, often with tenant or sharecropping arrangements. During the first half of the century, small holders and villages often bargained successfully with large estates to maintain their boundaries and autonomy, while the estates experienced downturns because of the damages inflicted by war. In the last decades of the century, however, the value of land rose because markets for agricultural commodities expanded. Land became more valuable. The balance of power shifted to the large estates. Plantations endured cycles. After a long decline, sugar in Brazil recovered in the wake of the Haitian Revolution in 1792. Coffee production in Brazil expanded rapidly, as did sugar production in Cuba. There were, however, periodic ups and downs in the markets for agricultural commodities.

Everyday life continued much as it had for centuries. It was hard to make a living. Farmers, large and small landowners, tenants, and sharecroppers alike, survived only precariously, at the mercy of the weather. Workers on the estates toiled long hours for meager pay. Most small farmers supplemented their incomes with work on the estates or with artisan production, mostly weaving, sewing, or pottery making by women. Toward the end of the century, men journeyed ever more frequently to cities, mines, or other countries to provide enough income just to struggle through.

COMMERCIAL AGRICULTURE

Englishman George Gardner traveled through Brazil in the 1840s, a time when coffee cultivation was on its way to becoming the dominant crop in Brazil. Gardner was a physician and botanist, who, like other foreign visitors, could be a keen observer. In the following, he puts forth a rather idyllic view of the plantations of the Paraiba Valley, the major coffee-producing region.

COFFEE FAZENDA, FROM GARDNER, *TRAVELS* . . .

The great coffee country is much further inland, on the banks of the Rio Parahiba. The trees are planted from six to eight feet apart. Those plants which have been taken from the nursery with balls of mould round their root are found to bear fruit in about two years, whereas those which have been detached from the earth do not produce till the third year, and a greater proportion of the plants die. They are planted when about a foot high, on the slopes of the hills, in the alluvial soil from whence the virgin forest has been cleared. They are only allowed to grow to the height of from ten to twelve feet, so that the crop may lie within reach. Till the trees are in full bearing, one negro can take charge of, and keep clean, two thousand plants; but afterwards only half that number is allotted him. Large healthy coffee trees have been found to produce as much as from eight to twelve pounds of coffee; the average produce, however, varies from a pound and a half to three pounds. When the berry is ripe, it is about the size and color of a cherry; and of these berries a negro can collect about thirty-two pounds daily. In the course of the year there are three gatherings, but the greater part of the crop ripens during the dry season. The berries are spread out to dry in the sun, on large slightly convex floors; the dry shell is afterwards removed, either by mills, or by a series of large wooden mortars. It is only in some few estates in Brazil that the pulper is seen . . . , for taking off the pulp from the fresh berries. Nothing is more beautiful than a coffee plantation in full bloom . . . .

George Gardner, *Travels Through the Interior of Brazil, Principally Through the Northern Provinces and the Gold Diamond Districts During the Years 1836–1841.* Boston: Longwood Press, 1977. (1846)

. . .

Louis Agassiz (1807–1873) was a European born and -educated Harvard professor, who had hypothesized the Ice Age through his geological discoveries. Agassiz visited Brazil to pursue his long-standing interest in fish. Agassiz, his wife, six assistants, and several volunteers embarked on the Thayer Expedition to Brazil between April 1865 and July 1866. By the 1860s, when Mrs. Louis Agassiz traveled to visit the Fazenda de Santa Anna in Minas Gerais, in the interior of Brazil, the coffee plantations had taken on a more prosperous and industrial look.

FAZENDA, FROM AGASSIZ, *A JOURNEY IN BRAZIL*

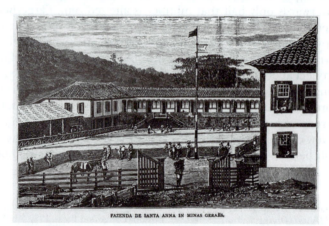

FAZENDA DE SANTA ANNA IN MINAS GERAËS.

FAZENDA DE SANTA ANNA IN MINAS GERAËS
Louis Agassiz, *A Journey in Brazil.* Boston:
Houghton Mifflin & Company, 1909.

Captain Richard F. Burton traveled 2,000 miles through Brazil, much of the journey by canoe, from June to November 1867 as part of a three-year stay in the country. A former president of the Anthropological Society of London, Burton was a meticulous observer.

LIFE OF A PLANTER, FROM BURTON, *EXPLORATIONS OF THE HIGHLAND OF BRAZIL*

The life of the planter is easily told. He rises at dawn, and his slave-valet brings him coffee and wash-hand basin with ewer, both of solid silver. After strolling about the mill, which often begins at 2 A.M., and riding over the estate to see that the hands are not idling, he returns between 9 and 11 with his family, and if a bachelor with his head men, to breakfast. The sunny hours are passed either in a siesta, aided by a glass of English ale—there is often nothing English in it but the name—in reading the newspapers, or in receiving visits. The dinner is between 3 P.M. and 4 P.M.—sometimes later; it is invariably followed by coffee and tobacco. Often there is another relay of coffee before setting down to tea, biscuits and butter or conserves, and the day ends with chat in some cool place. The monotony of this Vida de Frade—Friar's life—is broken by an occasional visit to a neighbor, or to the nearest country town. Almost all are excellent sportsmen, good riders, and very fond of shooting and fishing. They are also doctors, great at administering salsaparilla and other simples, and at prescribing diet. In Gardner's time Buchan's "Domestic Medicine", translated into Portuguese, was the book; now the Formulary of Chernoviz must have made a little fortune; it is part of our grandfathers. Homœopathy throughout the Brazil is in high favour, and generally preferred to the "old school" and the "regular mode of practice". The choice is the result, I presume, of easy action upon the high nervous temperament of the race, and the chemist who deals in the similia similibus, makes more money than his brother the allopath.

* This is still the custom of Turkey, Egypt, and Persia. On the Rio das Velhas metal is preferred to the more frangible material; for everywhere in the Brazil negroes break whatever they handle.

** The establisher of homœopathy in the Brazil, who corresponds with Dr. B. Mure, a Frenchman, a most active and energetic proselytizer, who worked the press with unwearied energy. "You and I are the only men who love homœopathy for its own sake," Hahnemann said to him. He died I believe on the Red Sea, riding his favourite hobby-horse towards and for the benefit of India. The "Instituto Homeopatico do Brasil" published his "Practica Elementar," and it has reached several editions.

Richard F. Burton, *Explorations of the Highlands of Brazil with a Full Account of the Gold and Diamond Mines.* Vol. II: Greenwood, 1969. London: Tinsley Brothers, 1869.

• • •

SUBSISTENCE AGRICULTURE

Manioc was the staple crop of Northeastern Brazil. It was a rather hearty plant, but the process of cultivating it and making it edible was difficult. Producers had to exercise care in processing the manioc, for the plant was poisonous unless treated properly. It was nonetheless a staple food of Brazilians. Daniel P. Kidder traveled extensively in Brazil during the 1840s, visiting most of the big cities. His goal was to inform Americans about Brazil, a country about which his audience knew little.

MANIOC, FROM KIDDER, *BRAZIL AND THE BRAZILIANS*

Mandioca is difficult of cultivation,—the more common species requiring from twelve to eighteen months to ripen. Its roots have a great tendency to spread. Cut slips of the plant are inserted in large hills, which at the same time counteract this tendency, and furnish it with a dry soil, which the mandioca prefers. The roots, when dug, are a fibrous texture, corresponding in appearance to those of the long parsnip. The process of preparation is first to boil them, then remove the rind, after which the pieces are held by the hand in contact with a circular grater turned by water-power. The pulverized material is then placed in sacks, several of which, thus filled, are subjected to the action of a screw-press for the expulsion of the poisonous liquid. The masses thus solidified by pressure are beaten fine in mortars. The substance is next transferred to open ovens, or concave plates, heated beneath, where it is constantly and rapidly stirred until quite dry. The appearance of the farinha, when well prepared, is very white and beautiful, although its particles are rather coarse. It is found upon every Brazilian table, and forms a great variety of healthy and palatable dishes. The fine substance deposited by the juice of the mandioca, when preserved, standing a short time, constitutes the *tapioca* of commerce, so well known in the culinary departments of North America and Europe, and is now a valuable export from Brazil.

Another species, called the Aipim (manihot Aipim) is common. It is destitute of all poisonous qualities, and is boiled or roasted, and is but little inferior to the potato or the large Italian chestnut. It has further the advantage of requiring but eight months to ripen, although it cannot be converted into farinha.

Daniel P. Kidder, *Brazil and the Brazillians*. Philadelphia: Childs & Peterson, 1857, p. 102.

• • •

EVERYDAY LIFE

The daily chores were the same for women in the country and the city. The women all had to clean the family's clothes. Daniel Kidder here observes women from Rio de Janeiro washing in an idyllic stream. It was hard work despite the picturesque scene.

LAUNDRY, FROM KIDDER, *BRAZIL AND THE BRAZILIANS*

A shallow but limpid brook gurgles along a wide and deep ravine, lying between two precipitous spurs of the Corcovado Mountain. Passing up its banks, you see scores of *lavandeiras*, or washer women, standing in the stream and beating their clothes upon the boulders of rock which lie scattered along the bottom. Many of these washerwomen go from the city early in the morning, carrying their huge bundles of solid linen on their heads, and at evening return with them, purified in the stream and bleached in the sun. fires are smoking in various places, where they cook their meals; and groups of infant children are seen playing around, some of whom are large enough to have toddled after their mothers; but most of them have been carried there on the backs of the heavily-burdened servants. Female slaves, of every occupation, may be seen carrying about their children . . . .

Daniel P. Kidder, *Brazil and the Brazilians*. Philadelphia: Childs & Peterson, 1857, p. 102.

Traveler Henry Koster describes the tribulations country people endured at the hands of arbitrary local authorities. Henry Koster, an Englishman born and brought up in Portugal and fluent in Portuguese, went to Brazil in 1809 and stayed for six years. Koster journeyed all over the then Portuguese colony. He went into the Northeast, all along the coast, visiting many of the secondary cities of the colony.

INDIANS, FROM KOSTER, *TRAVELS IN BRAZIL*

The Indians of these villages, and indeed of all those which I passed through, are Christians; though it is said that some few of them follow in secret their own heathenish rites, paying adoration to the *maracá*, and practicing all the customs of their religion. When the Roman Catholic religion does take root in them, it of necessity degenerates into the most abject superstition. An adherence to superstitious rites, whether of Roman Catholic ordination or prescribed by their own undefined faith, appears to be the only part of their character in which they show any constancy. Each village has its priest, who is oftentimes a vicar, and resident for life upon the spot. A director is also attached to each village, who is supposed to be a white man; he has great power over the persons within his jurisdiction. If a proprietor of land is in want of workmen he applies to the director, who agrees for the price at which the daily labor is to be paid, and he commands one of his chief Indians to take so many men, and proceed with them to the estate for which they are hired. The laborers receive the money themselves, and expend it as they please; but the bargains thus made are usually below the regular price of labor. Each village has two *juízes ordinaries* or mayors, who act for one year. One *juíz* is a white man, and the other an Indian; but it may easily be supposed that the former has, in fact, the management. These *juízes* have the power of putting suspicious persons into confinement, and of punishing for small crimes; those of more importance wait for the *correição* or circuit of the *ouvidor* of the captaincy. Each village contains a town hall and prison. The administration of justice in the sertão is generally spoken of as most wretchedly bad; every crime obtains impunity by the payment of a sum of money. An innocent person is sometimes punished through the interest of a great man, whom he may have offended, and the murderer escapes who has the good fortune to be under the protection of a powerful patron. This proceeds still more from the feudal state of the country than from the corruption of the magistrates, who might often be inclined to do their duty, and yet be aware that their exertions would be of no avail, and would possibly prove fatal to themselves. The Indians have likewise their *capitães-móres*, and this title is conferred for life; it gives the holder some power over his fellows, but as it is among them unaccompanied by the possession of property. . . .

The Indians . . . lives are certainly not passed in a pleasant manner under the eye of a director, by whom they are imperiously treated; consequently it is not surprising that they should do all in their power to leave their villages, and be free from an immediate superior; but even when they have escaped from the irksome dominion of the director, they never settle in one place. The Indian scarcely ever plants for himself, or if he does, rarely waits the crop; he sells his maize or manioc for half its value, before it is fit to be gathered, and removes to some other district. His favorite pursuits are fishing and hunting; a lake or rivulet will alone induce him to be stationary for any length of time. He has a sort of independent feeling, which makes him spurn at any thing like a wash to deprive him of his own free agency; to the director he submits, because it is out of his power to resist. An Indian can never be persuaded to address the master to whom he may have hired himself, by the turn of Senhor, though it is made use of by the whites in speaking to each other, and by all other free people in the country; but the Negros also use it in speaking to their masters, therefore the Indian will not; he addresses his temporary master by the term of *amo* or *partão*, protector or patron. The reluctance to use the term of Senhor may perhaps have commenced with the immediate descendants of those who were in slavery, and thus the objection may have become traditional. They may refuse to give by courtesy what was once required from them by law. However, if it began in this manner, it is not now continued for the same reason, as none of those with whom I conversed, and they were very many, appeared to know that their ancestors had been obliged to work as slaves.

The women however do not, among these semi-barbarians, perform the principal drudgery; if the husband is at home, he fetches water from the rivulet and fuel from the wood; he builds the hut while his wife takes shelter in some neighbor's shed. But if they travel, she has her young children to carry, the pots, the baskets, and the excavated gourds, while the husband takes his wallet of goatskin and his hammock rolled up upon his back, his fishing net and his arms, and walks in the rear. The children are washed on the day of their birth in the nearest brook or pool of water. Both men and the women are cleanly in many of their habits, and particularly in those relating to their persons.

Henry Koster, *Travels in Brazil.* Carbondale: Southern University Press, 1966. London, 1816.

German Carl Sartorius (1796–1872) migrated to Mexico in 1824, eventually settling in the state of Veracruz, where he owned a sugar plantation. He became an avid observer of the plants and animals of the region with connections to the Smithsonian Institution in Washington, D.C. He wrote the book, in 1850, from which we have taken a number of selections. Sartorius was not one to present a favorable picture of the lower classes. But in his description of the modest Indian dwelling, one can almost detect admiration.

INDIAN DWELLING, FROM SARTORIUS, *MEXICO ABOUT 1850*

The Indian's dwelling is in keeping with his simple person. In the warmer, well-wooded regions he generally builds his hut of wood. Unhewn logs support the beams and roof, are driven into the ground, and creeping plants which twine around them, supply the place of frame-work. Straw or palm-leaves constitute the roofing; the walls are made of sticks of bamboo, or slender stakes which afford the light free ingress to the interior. The roof on one side is commonly prolonged into a porch, supported upon posts. This main building is ordinarily about twenty five feet long, and fifteen wide, without partitions within. A smaller one is often joined to this to answer the purpose of kitchen.

Upon the higher table-lands the houses are built of unburnt brick (also of stones plastered with mud) with a flat roof constructed of beams laid close together with a covering of finely washed clay, which is stamped with great care. In the mountains one often sees roofs covered with shingles, and in the plains where the agave abounds, the flower-stalks and leaves of this plant are used for the purpose, while the walls—so-called dry walls—are built of stone without mortar.

Inside the hut, upon a floor of earth just as nature formed it, burns day and night the sacred fire of the domestic hearth. Near it, stand the *metate* and *metalpile*, a flat and a cylindrical stone for crushing the maize, and the earthen pan (*comale*) for baking the maize bread. A few unglazed earthen pots and dishes, a large water pitcher, a drinking cup and dipper of gourd-shell constitute the whole wealth of the Indian's cottage, a few rude carvings, representing saints, the decoration. Neither table nor benches cumber the room within, mass of rushes or palm-leaves answer both for seat and table. They serve as beds too for their rest at night, and for their final rest in the grave.

The utensils of the man, as a mattock and a hoe, together with a few strings and nets, hang upon the wall, and close by, the weaving apparatus of the women, consisting only of a few simple rods. A number of baskets of woven palm-leaves suspended from the beams above by grass-cordage, contain the scanty provision of all kinds, salt, beans, rice, eggs, cotton, soap etc. These baskets take the place of chests and cupboards, and are thus hung aloft to protect the contents from the inroads of dogs, ants and children. Upon a longer line hangs a contrivance somewhat larger, perhaps three feet long by two wide, of twigs bound together, in construction similar to the traps in which boys catch titmice. The inside is covered with a piece of matting. Its purpose does not long remain a mystery, for a half naked Indian baby now and then lets his voice be heard; whereupon a push sets the basket in motion like a swing; and the little aeronaut is again brought to a state of slumber.

Carl Sartorius, *Mexico About 1850.* (*Mexico. Landscapes and Popular Sketches.* 1858) Reprint. Stuttgart: FA Brockhaus Komm, 1961.

Brantz Mayer (1809–1879), a lawyer and later a prolific author, was secretary of the legation of the U.S. diplomatic mission to Mexico in 1843. Mexico as it was and as it is evidently stirred some controversy over its analysis of the Mexicans. Nonetheless, he provides a meticulously detailed description of a modest home in central Mexico.

HOUSE IN THE COUNTRYSIDE, FROM MAYER, *MEXICO AS IT WAS AND AS IT IS*

The house is built of mud and reeds, matted together; that is, there are four walls without other aperture but a door, while a thatch, supported on poles, spreads on either side from the roof-tree, forming a porch in front. This thatch is not allowed to touch the tops of the walls, but between them and it, all around the house, a space of five or six feet has been left, my means of which a free circulation of air is kept up within. The interior (of one room,) is in perfect keeping with this aboriginal simplicity. Along the western wall there are a number of wretched engravings of saints, with inscriptions and verses beneath them; next, a huge picture of the Virgin of Guadalupe, with tarnished gilded rays, blaze in the center; and near the corner is nailed a massive cross, with the figure of our Saviour apparently bleeding at every pore. A reed and spear are crossed below it, and large wreaths and festoons of marigolds are hung around. Six tressels, with reeds spread over them, stand against the wall; and in one corner a dilapidated canopy, with a tattered curtain, rears its pretentious head to do the honors of state-bedstead. The floor is of earth, and, in a corner, are safely stowed our saddles, bridles, guns, pistols, holsters, swords and spurs—so that taking a sidelong glance at the whole establishment, you might well doubt whether you were in a stable, church, sleeping-room or chicken-coop!

Don Miguel Benito—the owner and proprietor of this valuable catalogue of domestic comforts—received us with great cordiality. He is a man some fifty years of age; delights in a shirt, the sleeves of which have been so long rolled up, that there is no longer anything to roll down; and a pair of those elastic leather-breeches that last one's life-time in Mexico, and grow to any size that may be required, as the fortunate owner happens to fatten with his years. Not the least curious part of Don Miguel's household, is his female establishment . . . . As not less than a dozen women, of all colors and complexions, hover about his dwellings; while at least an equal number of little urchins, with light hair and dark, (but all with an extraordinary resemblance to the Don,) roll over the mud floors of the neighboring huts or amuse themselves by *lassoing* the chickens.

G——, the caterer of our mess, thought it but a due compliment to Don Miguel (who does not disdain to receive your money) to order supper—though we resolved to fall back in case of necessity upon our own stores and accordingly, unpacked some pots of soup and sardines.

In the course of an hour, a board was spread upon four sticks, and in the middle of it was placed a massive brown earthen platter, with the stew. At the same time, a dirty copper spoon and a hot tortillia were laid before each of us. Although we had determined to hold ourselves in reserve for our soups, yet there was but little left of the savory mess. Our turtle, flanked with lemons and claret, then came into play; and the repast was ended by another smoking platter of the universal frijoles.

Wild and primitive as was the scene among these simple Indians, I have seldom passed a pleasanter evening, enlivened with song and wit. When we crept to our reed tressels and serapes, at eleven o'clock, I found that the state-bed was already occupied by a smart-looking fellow from the West Coast, (who I take to have been rather deeply engaged in the contraband), and his young wife—a lively looking lass, rather whiter than the rest of the brood—who had spruced herself up on our arrival. Twelve of our party lodged together in that capacious apartment, while Don Miguel betook himself, with the rest of his household, to mats under the porch.

Brantz Mayer, *Mexico As It Was and As It Is.* New York: J. Winchester, New World Press, 1844.

The sertão, the name for much of the Northeast of Brazil, nowadays the most desperately poor area of the country, was difficult terrain. Koster traveled during the rainy season.

SERTÃO, FROM KOSTER, *TRAVELS IN BRAZIL*

Unlike the peons of the country in the vicinity of the river Plata, the sertanejo has about him his wife and family, and lives in comparative comfort. The cottages are small and are built of mud, but afford quite sufficient shelter in so fine a climate; they are covered with tiles where they are to be had, or, as is more general, with the leaves of the carnaúba. Hammocks usually supply the place of beds, and are by far more comfortable, and these are likewise frequently used as chairs. Most of the better sort of cottages contain a table, but the usual practice is for the family to squat down upon a mat in a circle, with the bowls, dishes, or gourds in the center, thus to eat their meals upon the floor. Knives and forks are not much known, and are not at all made use of by the lower orders. It is the custom in every house, from the highest to the lowest, as in former times, and indeed the same practice prevails in all the parts of the country which I visited, for a liver basin, or one of earthenware, or a *cuia*, and a fringed cambric towel, or one that is made of the coarse cotton cloth of the country, to be handed round, that all those who are going to sit down and eat may wash their hands; and the same ceremony takes place again after the meal is finished. Of the gourds great use is made in domestic arrangements; they're cut in two, and the pulp is scooped out, the rind is dried, and these rude vessels serve almost every purpose of earthenware—water is carried in them, etc. and they are likewise used as measures. They vary from six inches in circumference to about three feet, and are usually rather of an oval shape. The gourd when whole is called *cabaça*, and the half of the rind is called *cuia*. It is a creeping plant, and grows spontaneously in many parts, but in others the people plant it among the manioc.

The conversation of the sertanejos usually turns upon the state of their cattle or of women, and, occasionally, accounts of adventures which took place at Recife or at some other town. The merits or demerits of the priests with whom they happen to be acquainted are likewise discussed, and their irregular practices are made a subject of ridicule. The dress of the men has already been described, but when they are at home a shirt and drawers alone remain. The women their only dress is a shift and petticoat, no stockings, and oftentimes no shoes; but when they leave home, which is very seldom, an addition is made of a large piece of coarse white cloth, either of their own or of European manufacture, and this is thrown over the head and shoulders; a pair of shoes is likewise then put on. They are good horsewomen, and the high Portuguese saddle serves the purpose of a sidesaddle very completely. I never saw any Brazilian woman riding, as is the case occasionally in Portugal, in the manner that men do. Their employment consists in household arrangements entirely, for the men even milk the cows and goats; the women spin and work with the needle. No females of free birth are ever seen employed in any kind of labor in the open air, excepting in that of occasionally fetching wood or water, if the men are not at home. The children generally run about naked until a certain age, but this is often seen even in Recife; to the age of six or seven years, boys are allowed to run about without any clothing. Formerly, I mean before the commencement of a direct trade with England, both sexes dressed in the coarse cotton cloth which is made in the country the petticoats of this cloth were sometimes tinged with a red dye, which was obtained from the bark of the *cuipina* tree, a native of their woods; and even now this dye is used for tinging fishing nets, as it is said that those which have undergone this process last longer.

In those times, a dress of the common printed cotton of English or Portuguese manufacture cost from eight to twelve *mil reis*, from two to three guineas, owing to the monopoly of the trade, by which the merchants of Recife put what price they pleased upon their commodities; other things were in proportion. Owing to the enormous prices, European articles of dress could of course only be possessed by the rich people. However, since the opening of the ports to foreign trade, English goods are finding their way all over the country, and the hawkers are now a numerous body of men.

The women seldom appear, and when they are seen do not take any part in the conversation, unless it be some one good wife who rules the roost; if they are present at all when the men are talking, they stand or squat down upon the ground, in the doorway leading to the interior of the house and merely listen.

The food of the inhabitants of the sertão consists chiefly of meat, of which they make three meals; and to this is added the flour of the manioc stirred up into paste, or rice sometimes supplies its place. The bean, which is commonly called in England and French bean, is a favorite food; it is suffered to run to seed, and is only plucked up when quite dry and hard. I have often been surprised to see how little service maize is to them as food, but yet it is occasionally used. In default of these, the paste of the carnaúba is made; and I have seen meat eaten with curds. Of green vegetables they know nothing, and they laugh at the idea of eating any kind of salad. The wild fruits are numerous, and to be obtained in any quantities, but few species are cultivated; among the latter are the watermelon and the plantain. The cheese of the sertão, when it is fresh, is excellent; but after four or five weeks, it becomes hard and tough. On the towns even of the sertão, rancid Irish butter is the only kind which is to be obtained. Wherever the lands admit of it, these people plant manioc, rice, etc. but much, I may say the greater part of the vegetable portion of their food, is brought either from more fertile districts near to the coast, or from the settlements still further back—the valleys and skirts of the Cariris, Serra do Teixeira, and other inland mountains.

The trade of the sertão consists in receiving small quantities of European manufactured goods; the cotton cloth of the country, of which they make some among themselves; a small portion of European white earthenware, and considerable quantities of the dark brown ware of the country, which is made for the most part by the Indians who live in the districts that contain the proper kind of clay; rum in small casks; butter, tobacco, snuff, sugar or treacle made up in cakes, spurs, bits of bridles, and other gear for their horses, excepting the saddles, of which the greater part are made in their own districts; gold and silver ornaments also find a market to a certain amount. The peddlers travel about from village to village, and from one estate to another, bartering their commodities for cattle of all kinds, cheese, and hides of horned cattle. A colt of from two to three years sells for about one guinea; a horse broken in for the packsaddle, for two or three guineas; a horse broken in for mounting, from five to six guineas. A bullock of two years, ten shillings; a full grown ox, one guinea and a half; a cow varies much, according to the quantity of milk, from one guinea to five guineas. A sheep, from two to three shillings; a goat for slaughter is worth even less, but a good milk goat is valued at one guinea, and sometimes higher. Children are frequently suckled by goats, which increases the value of these animals. The goat that has been so employed always obtains the name of *comadre*, the term which is made use of between the mother and godmother of a child; and so general is this, the she-goats are frequently called *comadres*, without having had the honor of suckling a young master or mistress. Dogs are sometimes valued at from one to two guineas, and even higher, if they are good sporting, or good house and baggage dogs. A fowl is as dear as a sheep or goat; and in one instance I paid four times the money for one of these birds that I had given for a kid. The hawkers seldom obtain money in exchange for their wares; they take whatever is offered, and hire people to assist in conveying the cattle or produce to a market, where they are exchanged for goods, and then the owner again returns. A twelve-month is sometimes passed in turning over the property once; but the profits are usually enormous, two or three hundred per cent.

Henry Koster, *Travels in Brazil.* Carbondale: Southern University Press, 1966. London, 1816.

Sartorius in this passage took pains to differentiate between mestizo and Indians. It was, perhaps, his attempt to explore the interrelationship between race and class in Mexico. People often were labeled by their dress, language, wealth, and habits more than the color of their skin.

MESTIZO DWELLING, FROM SARTORIUS, *MEXICO ABOUT 1850*

The Mestizo lives in general more simply than the Creole; indeed the majority have nearly the same mode of life as the Indians, but with somewhat more comfort and convenience in their houses. We commonly find, however, simply a bench and a table, and some board bedsteads covered with mats, and having a few sheep-skins for pillows and bolsters. One usually meets with a kitchen detached from the house, where the family take their three meals a day, in order that they may have their maize bread warm from the fire. At meals the men sit upon low stools and take the plate upon their knees; the women sit upon mats. Knives and forks are not used. The food of the Mestizoes is distinguished from that of the Indians, by consisting chiefly of meat. The cooking is very greasy, and they eat in general much pork. On festive occasions there is a great slaughter of hens and turkies, for the Mestizoes raise poultry in abundance, and greatly enjoy eggs with their beans at breakfast; fruits and confectionary are a necessity with them, and after every meal a lump of sugar is eaten to prepare them for drinking copious draughts of water.

The manners of the white Creoles have for the most part passed over to the Mestizoes; among the wealthier, one will hardly find a difference, while the poorer portion more nearly resemble the Indians in simplicity of life and household arrangements. This lies in the nature of the case, since the Mestizo constitutes a connecting link between the two dissimilar races, an organ through which the white race gradually assimilates itself to the brown.

Carl Sartorius, *Mexico About 1850.* (*Mexico. Landscapes and Popular Sketches.* 1858) Reprint. Stuttgart: FA Brockhaus Komm, 1961.

Cowboys, called gauchos in Argentina, Uruguay, and Brazil, llaneros in Venezuela, and vaqueros in Mexico, were to outsiders the most colorful residents of the countryside. Charged with collecting cattle in scarcely populated regions, often working autonomously, they were legendarily independent of spirit. They were, because of their skill and mobility (they could leave employment in an instant on horseback), usually the highest paid rural workers. Despite their relative freedom and high pay, they led hardscrabble lives. They had few possessions and traveled light.

GAUCHO, FROM HEAD, *JOURNEYS ACROSS THE PAMPAS*

The situation of the gaucho is naturally independent of the political troubles which engross the attention of the inhabitants of the towns. The population or number of these gauchos is very small, and a great distances from each other: they are scattered here and there over the face of the country. Many of these people are descended from the best families in Spain; they possess good manners, and often very noble sentiments: the life they lead is very interesting—they generally inhabit the hut in which they were born, and in which their fathers and grandfathers lived before them, although it appears to the stranger to possess few of the allurements of *dulce domum.* The huts are built in the same simple form; for although luxury has ten thousand plans and elevations for the frail abode of its more frail tenant, yet the hut in all countries is the same, and therefore there is no difference between that of the South American gaucho, and the Highlander of Scotland, excepting that the former is built of mud, and covered with long yellow grass, while the other is formed of stones, and thatched with heather. The materials of both are the immediate produce of the soil, and both are so blended in color with the face of the country, that it is often difficult to distinguish them; and as the pace at which one gallops in south America is rapid, and the country flat, one scarcely discovers the dwelling before one is at the door.

The corral is about fifty or hundred yards in diameter, enclosed by a number of strong rough posts, the ends of which are struck into the ground . . . . The ground around the hut and corral is covered with bones and carcasses of horses, bullocks' horns, wool, &c., which give it the smell and appearance of an ill-kept dog-kennel in England.

The hut consists generally of one room, in which all the family live, boys, girls, men, women, and children, all huddled together. The kitchen is a detached shed a few yards off: there are always holes, both in the walls and in the roof of the hut, which one at first considers as singular marks of the indolence of the people. In the summer this abode is so filled with fleas and vinchucas (which are bugs as large as black beetles) that the whole family sleep on the ground in front of their dwelling; and when the traveler arrives at night, and after unsaddling his horse walks among this sleeping community, he may place the saddle or recado on which he is to sleep close to the companion most suited to his fancy:—an admirer of innocence may lie down by the side of a sleeping infant; a melancholy may slumber near an old black woman; and one who admires the fairer beauties of creation may very demurely lay his head on his saddle, within a few inches of the idol he adores. However, there is nothing to assist the judgment but bare feet and ankles of all the slumbering group, for their heads and bodies are covered and disguised by the skin and poncho which cover them.

In winter the people sleep in the hut, and the scene is a very singular one. As soon as the traveler's supper is ready, the great iron spit on which the beef has been roasted is brought into the hut, and the point is struck into the ground; the gaucho then offers his guest the skeleton of a horse's head, and he and several of the family, on similar seats, sit round the spit, from which with their long knives they cut very large mouthfuls.

The hut is lighted by a feeble lamp, made of bullock's tallow; and it is warmed by a fire of charcoal: on the walls of the hut are hung, upon bones, two or three bridles and spurs, and several lassos and balls: on the ground are several dark-looking heaps, which one can never clearly distinguish; on sitting down upon these when tired, I have often heard a child scream underneath me, and have occasionally been mildly asked by a young woman, what I wanted?—at other times up has jumped an immense dog! While I was once warming my hands at the fire of charcoal, seated on a horse's head, looking at the black roof in a reverie, and fancying I was quite by myself, I felt something touch me, and saw two naked black children leaning over the charcoal in the attitude of two toads: they had crept from under some of the ponchos, and afterwards found that many other persons, as well as some hens sitting upon eggs, were also in the hut. In sleeping in these huts, the cock has often hopped upon my back to crow in the morning; however, as soon as it is daylight, everybody gets up.

The life of the gaucho is very interesting. Born in the rude hut, the infant gaucho receives little attention, but is left to swing from the roof in a bullock's hide, the corners of which are drawn towards each other by four strips of hide. In the first year of his life he crawls about without clothes, and I have more than once seen a mother give a child of this age a sharp knife, a foot long, to play with. As soon as he walks, his infantine amusements are those which prepare him for the occupations of his future life: with a lasso made of twine he tries to catch little birds, or the dogs, as they walk in and out of the hut. By the time he is four years old he is on horseback, and immediately becomes useful by assisting to drive the cattle into the corral.

His amusements and his occupations soon become more manly—careless of the vizcacheras (the holes of an animal called vizcacha) which undermine the plains, and which are very dangerous, he gallops after the ostrich, the gama, the lion, and the tiger; he catches them with his balls; and with his lasso he daily assists in catching the wild cattle, and in dragging them to the hut either for slaughter, or to be marked. He breaks in the young horses in the manner which I have described, and in these occupations is often away from his hut many days, changing his horse as soon as the animal is tired, and sleeping on the ground. As his constant food is beef and water, his constitution is so strong that he is able to endure great fatigue; and the distances he will ride, and the number of hours that he will remain on horseback, would hardly be credited. The unrestrained freedom of such a life he fully appreciates; and, unacquainted with subjection of any sort, his mind is often filled with sentiments of liberty, which are as noble as they are harmless, although they of course partake of the wild habits of his life.

The gaucho has by many people been accused of indolence; those who visit his hut find him at the door with his arms folded, and his poncho thrown over his left shoulder like a Spanish cloak; his hut is in holes, and would evidently be made more comfortable by a few hours' labor: in a beautiful climate, he is without fruit or vegetables; surrounded by cattle, he is often without milk; he lives without bread, and he has no food but beef and water and anyone who will live with the gaucho, and will follow him through his exertions, will find that he is anything but indolent, and his surprise will be that he is able to continue a life of so much fatigue. It is true that the gaucho has no luxuries, but the great feature of his character is that he is a person without wants: accustomed constantly to live in the open air, and to sleep on the ground, he does not consider that a few holes in his hut deprive of its comfort. It is not that he does not like the taste of milk, but he prefers being without it to the everyday occupation of going in search of it. He might, it is true, make cheese, and sell it for money, but if he has got a good saddle and good spurs, he does not consider that money has much value: in fact, he is contented with his lot; and when one reflects that, in the increasing series of human luxuries, there is no point that produces contentment, one cannot but feel that there is perhaps as much philosophy as folly in the gaucho's determination to exist without wants; and the life he leads is certainly more noble than if he was slaving from morning till night to get other food for his body or other garments to cover it.

The character of the gaucho is often very estimable; he is always hospitable—at his hut the traveler will always find friendly welcome, and he will often be received with a natural dignity of manner which is very remarkable, and which he scarcely expects to meet with in such a miserable-looking hovel. On entering the hut, the gaucho has constantly risen to offer me his seat, which I have declined, and many compliments and bows have passed, until I have accepted his offer, which is the skeleton of a horse's head. It is curious to see them invariably take off their hats to each other as they enter into a room which has no window, a bullock's hide for a door, and but little roof.

The habits of the women are very curious: they have literally nothing to do; the great plains which surround them offer them no motive to walk, they seldom ride, and their lives certainly are very indolent and inactive. They have all, however, families, whether married or not; and once when I inquired of a young woman employed in nursing a very pretty child, who was the father of the "criatura", she replied, "Quién sabe?".

The religion which is professed throughout the provinces of the Rio de la Plata is the Roman Catholic, but it is very different in different places. During the reign of the Spaniards, the monks and priests had everywhere very great influence; and the dimensions of the churches at Buenos Aires, Luján, Mendoza, &c., show the power and riches they possessed, and the greedy ambition which governed them. It is a sad picture to see a number of small, wretched-looking huts surrounding a church whose haughty elevation is altogether inapplicable to the humility of the Christian religion;

Once a year the men and women are called upon to live for nine days in a sort of barrack, which, as a great favor, I was allowed to visit. It is filled with little cells, and the men and women, at different times, are literally shut up in these holes, to fast and whip themselves. I asked several people seriously whether this punishment was bona fide performed, and they assured me that most of them whipped themselves till they brought blood. One day, I was talking very earnestly to a person at Mendoza, at the hotel, when a poor-looking monk arrived with a little image surrounded with flowers: this image my friend was obliged to kiss, and the monk then took it to every individual in the hotel—to the landlord, his servants, and even to the black cook, who all kissed it, and then of course paid for the honor. The cook gave the monk two eggs.

Francis Bond Head, *Journeys Across the Pampas and Among the Andes.* Carbondale: Southern Illinois University Press, 1967. Originally published in 1866.

· · ·

Although Latin Americans often lived beyond the reach of priests, many of whom were loath to venture into the discomfort of the countryside, they were religious in their own ways. Country Catholicism was not always the same as that practiced in the cities. Many folk customs melded into church traditions. Religious festivals and other religious rites such as baptism, marriage, and funerals formed the heart of village social life and entertainment.

RELIGIOUS FESTIVAL, FROM KIDDER,
SKETCHES OF A RESIDENCE

FESTIVAL IN THE VILLAGE

"On the 3rd of July, 1793, Souza Coutinho, the twenty-fifth captain-general of the Gran Pará and Rio negro, decreed that there should annually be held on this spot a general festival in honor of our Lady of Nazareth. The brotherhood of the church was instructed thenceforward to solemnize the occasion with a novena, a chanted mass, and a procession. The image should be deposited in the chapel of the government palace, on the eve of the first day of the novena, so as on the following day to be conveyed, in public procession, to the church."

Such an institution accorded too well with the religious genius of the people, not to be zealously observed and handed down to their children. Preparations were made on an extensive scale some time in advance of the festa. The road leading from the city to the church extends most of the way through a forest, and requires every year to be cleaned of its shrubbery afresh. The church stands at one corner of the square mentioned above. This square is the only cleared ground in the neighborhood. As in the road, the surface of this opening needs to have the weeds and brushwood annually cleared off. Parts of it are generally burned over. Around the area, barracas, a species of board tents, are constructed, for the accommodations of families who wish to remove to the spot during these holidays. Towards evening of the day fixed upon for opening the festivities, a long procession, bearing the image, moved slowly out of the city towards the hermitage, or church in the woods.

First preceded a company of outriders, military officers, and citizens on horseback; then followed a cart, called the car of triumph, drawn by two oxen, and surmounted by large fantastic frame-work, covered with painted cloth. Within the vehicle was a knot of boys, whose dignified office it was to edify the multitude by firing off rockets, of which they had a large supply.

Next came a band of martial music, and a company of cavalry with drawn swords. The civil escort was now in order. It consisted of some twenty-five persons on horseback, and eight or ten carriages, which were understood to be nearly all the city could muster. Finally came the president of the province, in full uniform, and after him a sege, bearing a single priest, with the image of Nossa Senhora in his lap. It was not more than two feet high, but was dressed out with a great array of finery. Several foot companies of military closed up the procession, while hundreds of people thronged around as spectators. The chief peculiarity that I observed in the crowd, as compared with collections of people seen in other cities of Brazil, was the unusual number of females, of different shades of color, between black and yellow, who were gaily dressed, and ornamented with gold and jewelry in the greatest profusion. Many of these females carried trays of sugar toys upon their heads, and little stools in their hands, upon which they occasionally sat down to vend their commodities.

The people were generally quite well dressed, and very orderly in their appearance. The image once deposited in the church the novena commenced, and was continued on the eight successive evenings. This was the chief religious exercise of the occasion. It was enlivened by the performances of a band of instrumental music, being, as one would expect, preceded and followed by a deafening discharge of sky-rockets.

Masses of people crowd around the church during this service, and join in singing the litany to the saints and the Virgin. They afterward disperse, and stroll about the grounds, or resort to parties, balls, and gaming clubs. I was sorry to observe that of all the other amusements, gaming seemed to attract most attention, and excite most interest.

On the splendid moonlight nights of the season the city would be nearly emptied of people, and multitudes, *todo o mundo,* would crowd to the Nazareth feast; how few of them all had any proper idea of the character of Him who came out of Nazareth to take away the sins of his people!

The church on this spot was quite small, and constructed so much like a dwelling-house as to have a double veranda, above and below, on three of its sides. In the upper veranda hung the hammocks of the soldiers on guard. In front stood a species of alpendre, or rancho, with a tiled roof. Within the mass-house were two altars—that surrounded by the image borne in the procession stood on the right, and was unusually elevated. One would have supposed that this image came from France, for its tout ensemble reminded the beholder of toy-shop dolls of the largest size. Two wide ribbons, one green and the other red, extended from the dress over the altar, and hung down towards the floor. Hundreds of people crowded around to enjoy, in turn, the privilege of kneeling down and kissing these ribbons! On the opposite wall hung a collection of plaster forms, representing all manner of ulcerated limbs and diseased members, that were said to have been miraculously cured by our Lady. Near these hung a rude painting, designed to show an apparition of said Lady to a sick person, who, of course, recovered. Lest this event should not be comprehended it was explained in the vulgar tongue—*Milagre que fez Nossa Senhora de Nazaré!*

How changed in appearance was this whole scene when visited in the morning at early dawn. The crowd had disappeared. Here and there an individual might be seen sleeping on the ground—others were taking rest in their unopened barracas. No romance of moonbeams, or glimmering tapers, now lend enchantment to the half-defined objects that address the sight. The artificial decorations so profusely displayed, are now seen in their true colors. Hangings of matting, of muslin, and of calico, together with national and signal flags, are suspended around the barracas, and occasionally seen elevated on poles, but every thing is lifeless and dull, indicating the results that might be expected to follow the stupid amusements and general debauch of the preceding night. I often observed that the stars and stripes of the United States seemed to be a favorite ornament on such occasions as this, and here a single establishment displayed two United States' flags.

General reflections upon the character and tendency of such a scene of festivities, so absorbing to a whole community, and so long continued, seem unnecessary. If it had no religious pretensions it would be less exceptionable. But for a people to be made to think themselves doing God's service, while mingling in such amusements and follies, is painfully lamentable.

The whole feast, indeed, passed off without any public disorder. But who was the wiser, the better, or the happier for it? It would not have been difficult to find those who were more debauched, and more miserable; and it was melancholy to reflect that many might have there commenced a career of gambling, of prostitution, or of some other vice, which would end in their utter ruin. While these results could hardly fail to occur, nothing like a sermon was delivered during the whole ten days, or any effort made to instruct or moralize the community.

The evening and morning scenes that may be enjoyed at Pará are indescribably beautiful.

Daniel P, Kidder, *Sketches of a Residence and Travels in Brazil.* Vol. II. Philadelphia: Sorin and Hall, 1845.

Priests who lived in the countryside were often the defacto leaders of the community. As Gardner points out, to his astonishment country priests did not always adhere to vows of chastity or devote their days to prayer and contemplation.

PRIESTS, FROM GARDNER, *TRAVELS IN THE INTERIOR OF BRAZIL*

When we arrived, there were three priests in the Villa, one of whom died during our stay. These like most others I met with, instead of being examples of morality to the people, were immoral to an extent almost past belief. The one who died, was an old man upwards of seventy-four years of age; he was a native of Santos in the province of San Paolo, and a cousin of the celebrated José Bonifacio de Andrade. Although a man of a very humane and benevolent disposition, and well educated, he left behind him a family of a dozen children by his own slaves, most of whom, with their mothers, were left in bondage, and were afterwards sold with his other effects for the payment of his debts. The Vigario Geral was a half cast, upwards of forty years of age, who had only been ordained a few years before; up to that time he was and still continues to be, the largest cattle farmer in the district. Having acquired as much Latin from the old priest, as would enable him to mumble over the service of the church, but without the least knowledge of theology, he went to the city of Goyaz, to purchase his ordination from the bishop; a short time afterwards he obtained by another purchase the vicar generalship of the district. About a month after my arrival in the Villa, I was sent for to attend a young slave belonging to him, a fine girl about sixteen years of age, who died of puerperal fever, a few days after giving birth to a child, of which he was the father; by the inhabitants, this man was as much detested, as the old priest had been loved and esteemed.

George Gardner, *Travels Through the Interior of Brazil, Principally Through the Northern Provinces and the Gold Diamond Districts During the Years 1836–1841.* Boston: Longwood Press, 1977. (1846)

MINING

The Portuguese discovered diamonds in Minas Gerais in the interior of Brazil during the seventeenth century. The industry continues to the present. Extracting the gems from the ground is excruciating work in often unbearable conditions.

MINING, FROM BURTON, *HIGHLANDS OF BRAZIL*

Prospecting for diamonds is done as follows: The vegetable humus, the underlying clay, and the desmonte, or inundation sand, are removed with the almocafre, till the labourers reach the gem-bearing "cascalho", or "gurgulho". This first work is usually an open cut a few feet square. The larger fragments of quartz are then removed by the hand, the gravel is washed in a "báco", "canôa," or "cuyaca", and finally, the batêa is used.

After the prospecting (provas) a concession to work diamantine ground is directed to, and is easily obtained in these days from Government. The applicant specifies the limits of the extent which he proposes to exploit. The land is put up at public auction, any one may bid, and it is knocked down to the highest offer. The owner of the soil has the right of pre-emption, and if only 0$200 per braça (Brazilian fathom) be called, the proprietor can take it. After the death of the concessionee, the digging in inherited by his wife, his children, or, in default of other heirs, by his brother.

Richard F. Burton, *Explorations of the Highlands of Brazil with a Full Account of the Gold and Diamond Mines.* Vol. II: Greenwood, 1969. London: Tinsley Brothers, 1869.

QUESTIONS

1. Do you think that the descriptions of plantation life proffered by Gardner, Agassiz, and Burton represent the realities of agricultural life?
2. Why is manioc so difficult to produce?
3. What conclusions can we draw from Daniel Kidder's description of the washerwomen?
4. Koster is very critical of harsh local authorities in Brazil. Why do you think that country people did not protest or even rebel against them?
5. Sartorius seems almost kind in his description of Indian dwellings. Why do you think he is uncritical, in light of his harsh words elsewhere in evaluating other aspects of indigenous life?
6. Contrast the descriptions of country homes presented by Sartorius and Mayer. What strikes you about the discrepancies?
7. Compare Henry Koster's depiction of the lives of the people of the sertão with that of other country people by other authors?
8. What do the gauchos have in common with the people of the sertão?
9. Do you think that the authors whose descriptions we have excerpted attempt to make their subjects appear more exotic than they are? Do you think the authors try to pick up on whatever customs and practices are furthest from those of the Europeans to make their books more salable?
10. Does religion seem to be important in the lives of country people? If what ways?

5   SLAVES

INTRODUCTION

The revolution that swept Haiti in the early 1790s effectively ended its reign as the world's largest sugar producer, resulting in the emergence of Cuba and the reemergence of Brazil as major exporters. Since sugar depended entirely on slaves for labor, the first half of the nineteenth century became an economic golden age for both slavery and sugar. At the same time, for economic and moral reasons, the British Empire sought the abolition of the slave trade and ultimately of slavery itself, and abolitionist sentiment grew in the Caribbean and Brazil. In this context, historians have tried to reconstruct what life was like for the slave population. Most recently they have emphasized that slaves built lives, despite their oppression, through subtle, complicated negotiations with their masters. Nonetheless, although slaves married, celebrated, survived, worshipped, and led complex lives, the vast majority were subjected to the harsh regimen of the field. In the selections that follow we will observe the lives of slaves, sometimes rather benign, but often brutalized and dehumanized.

All slaves were, of course, deprived of their liberty and often their humanity. Their everyday lives, however, varied considerably. First, the experiences of slaves born in Africa differed from those who were born in Brazil or elsewhere in the Americas. Slaves who had recently arrived from Africa entered into their new environment with no knowledge of their captors' language, nor were they familiar with Iberian or Christian customs. Importantly, too, the new slaves, badly weakened by the exigencies of the transatlantic passage, horrifying at its best, often fell victim to diseases for which their bodies had no immunities. Perhaps worst of all, they remembered what it had been like to be free. Slaves born in the Americas learned the local language and customs as children. They were not used to any other way of life or to freedom. Second, there were substantial differences between the lives of slaves in the cities and on the plantations. Urban slaves were either domestics or hired out by their owners to other employers. These urban slaves sometimes acquired skilled occupations or worked as factory hands. There were cases when slaves accumulated enough money on their own to buy freedom. Other slaves worked in the gold and diamond mines in the interior of Brazil. Lastly, there were wide variations between the experiences among plantation slaves. Those who worked in the fields endured long hours and hard labor. Those who had skilled occupations and those who worked in the owner's home experienced less harsh conditions. Work on the sugar plantation could be quite dangerous. Cutting the sugar cane with sharp machetes risked life and limb. Feeding the harvested cane into the pressing machines and handling the scalding sugar from boiling pots to molds were highly dangerous undertakings requiring much skill.

THE SLAVE'S LIFE

Esteban Montejo was born in 1860 into slavery in Cuba. He spent the first years of his life on a plantation. He describes his life as hard, but not without amusement. Montejo subsequently escaped, later returned to work on a plantation after the abolition of slavery, and then fought for Cuban independence against the Spanish in 1895.

MONTEJO, *THE AUTOBIOGRAPHY OF A RUNAWAY SLAVE*

At the Flor de Sagua I started work on the *bagasse* wagons. I sat on the box and drove the mule. If the wagon was very full I stopped the mule, got down and led it by the rein. The mules were hardmouthed and you had to bear down on the reins like the devil. Your back began to grow hunched. A lot of people are walking around now almost hunchbacked because of those mules. The wagons went out piled to the top. They were always unloaded in the sugar-mill town, and the *bagasse* had to be spread out to dry. It was scattered with a hook, then it was taken, dried, to the furnaces. This was done to make steam. I suppose that was the first work I did. At least, that's what my memory tells me.

All the indoor parts of the plantation were primitive; not like today with their lights and fast machinery. They were called *cachimbos*, because that is the word for a small sugar-mill. In them the sugar was evaporated and drained. There were some which did not make sugar, but syrup and pan sugar. Almost all of them belonged to a single owner; these were called *trapiches*. There were three sugar-boilers in the *cachimbos*—big copper ones with wide mouths. The first cooked the cane-juice, in the next the froth was taken off, and in the third the treacle was boiled till ready. *Cachaza* was what we called the froth which was left over from the cane-juice. It came off in a hard crust and was very good for pigs. When the treacle was ready, you took a ladle with a long wooden handle and poured it into a trough and from there into the sugar-locker, which stood a short distance from the boilers. That was where they drained the *muscovade*, or unrefined sugar, which had most of the syrup left in it. In those days the centrifuge, as they call it, did not exist.

Once the sugar in the locker had cooled, you had to go in barefoot with spade and shovel and a hand barrow. One Negro always went in front and another behind. The barrow was to take the hogsheads to the *tinglado*, along shed with two beams where the hogsheads were stacked to drain the sugar. The syrup which drained off the hogsheads was given to the mill-town people and was given to the pigs and sheep. They got very fat on it.

To make refined sugar there were some big funnels into which the raw sugar was poured to be refined. That sugar looked like the sort we have today, white sugar. The funnels were known as 'moulds'.

I know that part of sugar-making better than most people who only know the cane as it is outside, in the fields. And to tell the truth I preferred the inside part, it was easier. At Flor de Sagua I worked in the sugar-locker, but this was after I had got experience working with *bagasse*. That was spade-and-shovel work. To my mind even cane-cutting was preferable. I must have been ten years old then, and that was why they had not sent me to work in the fields. But ten then was like thirty now, because boys worked like oxen.

If a boy was pretty and lively he was sent inside, to the master's house. And there they started softening him up and . . . well, I don't know! They used to give the boy a long palm-leaf and make him stand at one end of the table while they ate. And they said, 'Now, see that no flies get in the food!' If a fly did, they scolded him severely and even whipped him. I never did this work because I never wanted to be on closer terms with the masters. I was a runaway from birth.

All the slaves lived in barracoons. These dwelling-places no longer exist, so one cannot see them. But I saw them and I never thought well of them. The masters, of course, said they were as clean as new pins. The slaves disliked living under those conditions: being locked up stifled them. The barracoons were large, though some plantations had smaller ones; it depended on the number of slaves in the settlement. Around two hundred slaves of all colors lived in the Flor de Sagua barracoon. This was laid out in rows: two rows facing each other with a door in the middle and a massive padlock to shut the slaves in at night. There were barracoons of wood and barracoons of masonry with tiled roofs. Both types had mud floors and were as dirty as hell. And there was no modern ventilation there! Just a hole in the wall or a small barred window. The result was that the place swarmed with fleas and ticks, which made the inmates ill with infections and evil spells, for those ticks were witches. The only way to get rid of them was with hot wax, and sometimes even that did not work. The masters wanted the barracoons to look clean outside, so they were whitewashed. The job was given to the Negroes themselves. The master would say, "Get some whitewash and spread it on evenly.' They prepared the whitewash in large pots inside the barracoons, in the central courtyard.

Horses and goats did not go inside the barracoons, but there was always some mongrel sniffing about the place for food. People stayed inside the rooms, which were small and hot. One says rooms, but they were really ovens. They had doors with latchkeys to prevent stealing. You had to be particularly wary of the *criolitos*, who were born thieving little rascals. They learned to steal like monkeys.

In the central patio the women washed their own, their husband's and their children's clothes in tubs. Those tubs were not like the ones people use now, they were much cruder. And they had to be taken first to the river to swell the wood, because they were made out of fish-crates the big ones.

There were no trees either outside or inside the barracoons, just empty solitary spaces. The Negroes could never get used to this. The Negro likes trees, forests. But the Chinese! Africa was full of trees, god-trees, banyans, cedars. But not China— there they have weeds, purslaine, morning-glory, the sort of thing that creeps along. As the rooms were so small the slaves relieved themselves in a so-called toilet standing in one corner of the barracoon. Everyone used it. And to wipe your arse afterwards you had to pick leaves and maize husks.

The bell was at the entrance to the mill. The deputy overseer used to ring it. At four-thirty in the morning they rang the Ave Maria—I think there were nine strokes of the bell—and one had to get up immediately; at six they rang another bell called the line-up bell, and everyone had to form up in a place just outside the barracoon, men one side, women the other. Then off to the canefields till eleven, when we ate jerked beef, vegetables and bread. Then, at sunset, came the prayer bell. At half-past eight they rang the last bell for everyone to go to sleep, the silence bell.

The deputy overseer slept inside the barracoon and kept watch. In the mill town there was a white watchman, a Spaniard, to keep an eye on things. Everything was based on watchfulness and the whip. When time passed and the *esquifación*, the slaves' issue of clothing, began to wear out, they would be given a new one. The men's clothes were made of Russian cloth, a coarse linen, sturdy and good for work in the fields—trousers which had large pockets and stood up stiff, a shirt, and a wool cap for the cold. The shoes were generally of rawhide, low-cut with little straps to keep them on. The old men wore sandals, flat-soled with a thong around the big toe. This has always been an African fashion, though white women wear them now and call them mules or slippers. The women were given blouses, skirts and petticoats, and if they owned plots of land they bought their own petticoats, white ones, which were prettier and smarter.

These plots of land were the salvation of many slaves, where they got their real nourishment from. Almost all of them had their little strips of land to be sown close to the barracoons, almost behind them. Everything grew there: sweet potatoes, gourds, okra, kidney beans, which were like lima beans, yucca and peanuts. They also raised pigs. And they sold all these products to the whites who came out from the villages. The Negros were honest, it was natural for them to be honest, not knowing much about things. They sold their goods very cheap. Whole pigs fetched a doubloon, or a doubloon and a half, in gold coin, as the money was then, but the blacks didn't like selling their vegetables. I learned to eat vegetables from the elders, because they said they were very healthy food, but during slavery pigs were the mainstay. Pigs gave more lard then than now, more natural life.

The taverns were near the plantations. There were more taverns than ticks in the forest. They were a sort of store where one could buy everything. The slaves themselves used to trade in the taverns, selling the jerked beef which they accumulated in the barracoons. They were usually allowed to visit the taverns during the daylight and sometimes even in the evenings, but this was not the rule in all the plantations. There was always some master who forbade the slaves to go. The Negroes went to the taverns for brandy. They drank a lot of it to keep their strength up. A glass of good brandy costs half a peso. The owners drank a lot brandy too, and the quarrels which brewed were no joke. Some of the tavern-keepers were old Spaniards, retired from the army on very little money, five or six pesos' pension.

Sunday was the liveliest day in the plantations. I don't know where the slaves found the energy for it. Their biggest fiestas were held on that day. On some plantations the drumming started at midday or one o'clock. At Flor de Sagua it began very early. The excitement, the games, and children rushing about started at sunrise. The barracoon came to life in a flash; it was like the end of the world. And in spite of work and everything the people woke up cheerful. The overseer and deputy overseer came into the barracoon and started chatting the black women. I noticed that the Chinese kept apart; those buggers had no ear for drums and they stayed in their little corners. But they thought a lot; to my mind they spent more time thinking than the blacks. No one took any notice of them, and people went on with their dances.

As soon as the drums started on Sunday the Negroes went down to the stream to bathe—there was always a little stream near every plantation. It sometimes happened that a woman lingered behind and met a man just as he was about to go into the water. Then they would go off together and get down to business. If not, they would go to the reservoirs, which were the pools they dug to store water. They also used to play hide-and-seek there, chasing women and trying to catch them.

The women who were not involved in this little game stayed in the barracoons and washed themselves in a tub. These tubs were very big and there were one or two for the whole settlement.

Shaving and cutting hair was done by the slaves themselves. They took a long knife and, like someone grooming a horse, they sliced off the wooly hair. There was always someone who liked to clip, and he became the expert. They cut hair the way they do now. And it never hurt, because hair is the most peculiar stuff; although you can see it growing and everything, it's dead. The women arranged their hair with curls and little partings. Their heads used to look like melon skins. They liked the excitement of fixing their hair one way one day and another way the next. One day it would have little partings, the next day ringlets, another day it would be combed flat. They cleaned their teeth with strips of soap-tree bark, and this made them very white. All this excitement was reserved for Sundays.

Everyone had a special outfit that day. The Negroes bought themselves rawhide boots, in a style I have not seen since, from nearby shops where they went with the master's permission. They wore red and green *vayajá* scarves around their necks, and round their heads and waists too, like in the *mani* dance. And they decked themselves with rings in their ears and rings on all their fingers, real gold. Some of them wore not gold but fine silver bracelets which came as high as their elbows, and patent leather shoes.

I knew of two African religions in the barracoons: the Lucumi and the Congolese. The Congolese was the more important. It was well known at the Flor da Sagua because their magic-men used to put spells on people and get possession of them, and their practice of sooth-saying won them the confidence of all the slaves. I got to know the elders of both religions after Abolition.

The other religion was the Catholic one. This was introduced by the priests, but nothing in the world would induce them to enter the slaves' quarters. They were fastidious people, with a solemn air which did not fit the barracoons—so solemn that there were Negroes who took everything they said literally. This had a bad effect on them. They read the catechism and read it to the others with all the words and prayers. Those Negroes who were household slaves as messengers of the priests and got together with the others, the field slaves, in the sugar-mill towns. The fact is I never learned that doctrine because I did not understand a thing about it. I don't think the household slaves did either, although, being so refined and well-treated, they all made out they were Christian. The household slaves were given rewards by the masters, and I never saw one of them badly punished. When they were ordered to go to the fields to cut cane or tend the pigs, they would pretend to be ill so they needn't work. For this reason the field slaves could not stand the sight of them. The household slaves sometimes came to the barracoons to visit relations and used to take back fruit and vegetables for the master's house; I don't know whether the slaves made them presents from their plots of land or whether they just took them. They caused a lot of trouble in the barracoons. The men came and tried to take liberties with the women. That was the source of the worst tensions. I was about twelve then, and I saw the whole rumpus.

There were other tensions. For instance, there was no love lost between the Congolese magic-men and the Congolese Christians, each of whom thought they were good and the others wicked. This still goes in Cuba. The Lucumi and Congolese did not get on either; it went back to the difference between saints and witchcraft.

The only ones who had no problems were the old men born in Africa. They were special people and had to be treated differently because they knew all religious matters.

Many brawls were avoided because the masters changed the slaves around. They kept them divided among themselves to prevent a rash of escapes. That was why the slaves of different plantations never got together with each other.

The Lucumis didn't like cutting cane, and many of them ran away. They were the most rebellious and courageous slaves. Not so the Congolese; they were cowardly as a rule, but strong workers who worked hard without complaining. There is a common rat called Congolese, and very cowardly it is too.

In the plantations there were Negroes from different countries, all different physically. The Congolese were black-skinned, though there were many of mixed blood with yellowish skins and light hair. They were usually small. The Mandingas were reddish-skinned, tall and very strong. I swear by my mother they were a bunch of crooks, too! They kept apart from the rest. The Gangas were nice people, rather short and freckled. Many of them became runaways. The Carabalís were like the Musungo Congolese, uncivilized brutes. They only killed pigs on Sundays and at Easter and, being good businessmen, they killed them to sell, not to eat themselves. From this comes a saying, 'Clever Carabalí, kills pig on Sunday,' I got to know all these people better after slavery was abolished.

All the plantations had an infirmary near the barracoon, a big wooden hut where they took the pregnant women. You were born there and stayed there till you were six or seven, when you went to live in the barracoons and began work, like the rest. There were Negro wet-nurses and cooks there to look after the criolitos and feed them. If anyone was injured in the fields or fell ill, these women would doctor him with herbs and brews. They could cure anything. Sometimes a criolito never saw his parents again because the boss moved them to another plantation, and so the wet-nurses would be in sole charge of the child. But who wants to bother with another person's child? They used to bath the children and cut their hair in the infirmaries too. A child of good stock cost five hundred pesos, that is the child of strong, tall parents. Tall Negroes were privileged. The masters picked them out to mate them with tall, healthy women and shut them up together in the barracoon and forced them to sleep together. The women had to produce healthy babies every year. I tell you, it was like breeding animals. Well, if the Negroes didn't produce as expected, the couple were separated and she was sent to work in the fields again. Women who were barren were unlucky because they had to go back to being beasts of burden again, but they were allowed to choose their own husbands. It often happened that a woman would be chasing one man with twenty more after her. The magic-men would settle these problems with their potions.

I saw many horrors in the way of punishment under slavery. That was why I didn't like the life. The stocks, which were in the boiler-house, were the cruelest. Some were for standing and others for lying down. They were made of thick planks with holes for the head, hands and feet. They would keep slaves fastened up like this for two or three months for some trivial offense. They whipped the pregnant women too, but lying face down with a hollow in the ground for their bellies. They whipped them hard, but they took good care not to damage the babies because they wanted as many of those as possible. The most common punishment was flogging; this was given by the overseer with a rawhide lash which made weals on the skin. They also had whips made of the fibres of some jungle plant which stung like the devil and flayed the skin off in strips. I saw many handsome big Negroes with raw backs. Afterwards the cuts were covered with compresses of tobacco leaves, urine and salt.

Life was hard and bodies wore out. Anyone who did not take to the hills as a runaway when he was young had to become a slave. It was preferable to be on your own on the loose than locked up in all that dirt and rottenness. In any event, life tended to be solitary because there were none too many women around. To have one of your own you had either to be over twenty-five or catch yourself one in the fields. The old men did not want the youths to have women. They said a man should wait until he was twenty-five to have experiences. Some men did not suffer much, being used to this life. Others had sex between themselves and did not want to know anything of women. This was their life—sodomy. The effeminate men washed the clothes and did the cooking too, if they had a 'husband'. They were good workers and occupied themselves with their plots of land, giving the produce to their 'husbands' to sell to the white farmers. It was after Abolition that the term 'effeminate' came into use, for the practice persisted. I don't think it can have come from Africa, because the old men hated it. They would have nothing to do with queers. To tell the truth, it never bothered me. I am of the opinion that a man can stick his arse where he wants.

Everyone wearied of the life, and the ones who got used to it were broken in spirit. Life in the forest was healthier. You caught lots of illnesses in the barracoons, in fact men got sicker there than anywhere else. It was not unusual to find a Negro with as many as three sicknesses at once. If it wasn't colic it was whooping cough. Colic gave you a pain in the gut which lasted a few hours and left you shagged. Whooping cough and measles were catching. But the worst sickness, which made a skeleton of everyone, were smallpox and the black sickness. Smallpox left men all swollen, and the black sickness took them by surprise; it struck suddenly and between one bout of vomiting and the next you ended up a corpse. There was one type of sickness the whites picked up, a sickness of the veins and male organs. It could only be got rid of with black women; if the man who had it slept with a Negress he was cured immediately.

There were no powerful medicines in those days and no doctors to be found anywhere. It was the nurses who were half witches who cured people with their home-made remedies. They often cured illnesses the doctors couldn't understand. The solution doesn't lie in feeling you and pinching your tongue; the secret is to trust the plants and herbs, which are the mother of medicine. Africans from other side, across the sea, are never sick because they have the necessary plants at hand.

If a slave caught an infectious disease, they would take him from his room and move him to the infirmary and try to cure him. If he died they put him in a big box and carried him off to the cemetery. The overseer usually came and gave instructions to the settlement to bury him. He would say, 'We are going to bury this Negro who has done his time.' And the slaves hurried along there, for when someone died everyone mourned.

The cemetery was in the plantation itself, about a hundred yards from the barracoon. To bury slaves, they dug a hole in the ground, filled it in and stuck a cross on top to keep away enemies and the Devil. Now they call it a crucifix. If anyone wears a cross around his neck it is because someone has tried to harm him.

A MORE BENIGN SLAVERY?

Englishman James Wetherell was a merchant in Brazil, who served as unpaid vice-consul in Bahia from 1843 to 1855. After his tragic death from a fall at age thirty-six, friends discovered and published a thin book of his observations of his time as consul. In this instance, he depicted a relatively benign slavery with slaves singing as they worked and the women in "gala dress."

WETHERELL, *STRAY NOTES FROM BAHIA*

The black carriers "Ganha dores", their only dress being the scantiest pair of coarse cotton drawers. They carry all the smaller things upon their heads, whilst large objects, such as pipes of wine, &c., are slung between two poles which are carried on the shoulders.

   During the time of carrying these heavy burdens through the streets they sing a kind of chorus, a very useful manner of warning persons to get out of the way, as the footfall is not heard in the surrounding bustle. This chorus generally consists of one of the blacks chanting a remark on anything he sees, and the others come in with a chorus of some ridiculous description, which is seldom varied, however much the recitative solo part may. Thus a kind of march, time and time, is kept up. . . . when the work is heavy, or the burden is being carried up hill, that they become much more vigorous in their shouts, aiding their labor and varying their song with an expressive longdrawn grunt. . . . From the constant custom of conveying things on the head, the carriage of the body is very upright. The women are particularly expert, . . . everything is placed upon the head, and thus the hands are left free. The things appear to be carried equally as safely if placed on the bare head as when placed on the handkerchief which serves as a turban.

   James Wetherell, *Brazil, Stray Notes from Bahia: Being Extracts from Letters, etc. during a Residence of Fifteen Years.* Liverpool: Webb and Hunt, 1860.

WETHERELL, *STRAY NOTES FROM BAHIA*

The gala dress of the black women is . . . very elegant. The upper part of the dress above the petticoat is made of fine muslin, plain or worked, sometimes so transparent as to form scarcely a cover for the body from the waist upwards. The part round the bust is edged with broad lace; small armlets, richly worked, are joined with a double gold button; this upper part of the dress is so loose that one shoulder of the woman almost always remains bare. The skirt of the dress is very voluminous, forming a complete circle when placed upon the ground; the lower edge is bordered with lace, or has a white arabesque pattern sewed upon it; the inner petticoat is likewise edged with lace. The feet, bare, are inserted into small shoes, which just cover the tips of the toes; and the heels, very high and small, do not reach the heel of the foot. The arms are covered with bracelets of coral and gold, beads, &c., the neck loaded with chains, and the hands with rings—principally the one which is most frequently exhibited from the folds of the shawl. A handsome coast cloth is thrown over the shoulder. These cloths are woven in small stripes of colored cotton from two to four inches wide in striped or checked patterns, and the slips sewed together form a shawl.

A black turban is scarcely ever worn by a black woman, only by a colored one. A large bunch of keys strung on a silver chain, from which also hangs silver coins, a boar's tusk or shark's tooth mounted in silver, and various other kind of charms are attached to one side of the dress, and a small coast basket more for ornament than use is sometimes carried on the head. During Lent the dress worn is generally of black stuff doubled together in small stiff plaits, which gathered together at the waist, open out as the dress expands towards the bottom. The shawl then worn is made of black cloth, lined with some light colored silk, each end being deeply edged with velvet or plush. The shawls are most gracefully worn, and in various and constantly varying modes. Spite of their ridiculous shoes the women walk in a very graceful manner, occasionally when handsomely dressed with no small amount of affection.

James Wetherell, *Brazil, Stray Notes from Bahia: Being Extracts from Letters, etc. during a Residence of Fifteen Years*. Liverpool: Webb and Hunt, 1960.

Capt. Richard F. Burton was a well-known soldier, explorer, and writer who was posted as a diplomat in Santos (the port for São Paulo), Brazil, in 1865. Before this, he had spent many years in Africa and the Mid-East. Evidently bored with the humdrum of life as a consular officer, he and his wife Isabel set off to the origins of the great São Francisco River. In the three excerpts below Burton paints a relatively benign picture of slavery. In the first he describes Sundays, the Sabbath, for slaves at Morro Velho, a large mining complex operated by the St. John del Rey Company, a British concern.

BURTON, *EXPLORATIONS OF THE HIGHLANDS OF BRAZIL*

A peculiar sight, and very fit for a photograph, is the Revista or muster of the Blacks, which takes place every second Sunday. When we were there about 1100 out of 1452 attended in the "Compound" fronting the "Casa Grande". Both sexes were bare-footed—everywhere in the Brazil a token of slavery. The women, fronted by a picket of twelve young girls, were ranged in columns of six companies. They were dressed in the "Sabbath" uniform, white cotton petticoats, with narrow red band round the lower third; cotton shawls striped blue and white, and a bright kerchief, generally scarlet, bound round the wool. On the proper right, perpendicular to the column, are the "good-conduct women". The first year's badge is a broad red band round the white hem, and replaced by narrow red stripes, one for each year, till the mystic number seven gives freedom. We saw ten women and as many men officially apply for the preliminaries to manumission.

Ranged behind the women, the men are clothed in white shirts, loose blue woolen pants, red caps—Turkish or Glengarry—and cotton trousers. The "jacket men", as the "good conducts" are called, stand on the proper left of, and at right angles with, the battalion of Amazons. They wear tailless coats of blue serge, bound with red cuffs and collars, white waistcoats, overalls with red stripes down the seams, and the usual bonnets; each has a medal with the Morro Velho stamp, the badge of approaching freedom. Children of an age to attend the Revista are clad in the same decent comfortable way; a great contrast they offer to the negrolings that sprawl about the land.

The slaves answer to the roll-call made by the heads of the respective departments. This done, the Superintendent, followed by the Manager and Assistant Manager of the Blacks, and the two medical officers, walks down the companies and minutely inspects each individual. I observed that almost all the "chattels" were country born; there was only one Munjolo, distinguished by the three scars of his race; the other "persons held to service" call him "Papagente" or man-eater.

After inspection, a pay-table was spread before the door, and the girls and small children received their allowance of pay and soap.

Muster over, both sexes and all ages are marched off to the church. The day is then their own. The industrious will look after house and garden, pigs and poultry; they will wash and sew, or fetch water, wood, or grass for sale.

Richard F. Burton, *Explorations of the Highlands of Brazil with a Full Account of the Gold and Diamond Mines.* Vol. II: Greenwood, 1969. London: Tinsley Brothers, 1869.

In the second selection, Burton delineates slaves' rights.

BURTON, *EXPLORATIONS OF THE HIGHLANDS OF BRAZIL*

In the present day the Brazilian negro need not envy the starving liberty of the poor in most parts of the civilized world.

The slave in the Brazil has, by the unwritten law, many of the rights of a freeman. He may educate himself, and he is urged to do so. He is regularly catechized, and in all large plantations there is a daily religious service. If assailed in life or limb he may defend himself against his master, or any white man, and an over-harsh proprietor or overseer always runs considerable risk of not dying in bed. He is legally married, and the chastity of his wife is defended against his owner. He has little fear of being separated from his family: the humane instincts and the religious tenets of the people are strongly opposed to this act of barbarity. He has every chance of becoming a free man: manumission is held to be a Catholic duty, priestly communities are ashamed of holding slaves, and whenever there is a war the African is bought and sent to fight by the side of white recruits. Old usage allows him to purchase his liberty by his labor, and to invest his property in manumitting his wife and children.

Richard F. Burton, *Explorations of the Highlands of Brazil with a Full Account of the Gold and Diamond Mines.* Vol. II: Greenwood, 1969. London: Tinsley Brothers, 1869.

A MINER'S LIFE

The discovery of gold and diamonds in Brazil during the colonial era shifted thousands of slaves from the declining sugar plantations to mines in the interior in the province of Minas Gerais. In the next excerpt Burton describes the everyday routines of slave miners also in Morro Velho.

BURTON, *EXPLORATIONS*
OF THE HIGHLANDS OF BRAZIL

I proceed now to give my account of the black miner as I found him at Morro Velho.

Without including 130 children of hired blacks, and who are not under contract, the establishment consists of 1450 head, thus distributed:

Company's blacks, 254 (109 men, 93 women, and 52 children); Cata Branca blacks, 245 (96 men, 87 women, and 62 children); blacks' hired under contract, 951.

Generally in the Brazil men are preferred upon the sugar plantations, women on those that grow coffee, and as they are wanted for domestic purpose it is not so easy to hire them.

The "Company's Blacks" consider themselves the aristocracy, and look down upon all their brethren. Both they and the Cata Brancas are known by the numbers on their clothing.

The figures given below will show the average of hire: clothing, food, and medical treatment are at the Company's expense. Usually the agreement is for three to five years, during which period the slave cannot be manumitted. As a rule the Superintendent employs only robust men who have passed a medical examination, but he will take in doubtful lives under annual contract. The slave is insured by a deduction of 10$000 to 20$000 per annum for a fixed period; and if he dies before the lease has expired the owner still receives his money—there are actually eighty-nine cases of this kind. Pay ceases only if the negro runs away: it is issued every third or sixth month, and the contractors can obtain one year's advance, at a discount of ten per cent.

As regards labor, all are classified according to their strength into first, second, and third-rate blacks. In 1847 permission to work overtime, that is to say, beyond nine hours forty-five minutes, was given to the first-rates. There is another division into surface and underground blacks. The former are smiths and mechanics, especially carpenters and masons, who work between 6 A.M. and 5 P.M., with one hour forty-five minutes of intermission for meals. The oldest and least robust are turned into gardeners, wood-fetchers, and grass-cutters. The regular working day at Morro Velho is as follows—

5 A.M. Reveillé sounded by the gong, and half an hour afterwards the Review.
6 A.M. Work
8.15 A.M. Breakfast
9 A.M. Work
12.30 P.M. Dinner
1.15 P.M. Work
2 P.M. Change guard. Blasting in the mine.
5.30 P.M. Mechanic's work ended.
8.30 P.M. Return to quarters. The slaves cook their own meals and eat supper at home.
　　Saturday is a half-holiday: they leave off work at 2.30 P.M., and retire at 9 P.M.

The underground laborers are borers, stope cleaners, trammers who push the wagons, kibble-filers, and timber-men: they are divided into three corps, who enter the mine at 6 A.M., 2 P.M. and 10 P.M. on Sunday the gangs shift places, so that only one week in three is night work. A rough estimate makes the number of the gang in the mine at the same time 620, including all hands. When work is over they proceed to the changing-house, and find a tepid bath at all hours. They put on their surface-clothes, and leave the mine suits either to be dried in the open air, or by flues during the rains. The precaution is absolutely necessary, though very difficult and troublesome to be enforced: the English miners shirk it, and the free Brazilians are the most restive, though they are well aware how fatal are wet garments.

The blacks lodge in the two villages situated half-way between the bottom of the river valley and the Morro Velho hill. Thus, while they escape malaria they are saved fatigue when going to, or coming from, work. They begin the day with coffee or Congonhas tea. Their weekly allowance, besides salt and vegetables, comprises 9 lb. of maize meal, 4 ½ —5 lb. of beans, 13 ½ oz. of lard, and 2 lb. of fresh beef. Meat of the best quality here averages 3$000 per arroba, or twopence a pound, and the laborers purchase, at cost prices, the heads and hoofs, the livers and internals of the bullocks killed for the use of the establishment. The industries have their gardens and clearings: they keep poultry and pigs, fattened with bran, which they receive gratis. Part they eat, the rest they sell to procure finery and small luxuries. "Carne Seca" and farinha are issued when the doctor orders. Nursing women have something added to the six-tenths of a plate of meal, one quarter of beans, and two ounces of lard, and children when weaned claim half rations. All the articles are of good quality, and if not a report is made to the Manager of Blacks.

Drink is not issued every day, nor may it be brought into the establishment. A well-conducted negro can obtain a dram once per diem with permission of the chief feitor or overseer. Each head of a department has a supply of "restilio", which he can distribute at discretion, and the mine captain can give a "tot" to any negro coming wet from duty. It is, however, difficult to correct the African's extreme fondness for distilled liquors, which in this light and exciting air readily affect his head, and soon prove fatal to him. He delights also in "Pángo," here called Ariri, the well-known Bhang (Cannabis sativa) of India, and of the east and west coast of Africa. He will readily pay as much as 1$000 for a handful of this poison.

I never saw negroes so well dressed. The men have two suits per annum—shirt, and overalls of cotton for the hot, and of woolen for the cold season; the "under-grounds" receive, besides these, a stout woolen shirt, and a strong hat to protect the head. Each has a cotton blanket, renewed yearly, and if his dress be worn or torn, the manager supplies another. The women work in shifts of thin woolen stuff, and petticoats of stronger material; they usually wear kerchiefs round their necks, thus covering the bosom, and one shoulder, after the fashion of African "Minas", is left bare. In winter capes or fed broad-cloth are added to the Review costume.

The slave laborer is rewarded with gifts of money; he is allowed leave out of bounds, even to Sabará; he is promoted to offices of trust and of increased pay; he is made an overseer or a captain over his own people; at the Review he wears stripes and badges of distinction, and he looks forward to liberty.

The chief punishments are fines, which negroes, like Hindus, especially hate; the penalties, which now amount to 400$000, have been transferred to charitable purposes, and swell a small reserved trust-fund, intended to support the old and infirm. Other pains are, not being allowed to sell pigs, poultry, and vegetables; arrest within the establishment or confinement in a dry cell, with boards like a soldier's guard-room; fugitives are put in irons. Formerly the manager and the head captain, who required implicit obedience from the 500 hands of the underground department, could order a flogging. This was abolished, not, I believe, with good effect. Every head of a department can still prescribe the "Palmatorio", but he must note and report the punishment to the Superintendent. Only the latter can administer a flogging with the Brazilian cat of split hide; and this is reserved for confirmed drunkenness, disobedience of orders, mutiny, or robbing fellow workmen. The punishment list is sent in every fortnight, and as a rule is small. I especially noticed the civil and respectful demeanor of the Morro Velho blacks, who invariably touch their hats to a white stranger, and extend their hands for a blessing. They are neither impudent, nor cringing, nor surly, and, in my opinion, there is no better proof that they are well and humanely treated. I would here formally retract an opinion which I once thoughtlessly adopted upon the worst of grounds, "general acceptation". The negro cannot live in the presence of the civilized man: the Brazil proves that unless recruited from home the black population is not more viable than the "Red Indian". His rule and "manifest destiny" are those of all savages.

Richard F. Burton, *Explorations of the Highlands of Brazil with a Full Account of the Gold and Diamond Mines.* Vol. II: Greenwood, 1969. London: Tinsley Brothers, 1869.

SLAVES ON THEIR OWN

Not all slave owners employed their slaves on their own plantations. Many slaves, particularly in the cities, worked at various occupations and returned part of their earnings to their owners. James Wetherell, the British Vice-Consul for Bahia and then Paraíba, observed this phenomenon during the 1850s.

WETHERELL, *STRAY NOTES FROM BAHIA*

A Brazilian has slaves, he sends them out to work as different trades—to cultivate the land, to sell vegetables, to hire as servants, as boatmen, &c.—in fact, employs them in every way that servants or workmen are required. The master directs the slave to pay him at the rate of, it may be, about one shilling a day; this frequently is the case, and all the slave can raise above that sum which his master demands, belongs to himself. In the process of time those who are industrious raise sufficient money to pay the price their master values them at, and when such is the case, the slave can claim his freedom. The produce of the labor of the slaves enables the master to live in idleness, and to call himself a gentleman in the proportion of his possessing two to three, twenty to thirty, two hundred to three hundred slaves. In a country like Brazil, which produces anything with a very small amount of labor, the land is comparatively neglected; because it is not absolutely required that it should be in a state of high cultivation, as the inhabitants can easily subsist without such, and its very cultivation would cause them trouble, labor, and work, all of which they detest. Thus, so long as the Brazilians can live at ease, without trouble to themselves, they are content with the present aspect of affairs, careless of the future. The abolition of slavery would sweep away all this, and so, of course, it is their interest, as far as personal feelings are concerned, to prevent it. These remarks apply in a less forcible degree to the slave trade.

James Wetherell, *Brazil, Stray Notes from Bahia: Being Extracts from Letters, etc. during a Residence of Fifteen Years.* Liverpool: Webb and Hunt, 1960.

THE SLAVE MARKET

The inhumanity of slavery was nowhere illustrated more vividly than in the markets where slaves were bought and sold, often put on display like livestock. The illustration below depicts a slave market in Pernambuco in Northeast Brazil. Notice the beatings and threatening by the guards and the distress of the Africans presumably recently arrived.

The document is an illustration from Maria Dundas Graham (Lady Maria Calcott) Journal of a Voyage to Brazil and Residence There During Part of the Years 1821, 1822, 1823. "Slave market in Pernambuco" is the illustration.

GATE & SLAVE MARKET AT PERNAMBUCO.

Maria Dundas Graham (Lady Maria Calcott), *Journal of a Voyage to Brazil and Residence There During Part of the Years 1821, 1822, 1823.* NY: Praeger, 1969.

C. S. Steward provides a written record of a slave sale.

SLAVE AUCTION, FROM STEWART, *PERSONAL RECORD...*

On one of these mornings, we entered a common auction-room for a moment, and accidentally stumbled on the humiliating and reproachful sight of a sale of men and women by a fellow man. Not the sale, as till within a few years past might here have been the case, of newly imported captives from Africa, but of natives of Rio, thus passing under the hammer from owner to owner like any article of merchandise. They were eight or ten in number of both sexes, varying in age from beyond and girlhood to years of maturity and middle life. They stood meekly and submissively, though evidently anxious and sad, under the interrogations and examinations of the bidders, and a rehearsal and laudation by the auctioneer of their different available working qualities and dispositions: their health, strength and power of endurance. All, in their turn were made to mount an elevated platform, to display their limbs almost to nakedness, and exhibit their muscular powers by various gymnastics, like a horse his movements and action, before the bidders at Tattersall's.

They were rapidly knocked down at prices varying from two hundred to a thousand and more milreis: that is, from one to five hundred and more dollars. As we turned away, the indignation of one of our party found vent in the exclamation: "Such a spectacle is a disgrace to human nature. It makes one sick at heart and ready to fear that in the retributive justice of the Almighty the time may come, when the blacks here will put up the whites for sale in the same manner!" And why not? Why should the blood boil at the mere suggestion of the thought in the one case, and yet flow coolly and tranquilly on, in view of the other?

C. S. Stewart, *The Personal Record of a Cruise.* New York: G. P. Putnam and Company 1856.

CORPORAL PUNISHMENT

Equally as inhumane was the harsh treatment meted out by some slave owners. Maria Dundas Graham described an instance or corporal punishment of slaves.

CORPORAL PUNISHMENT, FROM GRAHAM, *JOURNAL OF A VOYAGE TO BRAZIL*

28th — This morning before breakfast, looking from the balcony of Mr. S.'s house, I saw a white woman, or rather fiend, beating a young negress, and twisting her arms cruelly while the poor creature screamed in agony, till our gentlemen interfered. Good God! That such a traffic, such a practice as that of slavery, should exist. Near the house there are two or three depôts of slaves, all young; in one, I saw an infant of about two years old, for sale. Provisions are now so scarce that no bit of animal food ever seasons the paste of mandioc flour, which is the sustenance of slaves: and even of this, these poor children, by their projecting bones and hollow cheeks, show that they seldom get a sufficiency. Now, money also is so scarce, that a purchaser is not easily found, and one pang is added to slavery: the unavailing wish of finding a master! Scopes of these poor creatures are seen at different corners of the streets, in all the listlessness of despair—and if an infant attempt to crawl from among them, in search of infantile amusement, a look of pity is all the sympathy he excites. Are the patriots wrong? They have put arms into the hands of the new negroes, while the recollection of their own country, and of the slave-ship, and of the slave-market, is fresh in their memory.

Maria Dundas Graham (Lady Maria Calcott), *Journal of a Voyage to Brazil and Residence There During Part of the Years 1821, 1822, 1823.* New York: Praeger, 1969.

QUESTIONS

1. How would you assess a slave's life as described by Esteban Montejo?
2. Did all the slaves get along? What were the dividing lines?
3. How does Montejo describe Sundays?
4. Do you think that the singing related by James Wetherell was a sign of slave contentment? How does singing at work compare with Montejo's descriptions of Sundays?
5. When Wetherell writes about the dressed up black women, do you think he is trying to present a distorted view of slavery?
6. How does life at Morro Velho compare with that of the plantation?
7. Why do you think that slaves who worked independently did not run away?
8. What is the most noteworthy aspect of the "Gate and Slave Market at Pernambuco" the illustration in Graham?
9. What was Stewart's reaction to the slave auction? What is yours?
10. What is your reaction to Graham's rendition of the woman beating her slave?
11. How does prejudice enter into the assessment of the foreign travelers of the slaves' lives?

6   CITIES IN THE NINETEENTH CENTURY

INTRODUCTION

Latin American cities rivaled any in the world in size and beauty. Mexico City was the largest in the Western Hemisphere with 168,000 people when the Wars of Independence began in 1810, and the number of residents grew to more than 200,000 by mid-century. Rio de Janeiro's population was more than 200,000 by 1870. Buenos Aires quintupled in area in half a century to accommodate the influx of immigrants from Italy and Spain. The legacy of the colonial era left spectacular architecture. Rio's geographic setting by the ocean was truly magnificent. But the cities were, as elsewhere in the world, filthy, noisy, dangerous places. The stench of human wastes and garbage were often overwhelming and the clatter numbed the senses. Disease resulting from unsanitary conditions was rampant. The contrasts, too, were stark, for enormous wealth and conspicuous consumption existed next to heartbreaking poverty. The selections that follow will evoke the contrasts and tempo of everyday life in these teeming cities.

CONTRASTS

German Carl Sartorius (1796–1872) migrated to Mexico in 1824, eventually settling in the state of Veracruz, where he owned a sugar plantation. He became an avid observer of the plants and animals of the region with connections to the Smithsonian Institution in Washington, D.C. He wrote the book in 1850 from which we have taken a number of selections.

Sartorius provides us with this view of Mexico City as a teeming metropolis filled with great beauty and repulsive filth. It is startling both how little and how much the city changed over the succeeding century and a half.

MEXICO CITY, FROM SARTORIUS, *MEXICO ABOUT 1850*

In Mexico the suburbs are mean and dirty, and inhabited by the lowest classes. Refuse and filth, carcasses of animals and rubbish of buildings are found piled up at the entrances of the streets, by the side of wretched hovels, the abode of ragged vagabonds or half naked Indians. Lean hungry dogs, flocks of auras and Zopilotes (carrion vultures) beleaguer these loathsome, neglected precincts, and we hasten our pace in passing, to withdraw both nose and eyes from the unpleasant impression. Upon the table-lands this is almost universally the case, but, on the contrary, in the cities of the eastern coast, Jalapa, Orizava and Cordova, for instance, these suburbs are a labyrinth of fruit gardens, from among which the red-tiled roofs of the cottages look forth with remarkable cheerfulness.

On entering the city proper, one finds the streets paved, and at the sides a raised foot-pavement of well-fitted basalt flags furnishes an agreeable walk for the pedestrian. The houses of the wealthier people are of two, three or more stories, those of the humbler classes, in the majority of instances, only one. The architecture is Spanish, but the numerous churches are all in the French and Italian style of the seventeenth century. Many of them are imposing in extent, many have, in the interior, great simplicity and beauty of proportion, and since they are all of stone with vaulted roofs and lofty domes, they produce an impression of solemnity corresponding with their design.

First of all let us stroll out into the principal square, for this is always the grand focus of splendor in all Mexican cities. The great church always occupies one side of the stately quadrangle; the three remaining are composed of large houses whose lower story consists of broad colonnades running from end to end.

In these arcades are to be found the finest shops, warehouses, wine and coffee-houses. The building opposite the church is invariably the city-hall, or in chief towns the capitol. A beautiful fountain, or a column usually decorates the centre of the square, and many are also ornamented with rows of trees, which trees afford an agreeable promenade. In the smaller towns the weekly market is generally held in the principal square, which then offers a very lively picture by the contrast of its groups of people, and the multifarious wares exposed for sale. One could hardly see a finer sight for instance, than the market at Cordova, in the state of Vera Crus, offers on a clear Friday morning. One should choose a point of observation on the east side of the church. Here one overlooks the fine square surrounded by its stately portico. The vendors fill the whole area, arranging themselves in long rows like regular streets, so that articles of one kind can be found together. Whites and Indians, Mestizoes, mulattoes and negroes, all cleanly dressed, crowd themselves together, a medley of every color. Nowhere can be found such a mixture of different colored faces as here, just open the boundary between the temperate and torrid regions. In addition to this animated scene, we are surrounded by a splendid tropical landscape. Tall palm-trees and great-leaved bananas are waving in the mild air, and the stern masses of the mountains of Orizava, rising up with their cones of glittering snow, constitute the back-ground.

The public square (plaza) is to the Mexican what the forum was to the Roman. Every event is first heard of there, every festivity whether of state or church is to be witnessed upon the plaza. There elections take place and public speeches are made, the gensd'armes are mustered and fire-works and brilliant illuminations are displayed, and there under a gorgeous canopy the procession of Corpus-Christi is held. Before or after church-service, the people take a little walk under the arcades, here they loiter at evening in order to meet acquaintances, to hear the news or do business; and it is a legitimate part of every citizen's life once a day to smoke his cigar in these halls. As we have already remarked, the town-hall is invariably situated, as well as the court of justice, the offices of numerous lawyers and of the public notaries. Shops, coffee and drinking-houses are moreover the magnets which everywhere exercise their power of attraction. The noble profession of loungers and idlers is here finely represented; the leperos or lazzaroni of the cities are driven hither by instinct, because opportunity most readily offers itself of procuring something without great exertion, whether it be by relieving some one's pockets, or the more honorable method of doing some errand; porters or such-like evangelists recline against the pillars and communicate their oracles, muleteers seek for return freight, dealers in all sorts of trinkets carry about their finery in their hands, and praise it to the pretty Chinas (Mestizo girls), who gaze with bewitched eyes at the ear-rings and necklaces.

Carl Sartorius, *Mexico About 1850.* (*Mexico. Landscapes and Popular Sketches.* 1858) Reprint. Stuttgart: FA Brockhaus Komm, 1961.

RIO DE JANEIRO

Daniel P. Kidder traveled extensively in Brazil during the 1840s, visiting most of the big cities. His goal was to inform Americans about Brazil, a country about which his audience knew little. In this excerpt, he depicts Rio de Janeiro as a beautiful, bustling city.

RIO DE JANEIRO, FROM KIDDER, *BRAZIL AND THE BRAZILIANS*

The streets of the city are generally quite narrow; but the *Rua Direita*, which is seen in the above cut beyond the Largo do Paço, is wide, and well paved with small square blocks of stone which are brought from the Isle of Wight. The *Rua Direita* and many of the principal streets of Rio de Janeiro are now as well paved as the finest thoroughfares of London or Vienna, presenting a great contrast to the former irregular and miserable pavement, which was in use up to 1854. The *Rua Direita* and the *Largo de Rocio* are the points whence omnibuses start for every portion of the vast city and its suburbs.

The houses seldom exceed three or four stories; but four-story house at Rio is equal in height to one of five in New York. Formerly nearly all were occupied as dwellings, and even in the streets devoted to business the first floors only were appropriated to the storage and display of goods, while families resided above. But since 1850 this has greatly changed in the quarter where the wholesale houses are found: proprietors and clerks now reside in the picturesque suburbs of Botafogo, Engenho Velho, and across the bay at Praia Grande or San Domingo. Every evening presents an animated spectacle of crowded streamers, full omnibuses, and galloping horses and mules, all conveying the *negociantes* and *careiros* (bookkeepers) to their respective residences.

The distant steeples on our left are those of the Church of Candelaria, which is situated on a narrow street back from the Rua Direita. It is the largest church in the city, and presents taller spires and a handsomer front than any other.

The *Praca do Commercio*, or Exchange, occupies a prominent position in the Rua Direita. This building, formerly a part of the Custom-House, was ceded by Government for its present purposes in 1834. It contains a reading-room, supplied with Brazilian and foreign newspapers, and is subject to the usual regulations of such an establishment in other cities. Beneath its spacious portico the merchants of eight or nine different nations meet each other in the morning to interchange salutations and to negotiate their general business. The Exchange is not far from the Custom-House, which formerly had its main entrance adjoining the Praca.

Nothing can be more animated and peculiar than the scenes which are witnessed in this part of the Rua Direita during the business-hours of the day,—viz.: from nine A.M. to three P.M. It is in these hours only that vessels are permitted to discharge and receive their cargoes, and at the same time all goods and baggage must be dispatched at the Custom-House and removed there from. Consequent upon such arrangements, the utmost activity is required to remove the goods dispatched, and to embark those productions of the country that are daily required in the transactions of a vast commercial emporium. There are the black-coated merchants congregated about the Exchange, and here comes a negro dray. The *team* consists of five stalwart Africans pushing, pulling, steering, and shouting as they make their way amid the serried throng, unmindful of the Madeira Islanders, who, with an imprecation and a crack of his whip, urges on a thundering mule-cart laden with boxes. Now an omnibus thunders through the crowd, and a large four-wheeled wagon, belonging to some company for the transportation of "goods", crashes in its wake. Formerly all this labor was performed by human hands, and scarcely a cart or a dray was used in the city, unless, indeed, it was drawn by negroes. Carts and wagons propelled by horse-power are now quite common; but for the moving of light burdens and for the transportation of furniture, pianos, & c. the negro's head has not been superseded by any vehicle.

While we are almost stunned by the sounds of the multitude, we have new source of wonderment. Above all the confusion of the Rua Direita, we hear a stentorian chorus of voices responding in quick measure to the burden of a song. We behold, over the heads of the throng a line of white sacks rushing around the corner of the Rua de Alfandega *(Custom-House Street)*. We hasten to that portion of Rua Direita, and now see that these sacks have each a living ebony Hercules beneath. These are the far-famed coffee-carriers of Rio. They usually go in troops, numbering ten or twenty individual, of whom one takes the lead and is called the captain. These are generally the largest and strongest men that can be found. While at work they seldom wear any other garment than a pair of short pantaloons; their shirt is thrown aside for the time as an encumbrance. Each one takes a bag of coffee upon his head, weighing one hundred and sixty pounds, and, when all are ready, they start off upon a measured trot, which soon increases to a rapid run.

As one hand is sufficient to steady the load, several of them frequently carry musical instruments in the other, resembling children's rattle-boxes: these they shake to the double-quick time of some wild Ethiopian ditty, which they all join in singing as they run. Music has a powerful effect in exhilarating the spirits of the negro; and certainly no one should deny him the privilege of softening his hard lot by producing the harmony of sounds which are sweet to him, though uncouth to other ears. It is said, however, that an attempt was at one time made to secure greater quietness in the streets by forbidding them to sing. As a consequence, they performed little or no work; so the restriction was in a short time taken off. Certain it is that they now avail themselves of their vocal privileges at pleasure, whether in singing and shouting to each other as they run, or in proclaiming to the people the various articles they carry about for sale. The impression made upon the stranger by the mingled sound of their hundred voices falling upon his ear at once is not soon forgotten.

Daniel P. Kidder, *Brazil and the Brazilians.*

Maria Dundas Graham (1786–1844), later known as Lady Maria Calcott, traveled in Chile and Brazil during the 1820s. She accompanied her first husband, a British naval officer, to Chile in 1821 and after he died, she lived in Brazil, for a time tutoring Princess Maria, the daughter of Emperor Pedro I. She offers her views of Rio de Janeiro and Bahia.

RIO, FROM MARIA DUNDAS GRAHAM, *JOURNAL OF A VOYAGE TO BRAZIL*

The city of Rio is more like an European city than either Bahia or Pernambuvo; the houses are three or four stories high, with projecting roofs, and tolerably handsome. The streets are narrow, few being wider than that of the Corso at Rome, to which one or two bear a resemblance in their general air, and especially on days of festivals, when the windows and balconies are decorated with crimson, yellow, or green damask hangings. There are two very handsome squares, besides that of the palace. One, formerly the Roça is now that of the Constituçaõ, to which the theatre, some handsome barracks and fine houses, behind which the hills and mountains tower up on two sides, give a very noble appearance. The other, the Campo de Santa Anna, is exceedingly extensive, but unfinished. Two of the principal streets run across it, from the sea-side to the extremity of the new town, nearly a league, and new and wide streets are stretching out in every direction. But I was too tired with going about in the heat of the day to do more than take a cursory view of these things, and could not even persuade myself to look at the new fountain which is supplied by a new aqueduct.

There is in the city, an air of bustle and activity quite agreeable to our European eyes; yet the Portuguese all take their siesta after dinner. The negroes, whether free blacks or slaves, look cheerful and happy at their labor. There is such a demand for them, that they find full employment, and of course good pay, and remind one here as little as possible of their sad condition, unless, indeed, one passes the street of the Vallango; then the slave-trade comes in all its horrors before one's eyes. On either hand are magazines of new slaves, called here pieces; and there the wretched

Rio de Janeiro
RIO, FROM THE GLORIA HILL

creatures are subject to all the miseries of a new negro's life, scanty diet, brutal examination, and the lash.

Maria Dundas Graham (Lady Maria Calcott), *Journal of a Voyage to Brazil and Residence There During Part of the Years 1821, 1822, 1823.* New York: Praeger, 1969.

BAHIA, BRAZIL

Bahia was another stunningly beautiful, bustling Brazilian city. But Graham found it rather disgusting in some aspects as well.

BAHIA, FROM MARIA DUNDAS GRAHAM, *JOURNAL OF A VOYAGE TO BRAZIL*

Wed., 17th— This morning, at day-break, my eyes opened on one of the finest scenes they ever beheld. A city, magnificent in appearance from the sea, is placed along the ridge and on the declivity of a very high and steep hill: the richest vegetation breaks through the white houses at intervals, and beyond the city, reaches along to the outer point of land on which the picturesque church and convent of Sant Antonio da Barre is placed. Here and there the bright red soil shows itself in harmony with the tiling of the houses. The tracery of forts, the bustle of shipping, hills melting in the distance, and the very form of the bay, with its promontories and islands, altogether finish this charming picture.

.... Every thing is visibly either suspended or on the decline, and there will probably be no improvement, until the political state of Brazil is a little more settled. We find things here, though not quite so unquiet as at Pernambuco, yet tending the same way.

The street into which we proceed through the arsenal gate, forms at this place, the breadth of the whole lower town of Bahia, and is, without any exception, the filthiest place I ever was in. It is extremely narrow, yet all the working artificers bearing their benches, and tools into the street: in the interstices between them, along the walls, are fruit-sellers, venders of sausages, black-puddings, fried fish, oil and sugar cakes, negroes plaiting hats or mats, caderas, (a kind of sedan chair,) with their bearers, dogs, pigs, and poultry, without partition or distinction; and as the gutter runs in the middle of the street, every thing is thrown there from the different stalls, as well as from the windows; and there the animals live and feed! In this street are the warehouses and counting-houses of the merchants, both native and foreign. The buildings are high, but neither so handsome nor so airy as those of Pernambuco.

It was raining when we landed; therefore, as the streets leading out of the filthy lower town do not admit of the use of wheeled carriages, on account of the steepness of the ascent, we hired caderas.

As we ascended from the street, every step brought us in sight of some beautiful scene, generally terminated by the bay and shipping. There is something in the landscape here peculiarly agreeable. The verdure, the wood, the steep banks, and gently sloping lawns, generally opening to the sea or the lake behind the town, have a freshness and amenity that I scarcely remember seeing before. We saw but little of the upper city, but that little was handsome.

BAHIA, FROM MARIA DUNDAS GRAHAM,
JOURNAL OF A VOYAGE TO BRAZIL

Friday 19th—In the first place, the houses, for the most part, are disgustingly dirty: the lower story usually consists of cells for the slaves, stabling & c.; the staircases are narrow and dark; and, at more than one house, we waited in a passage while the servants ran to open the doors and windows of the sitting-rooms, and to call their mistresses, who were enjoying their undress in their own apartments. When they appeared, I could scarcely believe that one half were gentlewomen. As they wear neither stay nor bodice, the figure becomes almost indecently slovenly, after very early youth; and this is the most disgusting, as they are very thinly clad, wear no neck-handkerchiefs, and scarcely any sleeves. Then, in this hot climate, it is unpleasant to see dark cottons and stuffs, without any white linen, near the skin. Hair black, ill combed, and disheveled, or knotted unbecomingly, or still worse, en papillote, and the whole person having an unwashed appearance. When at any of the houses the bustle of opening the cobwebbed windows, and assembling the family was over, in two or three instances, the servants had to remove dishes of sugar, mandioc, and other provisions, which had been left in the best rooms to dry. There is usually a sofa at each end of the room, and to the right and left a long file of chairs, which look if as if they never could be moved out of their place. Between the two sets of seats is a space, which, I am told, is often used for dancing; and, in every house, I saw either a guitar or piano, and generally both. Prints and pictures, the latter the worst daubs I ever saw, decorate the walls pretty generally; and there are, besides, crucifixes and other things of the kind. Some houses, however, are more neatly arranged; one, I think belonging to a captain of the navy, was papered, the floors laid with mat, and the tables ornamented with pretty porcelain, Indian and French: the lady too was neatly dressed in a French wrapper. Another house belonging to one of the judges was also clean, and of a more stately appearance than the rest, though the inhabitant was neither richer nor of higher rank. Glass chandeliers were suspended from the roof; handsome mirrors were intermixed with the prints and pictures. A good deal of handsome china was displayed round the room; but the jars, as well as the chairs and tables, seemed to form an inseparable part of the walls. We were every where invited, after sitting a few moments on the sofa, to go to the balconies of the windows and enjoy the view and the breeze, or at least amuse ourselves with what was passing in the street. And yet they did not lack conversation: the principal topic, however, was praise of the beauty of Bahia; dress, children, and diseases, I think, made up the rest; and, to say the truth, their manner of talking on the latter subject is as disgusting as their dress, that is, in a morning: I am told they are different after dinner. They marry very early, and soon lose their bloom.

BAHIA, FROM MARIA DUNDAS GRAHAM,
JOURNAL OF A VOYAGE TO BRAZIL

The upper town is most beautifully situated on the ridge between the sea and the fresh water lake, and from its height, and the great slope of most of the streets, it is incomparably cleaner than the port. The cathedral dedicated to St. Salvador is a handsome building, and stands on one side of a square, where the palace, prison, and other public buildings are placed. The finest of these, the Jesuits' college, the marble columns of which came from Europe ready cut, is now converted into a barracks. The most useful is the hospital of Nossa Senhora da Misericordia, founded by Juan de Matinhos, whose statue in white marble, with a wig like Sir Cloudesley Shovel's in Westminster Abbey, stands at the first landing-place, and is the ugliest piece of carving I ever saw.

Maria Dundas Graham, *Journal of a Voyage to Brazil and Residence There during Part of the Years 1821, 1822, 1823*. New York: Praeger, 1961.

BUENOS AIRES

Nineteenth century Buenos Aires was a backwater, nothing like the elegant metropolis it would become in the early twentieth century.

BUENOS AIRES, STEWART, *THE PERSONAL RECORD OF A CRUISE*

Feb. 26th—The impressions made by Buenos Ayres in its external aspect, are increasingly favorable. The plan of the town is rectangular, like that of Philadelphia. Every street is of the same width, and every square of the same dimensions. The streets are narrow, just wide enough for two vehicles to pass each other, and the sidewalks comfortable only for those moving in Indian file. In walking two abreast, or arm in arm, there is a constant jostling against passers-by. In some parts of the town the sidewalks are elevated two or three feet above the level of the carriage-way. The city being a dead level, and the streets straight, long vistas in them are every where commanded. Some of these are striking, and where the domes and fine towers of the old Spanish churches come in as leading features, are quite European. These stately old structures are scattered about in various localities, and with the citadel on the highest rise of ground overlooking the river, are the chief, if not the only sombre objects in the architecture of the place: still retaining the natural color of the brick of which they are built, or exhibiting time stained surfaces of stone or stucco, and roofs covered with moss, lichens, and grass. Till within a few years, the houses were uniformly one story only in height. This is still the case in many quarters, but in others, successive blocks and almost entire streets are now composed of those of two stories. The general plan of all is the same: the Spanish, or rather Moorish quadrangle, upon which all the apartments open, with a cistern, and sometimes a fountain in the centre. In many of the establishments of the wealthy, there are a succession of these quadrangles. Filled with shrubbery and flowers, and often ornamented by a fountain, the view from the street through them, terminating not infrequently in an assimilating scene in fresco against a wall in the far perspective, is quite impressive is stage effect. The custom of constantly applying fresh whitewash to buildings new and old, gives to the whole city a clean and bright look. Here and there, however, in almost every street, a quaint and antiquated building is seen, contrasting with later structures. These are a single story in height, with slanting, instead of flat roofs, covered with tile. Over the central door, however, there is a kind of demi-tower, furnished with a window and projecting balcony, as a look-out and place of parley with an outsider whose motive for demanding admittance might be questioned. In many cases these look-outs are quite tasteful in their architecture, and pleasing to the eye from the air they bear of the "olden time."

Great improvements have been made of late years, both is the external architecture and internal arrangements of private dwellings. Many of the mansions recently erected would scarcely suffer, in point of richness and elegance, by comparison with some of the most luxurious of the Fifth Avenue by Gen. P——, the minister of war: though the lofty and massive entrance-gates, in complicated and artistic patterns of coast-iron bronzed, and the colonnades of Moorish arches surrounding its quadrangular courts within would not entirely harmonize with the prevailing architecture that street of palaces.

Every house here is necessarily a castle, having its window on the street barred and grated, with portals not easily to be forced, and parapets, upon the flat roof, capable of effective defense against assailants below. Being without cellars or basement-rooms, the level of the floors is elevated but little above that of the street, and as no railing or area intervenes between the side-walks and the large windows, which descend to the floors, the interior of the room is as open to the inspection of the passers by, as to the inmates themselves. In some residences of wealth and taste, a vista of room after room in long suites, richly furnished, is thus exposed to view. The apartments on the street, with scarcely an exception, are reception and drawing-rooms; and, in the afternoons and evenings, the promenades in the street are thus furnished with a succession of tableaux vivans of females—not occupied as with us in conversation, or reading, or fancy work, or other employments of leisure and taste, and grouped with husbands, and fathers, and brothers, and sons, and other male friends but seated in formal rows, or in a semicircle around the windows, in a greater or less degree of 'full dress', with little interchange of conversation among themselves, and evidently for the mere purpose of seeing and being seen. Every thing in their dress and manner shows the studied purpose of exciting admiration. These exhibitions, however, are only in hours of costume. Till late in the day the ladies of the country in general are invisible; very much in undress, lounging, and idling, and sipping Paraguay tea through the silver tube of the maté cup.

An American or Englishman cannot fail to be struck with the seemingly slight intercourse of the male and female members of a family. The latter are to all external appearance without husbands, fathers, brothers, or sons. You meet them in numbers in the morning, going to and returning from mass, followed by a servant or servants, but seldom, if ever, attended by a male relative. The evening is a favorite time for shopping, and the streets are often crowded in some sections, with ladies thus engage, but unattended by a gentleman in escort. And in the hundreds of parlors and drawing-rooms into which I have looked in passing, I do not recollect ever to have seen a gentleman, old or young, in the groupings of a family circle.

C. S. Stewart, *The Personal Record of a Cruise*. New York: G. P. Putnam and Company, 1856.

Francis Bond Head wrote what Argentines regard as one of the classic foreign travelers memoir of their country. Head, unlike most visitors of the nineteenth century, chose to write mostly about the less populated regions of the interior. He did not like the city and he found Buenos Aires especially unappealing.

BUENOS AIRES, FRANCIS BOND HEAD, *JOURNEYS ACROSS THE PAMAPS AND AMONG THE ANDES*

The town of Buenos Aires is far from being an agreeable residence for those who are accustomed to English comforts. The water is extremely impure, scarce, and consequently expensive. The town is badly paved and dirty, and the houses are the most comfortless abodes I ever entered. The walls, from the climate, are damp, mouldy, and discolored. The floors are badly paved with bricks, which are generally cracked, and often in holes. The roofs have no ceiling, and the families have no idea of warming themselves except by huddling round a fire of charcoal, which is put outside the door until the carbonic acid gas has rolled away.

Some of the principal families at Buenos Aires furnish their rooms in a very expensive, but comfortless manner: they put down upon the brick floor a brilliant Brussels carpet, hang a luster from the rafters, and place against the damp wall, which they whitewash, a number of tawdry North American chairs. They get an English pianoforte, and some marble vases, but they have no idea of grouping their furniture into a comfortable form: the ladies sit with their backs against the walls without any apparent means of employing themselves; and when a stranger calls upon them, he is much surprised to find that they have the uncourteous custom of never rising from their chairs. I had no time to enter into any society at Buenos Aires, and the rooms looked so comfortless, that, to tell the truth, I had little inclination. The society of Buenos Aires is composed of English and French merchants, with a German or two. The foreign merchants are generally the agents of European houses; and as the customs of the Spanish South Americans, their food, and the hours at which they eat, are different from those of the English and French, there does not appear to be much communication between them.

At Buenos Aires the men and women are rarely seen walking together; at the theater they are completely separated; and it is cheerless to see all the ladies sitting together in the boxes, while the men are in the pit—slaves, common sailors, soldiers, and merchants, all member of the same republic.

The town is furnished with provisions by the gauchos in a manner that shows a great want of attention to those arrangements which are generally met with in civilized communities. Milk, eggs, fruit, vegetables, and beef are brought into the town by individuals at a gallop, and they are only to be had when they choose to bring them. (One of the most striking pictures in and near Buenos Aires is the young gaucho who brings milk. The milk is carried in six or eight large earthen bottles, which hang on each side of the saddle. There is seldom room for the boy's legs, and he therefore generally turns his feet up behind him on the saddle, and sits like a frog. One meets these boys in squads of four or five, and the manner in which they gallop in their red cloth, caps, with their scarlet ponchos flying behind them, is a singular appearance. The butchers' shops are covered carts, which are not very agreeable objects. The beef, mangled in a most shocking manner, is swinging about; and I have constantly seen a large piece tied by a strip of hide to the tail of the cart, and dragged along the ground, with a dog trying to tear it.)

Francis Bond Head, *Journeys Across the Pampas and Among the Andes*. Carbondale: Southern Illinois University Press, 1967. Originally published in 1866.

SECONDARY CITIES

Henry Koster, an Englishman born and brought up in Portugal, fluent in Portuguese, went to Brazil in 1809 and stayed for six years. Koster journeyed all over the then Portuguese colony. He went into the Northeast, all along the coast, visiting many of the secondary cities of the colony. A shabby city in the tropics, São Luis represented the tier of secondary cities in Latin America lacking in the majestic architecture of the colonial era or the wealth of the Viceregal capitals. Neither it nor Fortaleza de Ceará was much more than a large village.

SÃO LUIS, FROM HENRY KOSTER, *TRAVELS IN BRAZIL*

The city of São Luis, situated upon the island of Maranhão, and the metropolis of the estado, or state of Maranhão, is the residence of a captain-general and the see of a bishop. It is built upon very unequal ground, commencing from the water's edge, and extending to the distance of about one mile and a half in a NE direction. The space which it covers ought to contain many more inhabitants than is actually the case; but the city is built in a straggling manner, and it comprises some broad streets and squares. This gives to it an airy appearance, which is particularly pleasant in so warm a climate. Its situation upon the western part of the island, and upon one side of a creek, almost excludes it from the sea breeze, by which means the place is rendered less healthy than if it was more exposed. The population may be computed at about 12,000 persons or more, including Negroes, of which the proportion is great, being much more considerable than at Pernambuco. The streets are mostly paved, but are out of repair. The houses are many of them neat and pretty, and one story in height; the lower part of them is appropriated to the servants, to shops without windows, to warehouses, and other purposes, as at Pernambuco. The family lives upon the upper story, and the windows of this reach down to the floor, and are ornamented with iron balconies. The churches are numerous, and there are likewise Franciscan, Carmelite and other convents. The places of worship are gaudily decorated in the inside; but no plan of architecture is aimed at in the formation of the buildings themselves, with the exception of the convents, which preserve the regular features appertaining to such edifices. The governor's palace stands upon rising ground, not far from the water-side, with the front toward the town. It is a long uniform stone building, of one story in height; the principal entrance is wide, but without a portico. The western end joins the town hall and prison, which appear to be part of the same edifice; and the oblong piece of ground in its front, covered with grass, gives to it on the whole a handsome and striking appearance. One end of this is open to the harbor and to a fort in the hollow, close to the water; the other extremity is nearly closed by the cathedral. One side is almost taken up with the palace and other public buildings, and the opposite space is occupied by dwelling houses and streets leading down into other parts of the city. The ground upon which the whole palace stands is composed of a soft red stone; so that the smaller streets leading from the town into the country, some of which are not paved, are full of gullies, through which the water runs in the rainy season. These streets are formed of houses consisting only of the ground floor, and having thatched roofs; the windows are without glass, and the dwellings have a most mean and shabby appearance. The city contains a customhouse and treasury; the former is small, but was quite large enough for the business of the place, until lately.

The importance of the province has increased very rapidly. Previous to the last sixty years no cotton was exported. The quantity of rice grown there is likewise great; but the sugar which is required for the consumption of the province is brought from the ports to the southward. Some sugar cane has lately been planted, but hitherto molasses only have been made. I heard many persons say that the lands are not adopted to the growth of the sugar cane. The cotton and rice are brought to São Luis in barks of about 25 or 30 tons burden. These come down the rivers with the stream from the plantations;

The province of Maranhão will not bear comparison with that of Pernambuco. It is still in an infant state; there still exist wild Indians, and the plantations upon the main land are still in danger from their attacks. The proportion of free persons is much smaller; the slaves very much preponderate, but this class can of necessity use but little of what is in any degree expensive, of what in such a climate is mere luxury. There exists at São Luis a great inequality of ranks; the chief riches of the place are in the hands of a few men who possess landed property to a great extent, numerous gangs of slaves, and are also merchants. The wealth of these persons and the characters of some of the individuals who enjoy it have raised them to great weight and consequence, and indeed one governor knows to his cost that without their concurrence it was useless to attempt the introduction of the innovations proposed, and impossible to trample long upon the rest of the community. But the great inequality of rank bespeaks the advancement of this place to have been less rapid than that of other settlements further south, where the society is more amalgamated, and property more divided. As a port of trade with Europe, São Luis may be accounted the fourth establishment upon the coast of Brazil in point of importance, giving precedence to Rio de Janeiro, Baía, and Pernambuco.

Another secondary city Koster visited was Fortaleza.

FORTALEZA, FROM HENRY KOSTER, *TRAVELS IN BRAZIL*

The town of the Fortress of Ceará is built upon heavy sand, in the form of a square, with four streets leading from it, and it has an additional long street on the north side of the square, which runs in a parallel direction, but is unconnected with it. The dwellings have only a ground floor, and the streets are not paved; but some of the houses have footpaths of brick in front. It contains three churches, the governor's palace, the town hall and prison, a customhouse, and the treasury. The number of inhabitants I judge to be from one thousand to twelve hundred. The fort, from which the place derives its name, stands upon a sand hill close to the town, and consists of a sand or earth rampart toward the sea, and of stakes driven into the ground on the land side; it contained four or five pieces of cannon of several sizes, which were pointed various ways; and I observed that the gun of heaviest metal was mounted on the land side. Those which pointed to the sea were not of sufficient caliber to have reached a vessel in the usual anchorage ground. The powder magazine is situated upon another part of the sand hill, in full view of the harbor.

Henry Koster, *Travels in Brazil.* Carbondale: Southern University Press, 1966. London, 1816.

Friedrich Hassaurek was the United States Minister to Ecuador for four years during the rule of long-term dictator Gabriel García Moreno, who dominated from 1860 to 1875. His memoir of the time was a best-seller.

QUITO, HASSAUREK, *FOUR YEARS AMONG THE ECUADORIANS*

Viewed from a distance, or from one of the surrounding hills, Quito resembles one of those spellbound towns in the Arabian Nights. But, as soon as we enter it, it presents a most lively appearance. On the principal streets and plazas hundreds of human beings are continually in motion. It is true, they are chiefly Indians and cholos, and you will meet twenty persons in ponchos and even in rags, barefoot or with alpargates (hemp sandals), before you meet one respectably dressed. But, nevertheless, the motley crowds of men in ponchos of all colors, beggars in rags, vagrants in sackcloth, women with red, green, brown, or blue pañuelones and rebozos, ladies with gay-colored silk shawls, monks with their immense hats, monks in white, monks in brown, monks in blue, and canons and curates in black, and Indians of a hundred different villages in every variety of costume—not even omitting the naked and painted Indian from the wilderness on the eastern side of the cordillera—present a most lively and interesting spectacle. There are but few carts in use, as I have already said; nevertheless, the streets are thronged from morning to evening with mules, horses, oxen, donkeys, and llamas with loads of every kind and description. Indians, men, and women, with loads on their backs, limp to and fro; soldiers in queer clown caps and with or without shoes, lazily saunter through the crowds; groups of merchants and their friends chat in front of their tiendas (stores); chagras (country people) on horseback dash through the streets; ladies will meet their lady friends and embrace and hug them, obstructing the narrow sidewalks; water carriers with immense jars on their backs, butchers or bakers with meat or bread in troughs on their heads, wend their way to the houses of their customers; children and dogs run about in all directions; mule drivers swear at their beasts; parrots chatter in the groceries and greenshops; in short, the life within the city favorably contrasts with its melancholy aspect from without.

The city is traversed from west to east by two deep ravines, through which Pinchincha sends down its torrents of melted snow. These quebradas are mostly covered with vaults and arches on which the houses rest, but where they are open, they disclose to the eye hideous abysses, the sides of which are overgrown with rank weeds. The territory over which the city extends being exceedingly uneven, as the slopes and spurs of the surrounding hills press down toward the Plaza Mayor from three different sides, a walk through Quito consists of continuous ascents and descents. The course of the streets, however, is generally regular, those running from east to west being intersected at right angles by others running from north to south. The gutters and sewers were formerly in the center of the streets, forming rivulets, through which the water was let down two or three times in twenty-four hours for purposes of public cleanliness; but in 1863 the municipality entered upon an extensive system of repaving; and the principal streets are now paved in modern style. The streets are not very wide; the sidewalks are exceedingly narrow. The houses are built mostly in the old Spanish or rather Moorish style, with the roofs projecting over the pavements so as to afford a partial protection against the frequent rains. There are but two or three buildings in Quito with two upper stories. Most of the houses have only one. Low and filthy houses of but a ground floor are found in great numbers, but only in the outskirts and suburbs.

The houses are generally built of adobe. The walls are exceedingly thick, forming deep embrasures for doors and windows. There are, strictly speaking, no windows, but glass doors leading to balconies overhanging the sidewalks. The roofs are covered with curved tiles of earthenware; two rows are first placed, the concave side upwards, the joint being covered with a third row reversed, so as to form channels for the water to flow off, which, from the main gutter, is thrown into the streets and courtyards by a number of projecting spouts. These precautions are necessary on account of the heaviness and long duration of the showers in the rainy season. The upper story is the dwelling part of a respectable house. The ground floor is occupied by the servants, or tenanted by poor people who cannot afford to pay high rents. The stores in front have no back doors and do not communicate with the interior of the houses to which they belong. They have no windows, and generally but one door, which must serve as entrance, exit, window, showcase, and all. There are but very few shops in Quito which have two doors. The stores consequently are but small; five or six customers, especially of the crinoline gender, will fill them completely. These stores are called tiendas, and are closed at early candlelight. They are naturally dark, and most of the business is done at or near the door. The houses have neither fireplaces nor chimneys, except in a few buildings of modern construction. The want of fireplaces is sometimes severely felt. The smoke arising from kitchen fires must make its way out of the kitchen door, and a few apertures above it. Kitchens, therefore, are black and dark; and as almost nothing but charcoal is used for cooking, they are noisome and uncomfortable. Stoves are not known. There being no flues connected with the hearths, cooking is quite a task, and the cook needs one, two, or more subordinates to fan the fires; to almost every pot a separate fire, and to two fires, one individual to fan them. Servants, however, are very cheap, although unreliable and lazy; but of his hereafter. The pots used for cooking have not a flat bottom like ours, but are pointed below, so that they cannot stand without being supported by some contrivance, or inserted into the holes which the hearth contains on purpose. The large jars in which water is carried have the same impracticable shape. They are put on wooden trestles, or into holes in a stone bench opposite or at the side of the hearth. The cook generally brings his family with him, allowing his dirty children to romp about the kitchen. A female cook will do her work with the baby tied to her back, or deposited by her side on the kitchen table. Hair in the meals is of frequent occurrence, without reference to an occasional flea, or a lot of vine fretters, which have communicated themselves to the soup from the unwashed vegetables.

Most of the houses have one or two spacious square courtyards paved and with drains. In the second, there is generally a covered place for horses, which is paved also. The stables of this country never have boards.

The street entrance is always high enough to admit a horseman with ease. In the upper story there is always a gallery resting on arches or pillars, and leading around the courtyard. All the rooms and galleries are floored with square tiles or bricks, on which mats or carpets are laid. The chinks between the bricks serve as hiding places for swarms of fleas; particularly troublesome after a room has remained shut up and uninhabited for some time; in which case it is not uncommon, especially on haciendas in the country, to drive a sheep through it first, in order to take up as many fleas as possible. The rooms, with the exception of the parlors, or salas, are generally but very indifferently furnished, with an incongruous mixture of antique and modern pieces, and kept in a pitiable state of uncleanliness, disorder, and confusion.

Not only is Quito a very healthy place, but it is without insects, except those against which cleanliness is a safe preventive, such as fleas and lice. In the country, niguas or piquis are sometimes, though rarely found; but it is chiefly the Indians, who, on account of going barefoot, are attacked by them. They are very diminutive, and generally introduce themselves into the cuticle below the nails; but the Indians, especially the women, are very skillful in taking them out, which painful operation is performed with a needle. For leagues around Quito, no snake is to be found. Mosquitoes are hardly known; scorpions and tarantulas have never been heard of. Flies, even, are very rare and do not molest at all. There are mice, but no rats; nor are there bats or lizards, or even bugs or beetles in the grass or on trees. In this respect the near neighborhood of Quito may be said to be paradise. The coolness of the weather is invigorating and refreshing, and has none of those relaxing and enervating effects which tropical climates produce. But as in the interior of Ecuador you may choose the temperature most suitable to your constitution or taste, so if you are dissatisfied with the autumnal coolness of Quito and its vicinity, a few hours' ride will lead you into regions where an eternal spring prevails, and where the products of all climates cluster around you—potatoes and clover by the side of the orange and the sugarcane.

Friedrich Hassaurek, *Four Years Among the Ecuadorians*. Carbondale: Southern Illinois University Press, 1967. Originally published as *Four Years Among the Spanish Americans in 1867*.

MENDOZA, FRANCIS BOND HEAD, *JOURNEYS ACROSS THE PAMPAS AND AMONG THE ANDES*

The town of Mendoza is situated at the foot of the Andes, and the country around it is irrigated by cuts from the Rio Mendoza. This river bounds the west side of the town, and from it, on the east side, there is a cut or canal about six feet wide, containing nearly as much water as would turn a large mill. This stream supplies the town with water, and at the same time adorns and refreshes the alameda or public walk. It waters the streets which descend from it to the river, and can also be conducted into those which are at right angles.

Mendoza is a neat small town, built upon the usual plan. The streets are all at right angles; there is a plaza or square, on one side of which is a large church, and several other churches and convents are scattered over the town. The houses are only one story high, and all the principal ones have a porte cochère, which enters a small court, round the four sides of which the house extends.

The houses are built of mud, and are roofed with the same. The walls are white-washed, which gives them a neat appearance, but the insides of the houses, until they are whitewashed, look like an English barn. The walls are of course very soft; occasionally a large piece of them comes off, and they are of that consistency that, in a very few moments, a person, either with a spade or a pickaxe, could cut his way through any wall in the town. Several of the principal houses have glass in the window sashes, but the greatest number have not. The houses are almost all little shops, and the goods displayed are principally English cottons.

Francis Bond Head, *Journeys Across the Pampas and Among the Andes.* Carbondale: Southern Illinois University Press, 1967. Originally published in 1866.

THE WEALTHY CLASS

Even in the mid-nineteenth century there were sharp contrasts between rich and poor in the great cities. In this excerpt from the travel memoir of German Carl Sartorius, we encounter the Creoles of Mexico City.

LIFE IN TOWN, FROM SARTORIUS

The creoles constitute the chief part of the population of the cities; they are government officials, physicians, lawyers, merchants, manufacturers, mining-proprietors, and artificers. The great landed proprietors, the country traders, and the higher orders of the clergy also belong to this class.

They are not distinguished by any national costume, but usually wear the European dress. In the country, only, the round jacket is still used in the house, over which, when in the open air, and especially when they go to church, the Spanish cloth cloak, trimmed with lace, is thrown. The short jacket is also worn on horseback. Poor and rich are much given to fine and clean linen. In their toilettes, the ladies are guided more by the Paris 'Journal des Modes' than the men. The newest patterns in silk, woolen and cotton-stuffs are seen sooner in Mexico than in Russia;

The female Creole, however, adheres to her morning-dress for the church, which is always black, with the graceful mantilla, trimmed with broad lace, attached to the back of the head and falling below the shoulders. In the country-towns and villages they go also in colored dresses to church, but the silk mantilla in invariably thrown over the head. In the country, too, the uncomfortable restraint of stays is less usual than in the large towns. Silk stockings and light silk shoes protect the little foot; the hand is provided with a fan, which is constantly in motion, and often serves to telegraph an interesting message across the street.

The wealthy Creole is a friend to luxury, he has showy equipages, beautiful saddle-horses, numerous servants, but no comfort in his house. In order to give an idea of the mode of living, I must describe the house itself.

From the street we enter through a great gate, beneath the archway of which is the porter's lodge, or the counting-house of the proprietor. We then arrive at a square yard, surrounded on all sides by a piazza; in the middle is usually a fountain, with flower-vases. The wide balustrade of the piazza is also mostly adorned with flowers. The doors of every room open on this fore-court. The chief apartment, the saloon, looks on the street, and is met with even in the villages, decorated with the best furniture, a looking-glass, corner-tables with flower-vases, the picture of a saint in a silver niche, or something else of the sort. One end of the saloon, the wall here having neither door nor window, is the seat of the ladies (estrado); it is frequently raised some inches, laid with carpets or mats, and furnished with low sofas. Numerous chairs are placed against the other walls. The saloon communicates either directly or through the corridor (piazza) with the other rooms, viz., the bed-rooms (recameras), the dinning-room, the kitchen etc. Opposite the entrance, a smaller gate usually conducts into the second yard, which is surrounded by the stable, coach-house, apartments for the men-servants etc. One-storied houses are mostly arranged in this manner; in large towns, the houses are generally two-storied, and frequently there is an 'entresol'. In this case the ground-floor is for warehouses, shops, or servants' rooms, whilst the family dwell in the first floor; the colonnade, however, is met with in the different stories, and the disposition of the apartments is in a great measure the same.

We will proceed to the house of a man, who has a tolerable income; there are many better, but also many worse; and therefore I make choice of one of a middling description. The floor of the whole house is paved with flags, carefully cemented. In the saloon and some of the rooms, the flags are painted so as to resemble mosaic. The walls are unpapered, plastered, and painted with arabesques; the ceiling is the same. The master's study or office, on the right, under the gateway, has a sufficiently smoky appearance, is full of bundles of deeds or acts (I believe he is a lawyer), whilst several clerks, with very subaltern faces, and important office-frowns, scribble away for their lives. The furniture is extremely simple, of course; but the adjoining cabinet, where the licentiate (here called Doctor, the usual title of a lawyer) himself works, has a handsome writing-table, a glass-case with books, and a few arm-chairs.

Let us enter the colonnade. The seat of honor is laid with fine mats, over which is a carpet, about four feet wide, before the sofa, which extends right across the upper end of the oblong apartment. Corner tables of japanned pine-wood are adorned with flower-vases, behind which we have here a 'mater dolorosa'; there an infant Christ in glazed niches. A modern sofa stands opposite the 'estrado'; several tables, and a few dozen chairs occupy the other walls. The windows reach to the ground, but are protected from without by iron bars, bent outwards, so that we can look on the street without inconvenience.

In an adjoining boudoir is some embroidery, a prayer-book, and one of Eugéne Sue's romances; a silver brazier with burning coals, and a bundle of paper cigars near it, indicate that the lady of the house is fond of smoking her 'cigarrito'. A half-opened door affords us a sight of the interior of a sleeping-apartment; a large bed stands against the wall, the head and foot of the bedstead are rounded off, and exhibits in oval panels, Adam and Eve, and the Landing of Noah's Ark, painted in oil. It seems to be an inviting place of repose, with a woolen damask counterpane, and pillows of embroidered muslin. A somewhat stout señora sits on the bed on a fringed tiger-skin, in the Turkish fashion (with her legs doubled up under her), enjoying a cup of chocolate, whilst a maid is seated before her on the ground, holding a silver plate, with a glass of water on it. The good lady has a cloth thrown over her head and shoulders; but the curious will not fail to remark that she wears no cap (invariably the case with the Creole ladies), but that her hair hangs down her back. Her morning- gown too is not plaited, but hangs about her much like a sack.

Merry peals of laughter in the next room lead us to the presumption that the young people are there. Sure enough they are the daughters, but strange to say, not one has her dress closed; one has her arms out of the sleeves even, which are tied round her waist, like a sash. Their plaited hair hangs down their backs, the feet are encased in silk slippers, but the stocking are wanting. Of what use would they be in so mild a climate? The blue and white cotton wrappers are worn; but they conceal little. The young people gaily smoke their cigars, whilst one of them is seated on a mat on the ground, having her long glossy hair combed by the maid. The room is not over tidy; the stocking lie about on the ground, on the bed are silk dresses, which are evidently for attending mass, on the chairs are crapes, and other articles of dress. There is no chest of drawers visible, but several boxes, standing against the wall on wooden tressles, replace the numerous cupboards etc. The dressing-table is not well supplied with brushes, soaps, essences etc., but with a complete assortment of rings, earrings, bracelets, brooches, chains, and pins.

It is a duty, I owe to the ladies, to add a few words about the housekeeping of the Creoles. I have already remarked, that they are not very early risers. About 8 o'clock a small cup of chocolate with sweet bread is taken. The family do not assemble for this refreshment, but each person receives it in his bedroom. At 10 o'clock there is a hot breakfast of roast or stewed meat, eggs, and with all classes the never-failing dish of beans (frijoles), which are first boiled soft, and then fried with fat and onions. At 3 o'clock in the afternoon dinner is served, which has certain unvarying dishes. First a cup of clear broth, then 'sopa', of rice, paste, or some kind of bread-fruit, cooked in broth, till the fluid has completely evaporated, and highly seasoned with tomatas. The 'olla' is the third dish, and is met with on every table. It consists of beef, mutton, a little pork, ham, fowl, small sausages, cabbage, French beans, parsnips, turnips, pear, banana, onions, celery, a little coriander and parsley, all cooked together. The vegetables are placed on the table apart from the meat, and each person helps himself according to his taste. The 'olla' is followed by some 'principios', mostly ragouts with strong-flavored broth of meat or fish; then comes a sweet dish, and finally some dried sweetmeats. Wine is rarely drunk at table: but the sweetmeats are succeeded by a large glass of water.

Most Creoles allow themselves a siesta after dinner. At 6 o'clock chocolate is drunk, or in hot weather, ice or fruit-jelly with water; a little walk, a ride or a drive is taken afterwards, and it is then time for the theatre and the 'tertullas'. The latter are the evening parties of the ladies, gentlemen being also frequently present. The guests sit round the saloon, which is wretchedly illuminated with two tallow candles. Here they smoke and chat. Sometimes there is music, or even dance; refreshments are rarely offered, unless it be perhaps a few sweetmeats and water.

Supper is usually taken about 10 o'clock, consisting of roast meat, salad, beans, and a sweet dish. Immediately after supper, the family goes to bed.

Invitations to dinner are seldom; if strange gentlemen only are invited, the ladies are frequently not present. The Mexican is hospitable, and it is a point of honor to entertain the guests well. The number of guests at country festivities, which are not unlike the feasts of the Homeric heroes, is often very great.

The ladies have thus fewer household labors, and many of the present generation devote the time to improving themselves by reading. In company they are amiable and animated, and whatever European ladies may have to object to, it is certain that the gentlemen who are masters of their beautiful language, will invariably find their society attractive, and praise their charms.

It would be wrong to conclude these cursory glances at the life of the Creoles, without alluding to a prominent feature, which does them much honor. This is the respect paid by the children to their parents. The sons remain under parental authority, until they have reestablished a family of their own, and even among the laboring classes, the son deposits his earnings in the father's hands, or at least makes no disposal of it, without his consent. A child never outrages his parents, or treats them with indifference; and this praiseworthy custom has been adopted even by the Mestins, being as strictly observed in the cottage as in the palace. From their tenderest youth upwards, the children when called by their parents, never ask: "What?" or, "What do you want?" but always: "What are your commands, Sir or Madam?" When they speak of their absent parents, they employ either the confidential: "my papa, my mama!" or they say "señor padre, señora madre", or even "Su Merced" (his honor). The son never permits himself to smoke tobacco in the presence of his father, not even when full-grown, or married. The mother, who always sits at home with her daughters, is more indulgent in this respect, perhaps even encourages them to smoke: but in presence of their father, they never venture it. The son takes off his hat, when his father speaks with him; if seated, he rises on either of his parents entering the room, and offers his chair; he avoids turning his back to them, and does not even pass in front of them, if it be possible to pass any other way, and when compelled to do so, he invariably says: "Pardon me!" or, "With your permission."

In Mexico there are no orphan-asylums, but the orphans are nevertheless provided for. At the christening, the god-parents undertake to care for the child, if it should have the misfortune to lose its parents. This is not an empty form as in Europe, but is literally observed. It is not necessary for the authorities to interfere in the matter; even the poor man fetches his orphan god-child, as soon as he learns the death of the parents, and brings him up as a member of his own family. If the god-parents are also dead, there is invariably a dispute between several families, as to who is to receive the child. Often have I heard poor people say: "I bring up a dog, or some other animal; should I not rather undertake the care of fellow-creature?"

This compassionate feature extends also to the suffering and indigent. In the war with North America, I saw persons tend and conceal their wounded enemies, incurring thereby great risk, and subsequently convey them back to their countrymen.

In the course of three centuries, this has been developed in a manner peculiar to the climate and soil, and the character of the Creole is no longer that of the Spaniard. A fertile country, producing abundance almost unasked, a clear sky, a mild climate, where the hardships of winter are unknown, have spoiled the Creole and rendered him more indolent and thoughtless than his transmarine relations; but he has retained liveliness, the excitability, and the romantic sentiments of the latter. The Spaniard is essentially conservative, the Mexican Creole is for progress; he is liberal and tolerant even in religious matters, whilst the Spaniard never quits the established forms in church and state. The Spaniard labors perseveringly, seeks also to profit in detail, and saves what he has earned for old age; the Mexican earns with facility, but just as easily lets it slip through his fingers; he seeks to enjoy the fleeting moment, and leaves Providence to care for the future.

I could easily continue these parallels, but an allusion to them is sufficient. Separate pictures of popular life will best complete the universal lineaments, and animate them with light and color.

Carl Sartorius, *Mexico About 1850.* (*Mexico. Landscapes and Popular Sketches.* 1858) Reprint. Stuttgart: FA Brockhaus Komm, 1961.

RELIGION

Various saints' days and other religious holidays comprised much of the enjoyment working people derived from their everyday lives. Particularly poignant was the Mexican relationship with death.

THE DAY OF THE DEAD OR ALL SAINT'S DAY, FROM SARTORIUS

All Saint's Day is everywhere preceded by vast purchases. On this day a new dress must be had, new ribands and shoes; the women buy new crockery of all kinds, fine, particolored mats, elegant little baskets of palm-leaves *(tompiatl),* and bright-colored schikales (the fruit of the *crescentia alata*). But above all the purchase of wax tapers causes much head-breaking in every house. For several weeks beforehand great activity is observed amongst the retail dealers. Every shopkeeper endeavors to procure wax at a reasonable figure, candle-makers work in his house preparing tapers of all sizes, and in the evening the whole family is occupied in ornamenting these tapers with strips of colored paper. There is no house, no cottage without some dollars' worth of tapers; the poorest laborer would rather go without bread, than without wax; and the Indians devote the earnings of weeks to its purchase.

In the large cities this is less known; the higher classes as they are called, withhold themselves as much as possible from plebeian habits, and we must wander to the villages, if we desire to see this festival in its ancient form.

Whoever is fortunate enough to have a godfather among the Indians—and one can easily attain this good fortune—should visit his *compadres* (god-parents) on the first of November. The street in front of the house is swept very clean, and before the door is a large cross covered with immortelles *(tagetes).* The Indian calls them *sempasochil* and always plants them near his cottage. The house is in festive order, the old saints on the wall are laden with flowers, a wreath of flowers is between them, and two tapers burn in clay candlesticks. No one is at home, but close by, in the kitchen, we distinctly hear the thumping and shaping of the tortillas. Let us look through the doorway into this sanctum of the women. Three stout lasses are preparing the maize on stones, but our *comadre* (godmother) stands there with a knife in her hand, happily, though, her victim is only a large turkey. Another, doomed to the same fate, is tied up in a corner; and close by are at least six fat hens, all ready for the pot. "Who would be so cruel, *comadre*", we exclaim, after saluting her: "what are you going to do with this mass of provision? Is one of the girls to be married?" The three look roguishly at each other and laugh. "*Ojala*", says the old woman chuckling,

"I should then be rid of one of my cares; but the fowls are for the dead, and you will afterwards do us the honor of trying the *tlatonile*."

Should the reader think of accepting the invitation, we must warn him not to fill his mouth the proffered dish before trying it; this *tlatonile* looks like a very innocent ragout, but burns like fire, being the genuine extract of unripe Spanish pepper, and none but mouths that are fire proof may venture on it. But we must now explain the meaning of the festival.

Neither the Indian nor the Mestizo knows the bitterness of sorrow; he does not fear death; the departure from life is not dreadful in his eyes, he does not crave for the goods he is leaving, and has no care for those who survive him, who have still fertile earth, and the mild sky. Is it indifference, is it frivolity which a rich tropical nature bestows on her children? I know not; but it is certain, that in the eyes of the people, death does not appear as a black, dismal specter, that sorrow for the dead does not absorb all the joys of life. The first outbreak of grief is violent, copious showers of tears are shed, but are soon dried. The Mexican says: "God has willed it, we must all die." Every Indian thinks thus, and regards it from the practical side. On the occasion of a death the relations and neighbors come and share in the grief, especially throughout the night; when the body remains in the house. The tribute offered is a taper, and something to drink. Prayers are offered up for the repose of the deceased, and the night is then passed in social games and merriment in the same apartment where the corpse lies on the floor surrounded with tapers. When death befalls a child under seven years (*parvulos*), it is celebrated as a day of rejoicing, because the soul ascends direct to heaven, without undergoing the transitory state of Purgatory. The little corpse is gaily decked with flowers and ribands, fastened to a board and placed upright in a corner of the cottage, in a sort of niche formed of branches and blossoms, and lighted up with many tapers. On the approach of evening, a few rockets proclaim the velorio, music resounds, and the whole night is passed in dancing and merry-making. The god-parents of the children do not altogether approve of it, as they have to pay the reckoning. At these wakes the company remain assembled till the morning (with children as with adults), and then proceed immediately to the churchyard. The bier is quickly formed of a few sticks, a mat serves for a coffin; if a priest is at hand, preceded by three cross-bearers he hastens to the spot, gives the benediction, and the body is lowered into the earth, to return to earth. Every one present casts in a handful of dust, the grave is filled in, and the mourners depart without any extraordinary impression being produced. If a mother is pitied for having lost her child, she replies: "I loved the little angel; but I am glad that he is happy, without having had to experience the bitterness of life."

Thus accustomed to make light of that which is inevitable, to dance about the yawning grave, we shall not be surprised to find, that the rites in honor of the departed have rather a joyous than a melancholy character. We repeat that only the Indian and the Mestizo observe this ancient practice, whereas the white Creole rarely imitates the Indian custom.

In the Indian villages the proceedings are as follows. On the evening of the last day of October, the house is put in the best order, and when it is dark, a new, parti-colored, woven mat is spread out on the floor of the dwelling. The whole family are assembled in the kitchen, waiting for the meal being prepared, which consists of chocolate, sweet maize porridge, stewed chickens and little tortillas. A portion of each is put if possible into new vessels, and conveyed by the members of the family into the house, where it is placed on the mat; to this is added a peculiar kind of maize-bread, called *elotlascale*, and death-bread, a kind of wheaten-bread without fat, sugar and salt, which is baked for this day only, shaped like a rabbit, a bird etc., and prettily ornamented. On clay candlesticks, corresponding with the number of dishes, thin wax-tapers are lighted, not much thicker than a quill; roses, marigolds, and the blossoms of the *datura grandiflora* are laid between the plates; and now the head of the family invites the dead children, that is to say those of his own immediate house (his own children, grandchildren, brothers and sisters) to come and regale themselves with the offering. The whole family now return to the kitchen to consume the remainder of the meal, which has been prepared abundantly enough to regale also the living. This is the offering of the children, and every child, according to the age it had attained, has its dish and its taper. Saucers with incense are placed around the mat, and fill the chamber with a dense cloud.

The following day offerings are prepared for the adults in a similar manner; but all on a larger scale, from the mat to the tapers. Other dishes, too, are added, which would be too hot for the children: turkey in red-pepper broth, tamales, and other highly seasoned dishes; there is moreover a good supply of drink in large mugs, brandy, pulque, castile and other favorite liquors of the Indians. With the adults less care is exhibited for adorning the room with flowers; but things are added which belonged to the deceased: their sandals, their straw-hat, or the hatchet with which they worked. The whole house is filled with incense, which is placed before the picture of the patron saints, who were undoubtedly introduced, three centuries ago, in place of the house idols.

The belief, that the souls of the departed visit the places that were dear to them in life, that they sometimes flutter about their dwelling as bright humming-birds, sometimes float above their former home as clouds, was doubtless handed down by the Toltecs to the subsequent lords of the soil, namely the Aztecs; and we may assume that it still obtains among the people, although we have never succeeded in gaining confirmation of the same from the mouth of an Indian. They are reserved in everything bearing reference to the religion of their fathers; perhaps, owing to their long subjection, their traditions are unconnected, and only here and there to be recognized.

The meal dedicated to the manes of the departed, is not usually consumed by those who offer it; but is sent to relations and neighbors, from whom a similar donation is reserved. In the villages where there is a mixed population, the young fellows on the look out for fun, go to the dwellings of the Indians, and offer to tell their beads for the repose of the souls. They are welcomed, and the offerings intended for the ghosts, are part devoured by the living. They laugh and jest at the silly Indians, who prepare a meal for those who are long since dead. "Do you recollect, Felipe, how we told our beads in old Mizcoatl's house, and had nearly burst with laughter when long Nicholas filched a glass of sweet liquor from the *ofrenta* (death-meal) and emptied it, and then made the old heathen believe, the shade of his son had drunk it?"—"To be sure", returned the other; "but last year he managed better, and would not admit us until all the liquids had been placed in safety. We made up for it, however, by carrying off a contribution from his fat *huajolete* (turkey), which was not to be despised; and there was drink enough at his neighbor's".

Talking in this way, the mischievous rogues knocked at the doors, and muttered prayers, feasted at the expense of the harmless superstition of the poor Indians, and in addition, carried away a tolerable supply of boiled and roast. We quit them, to do honor to the comadre's invitation, and are hospitably entertained. We there learned that only white ragouts were cooked for the children, which are but moderately spiced, but still burn like a decoction of pepper; further that few families spend less than from six to ten dollars for this feast, and that it is their greatest delight to consume all their favorite dishes on this day. The following day, the church-festival of All Souls, mass is attended, and the women light whole rows of little wax tapers which they stick on the floor before them. This is a harvest-day for the priests; for every Indian has a short prayer said for the souls of his departed after divine service, for which he has to depose two reals (about one shilling) on the altar.

In the evening the women and children proceed to the cemetery, strew the graves with flowers, sprinkle them with holy-water, burn incense, and light innumerable tapers, which are suffered to burn until they go out of themselves. In the clear, beautiful November nights, these grave illuminations afford a magical appearance, when the tapers light up the dark cypresses or orange-trees of the cemetery, and the gloomy walls of the chapel. All is hushed; no sound is heard near the abodes of the dead save the chirp of grasshoppers, like the breath of nature; whilst the expiring flame of the tapers reminds us of the soul quitting its frail earthly tenement.

Carl Sartorius, *Mexico About 1850*. (*Mexico. Landscapes and Popular Sketches*. 1858) Reprint. Stuttgart: FA Brockhaus Komm, 1961.

CORPUS CHRISTI

RELIGIOUS FESTIVAL, C.S. STEWART, *THE PERSONAL RECORD OF A CRUISE*

June 26th— It is to the Roman Church that we are here chiefly indebted for every thing in the way of spectacle. Two principal feast days have occurred within the week past: that of Corpus Christi on the 19th, and that of St. John the Baptist on the 24th inst. The fête of Corpus Christi was observed with great display. It was instituted by Urban IV., six hundred years ago, in honor of the then newly adopted doctrine of transubstantiation, and consequent adoration of the host. Its legendary origin is traced to Juliana, a nun of Liege, who, while looking at the full moon, saw a gap in its orb, and by peculiar revelation from heaven, learned that the moon represented the Christian Church, and the gap the want of a festival for the adoration of the body of Christ, in the consecrated wafer. This she was to begin to celebrate, and to announce to the world. The authorization of the festival by papal bull, was induced by the following miraculous incident. While a priest, who did not believe in the change of the bread into the body of Christ, was going through the ceremony of benediction, drops of blood fell upon his surplice, which, he endeavored to conceal them in the folds of his garment, were formed into bloody images of the host. His skepticism was thus overcome; and the bull of Urban, authorizing the adoration, was published. This occurred in 1264, and the bloody surplice is still shown at Civita Vecchia as a relic!

In Rio de Janeiro, as in all papal countries, Corpus Christi is a chief festival in the year. Its celebration was commenced at the dawn of day, by a general peal of the bells from every church and convent tower, by the booming of cannon along the shores, and the hissing and crackling of rockets in the sky. Flags were every where unfurled; draperies of silk and satin, of gold and silver tissue, of damask and velvet of every hue, were displayed, from the windows and balconies of the houses in the principal streets; and the windows of the palace ornamented on the outside with rich hangings of crimson damask. High mass was performed in the imperial chapel at 11 o'clock. This was now opened for the first time, after having been for a year undergoing thorough renovation, by regilding and new painting in fresco. The effect is rich and chaste. On either side of the nave, between the entrance and the transept, are the shrines of the apostolic saints, above which hang paintings of each, with the accustomed emblems of their individuality. "The Supper," by a master, ornaments the altar of a side chapel at one end of the transept, and a beautifully executed and classically draped effigy of St. Julian in wax, in a sarcophagus of glass, adorns the other. The altar-piece of the grand altar covers the entire end of the chapel within the chancel. The subject is the assumption of the Virgin. The royal family of Portugal—at the time of the immigration—in attitudes of adoration, occupy the foreground: the Queen mother, John VI and his wife, Carlota of Spain, and Don Pedro I., then a lad, being the chief figures.

The imperial body-guard in state dresses, with halberds at rest, early formed in lines on either side of the nave from the entrance to the transept. The intervening space, newly carpeted, was in reserve for the ministers of state, the officers of the household, and other dignitaries of the Empire. A procession of these soon made its appearance from a vesting-room communicating with the palace, and opened in file along the nave for the passage of the bishop and his ecclesiastical attendants to the chancel, and of the Emperor, who followed them, to a canopied throne near the high altar. The Empress and her ladies had already entered the imperial tribune facing the throne. The bishop was in full prelatic dress, wearing his mitre and bearing the gilded crosier emblematic of his office. When the chapel was thus filled, the coup d'œil presented a brilliant scene in the masses of rich embroideries in gold; the jeweled decorations of the dignitaries of state; and the court dresses of the different classes of the aristocracy. These last were chiefly of velvet in rich hues, lined with white silk—purple, maroon, mazarine and sky blue, light and dark green, and here and there a suit of the same of plain black.

The orchestra was full, and embraced the best performers of the opera company, both vocal and instrumental. As the service proceeded, the varied attitudes and groupings in the chancel and at the altar, of the officiating priests "Glaring in gems and gay in woven gold;" the floating incense; the harmony of the duo, the trio, and the quartette; the touching strains of the solo; and the burst of the full chorus, could scarcely fail to impress the senses. And when added to this general effect, at the elevation of the host each halberdier; with battle-axe reversed, dropped on his bended knee; every courtier bowed his forehead to the ground; the bishop humbled himself at the steps of the altar, and the Emperor kneeled on the platform of his throne; the whole tableau was one most striking in its dramatic show. Externally all was a profoundness of adoration, which, directed spiritually to the Godhead, would have been irresistibly impressive; but addressed to a mere wafer, and to be regarded as gross idolatry, it was both painful to the mind and saddening to the heart.

Long before the termination of the mass, a procession was marshaled in front of the chapel in the palace-square, awaiting the addition from the church of the ecclesiastics and the court, before moving through some of the principal streets. The leading group was unique; and apparently the most attractive part to the surrounding crowds. It consisted of a colossal effigy of St. George, in knightly armor, mounted upon a splendidly caparisoned charger from the Emperor's stud, led by a groom in oriental dress. An armor-bearer in black mail, and other attendants in characteristic costume, formed the suite; while a dozen led horses in housings of green cloth, stiff with the imperial arms in massive silver, completed the cortège of the pasteboard saint. All else in the show was purely ecclesiastic, with a great display of the varied costumes and emblematic devices of the Romish Church. At the end of the religious service, the dignitaries, both of Church and State, fell into the line, and were followed by the host, borne by the bishop beneath a fringed and tasseled canopy of cloth of gold, one of the gilt supporters of which was held by the Emperor with uncovered head

C. S. Stewart, *The Personal Record of a Cruise*. New York: G. P. Putnam and Company, 1856.

CARNAVÃO OR THE INTRUDO

Englishman James Wetherell was a merchant in Brazil, who served as unpaid vice-consul in Bahia from 1843 to 1855. After his tragic death from a fall at age thirty-six, friends discovered and published a thin book of his observations of his time as consul.

CARNIVAL, WETHERELL, BRAZIL:
STRAY NOTES FROM BAHIA

During the three days of the "Intrudo", the days of the carnival, a custom exists here of throwing water about and wetting one another. This singular custom is also carried out in other Catholic countries. The better classes use waxen balls made in the shape of fruit, and filled with water, which is sometimes scented, they are called "larangeiras" and "limas", these balls they throw at one another with great dexterity, and with the slightest contact they burst, covering the person with water. Amongst the lower classes large squirts are used; torrents of water, none of the cleanest, are thrown from the windows, and people are immersed in large troughs. All descriptions of practical jokes are carried out during these days of license, some not very agreeable; the blacks daub each other with red and white clay. During the three days it is quite impossible to move out without undergoing a thorough drenching, and the excitement is kept up unintermittingly. There are police laws prohibiting the practice, but the authorities have never been able to abate the nuisance. A relic of this curious custom exists at Howden, in Yorkshire, on the day before Ash Wednesday, the fire engines of the town are drawn round to the different public pumps, and all persons passing within range are well wetted, the supplies of water being exhausted, the engines are replaced, and a holiday is made of the rest of the day by the inhabitants.

James Wetherell, *Brazil, Stray Notes from Bahia: Being Extracts from Letters, etc. during a Residence of Fifteen Years*. Liverpool: Webb and Hunt, 1960.

FUNERALS

Funerals were religious spectacles. They also displayed the stark differences in status and wealth among Latin Americans.

FUNERALS, KIDDER, *SKETCHES OF RESIDENCE AND TRAVELS IN BRAZIL*

The funeral ceremonies of Rio have been repeatedly described. They exhibit the same fondness for parade and display which is manifest in other religious cere- monies, and moreover, afford one of the most common occasions of both. They are greatly varied in character, according to the age and condition of the person deceased. In the case of infants and young children the occasion is considered joyous, and the procession is one of triumph. White horses, gaily caparisoned and bearing white plumes upon their heads, draw an open coach, in which sits a priest in his most costly robes, with his head uncovered, and holding in his lap upon an open litter, the remains of the infant, adorned with tinsel, and ribbons, and roses. The torch-bearers if not dressed in white, have their coats trimmed with silver lace, and all the flambeaux are white.

In the case of adults, the contrast is the greatest imaginable. Night is generally chosen for the procession. On the day preceding, a funeral altar is set up in house of the deceased. The door is hung in black,—the horses, the hearse, the torch- bearers, are all dressed in black. The driver of the hearse wears black epaulettes on his shoulders, and on his head a chapeau de bras, with a nodding plume. The num- ber of torch-bearers is in proportion to the number of carriages in the train, on either side of which they form a line. They are frequently mounted, and their long black torches, flaming upon the darkness, create an imposing spectacle.

When the coffin reaches the church, it is transferred to a lofty pedestal, called a mausoleum, covered with black cloth, and surrounded with burning candles. Here it rests while the funeral services are performed. The body is then interred beneath some of the marble slabs by which the floor of the church is covered, or walled up in some of the catacumbas that have been constructed in the outer walls of the edifice.

The coffin used in the ceremony is not interred with the corpse, being kept by the church or brotherhood for the purpose of renting on such occasions. When the bodies are placed in the catacombs, quicklime is thrown upon them to hasten the process of decay; and, after the lapse of about twelve months, the cavity is opened, and the bones of the dead are taken out and cleansed. The friends of the deceased then cause the remains to be enclosed in a box, to remain at the church, or to be taken home at pleasure.

These boxes are generally left in the church, the families preserving the key; but an instance was mentioned to me of a gentleman who kept the house of his de- ceased wife in his own sleeping room.

The cases and boxes are of different sizes and shapes, but seldom have any re- semblance to coffins. Some are large, like mausoleums; others, with their ornamented exterior, resemble large dressing-cases. It seems highly incongruous to witness, in such a place the display of ornament; and yet some of these mortuary boxes are adorned with drapery of gold and silver tissue, wrought upon satin and velvet, to please the eye, and call forth the admiration of those who may visit the cloister.

How different form the funeral of ceremony, with its boasted "sumptuousness and magnificence," is that of the poor slave. Neither torches nor coffin are borne in his lonely procession. His body is placed in a hammock, the ends of which are fastened to a long pole, which is carried on the shoulders of two of his comrades. These may be seen early in the morning marching slowly, one after the other, towards the Misericordia. The cemetery connected with that institution consists of a small piece of ground, surrounded by a high wall, on which the figure of a death's head is emblazoned in different places.

Within this enclosure a grave is daily dug, in the form of a pit, seven feet square. In this are placed promiscuously the bodies of those who die in the hospital over night, and of the slaves and poor persons who are brought here to receive gratuitous interment. Thus, in the space of a year, the whole surface is dug over, and in successive years the same process continues to be repeated.

As the health of the city is manifestly endangered by these repeated and premature excavations, no less than by the practice of burying in churches, the Misericordia has recently purchased extensive grounds for a cemetery, on the Ponta do Cajú, a little north of S. Christovaõ, whither the dead are conveyed by water, and interred in permanent graves.

Great numbers of slaves are brought together at the Emperor's country seat, where they are permitted to follow the customs they prefer.

On looking out of the window, a negro was seen bearing on his head a wooden tray, on which was the corpse of a child, covered with a white cloth, decorated with flowers, a bunch of them being fastened to its hand. Behind him, in a promiscuous throng, were about twenty negresses, and a number of children, adorned most of them with flaunting stripes of red, white, and yellow. They were all chanting some Ethiopian dirge, to which they kept time by a slow trot; the bearer of the deceased child pausing, once in one or two rods, and whirling around on his toes like a dancer.

Among the foremost, the mother was distinguished as her excessive gesticulation, although it could hardly be determined by her actions, whether emotions of grief or joy were predominant. Thus they passed on to the church-yard, where the corpse was delivered up to the vigario and his sexton. The procession then returned, chanting and dancing, if possible, more wildly than when they came.

Daniel P. Kidder, *Sketches of a Residence and Travels in Brazil.* Vol. II. Philadelphia: Sorin and Hall, 1845.

QUESTIONS

1. Compare Sartorius's rather critical view of Mexican cities with Kidder's observations of Rio de Janeiro. What accounts for the differences?
2. Despite the beauty of Rio de Janeiro, what is it that Ms. Graham observes as an undercurrent of sadness?
3. Ms. Graham describes Bahia in somewhat dismal terms. What are her observations?
4. What are Stewart's observations about the women of Buenos Aires? Does Head concur?

5. Why do Stewart and Head find Buenos Aires disagreeable?
6. Of the smaller urban areas, São Luis, Fortaleza, Mendoza, and Quito, which seems most amenable? Where would you prefer to have lived? Why?
7. What is Sartorius's view of the Creoles of Mexico? Do you think he is particularly critical of the women?
8. What was the role of religion in urban life in nineteenth-century Latin America? How does this compare with the role of religion in the countryside?
9. What is the overall picture of Latin American cities presented by these observers? Do you think these foreign observers were prejudiced against Latin Americans?
10. How would you compare Latin American cities with those in the United States at the same time?

7

THE MILITARY

INTRODUCTION

In much of Latin America over the past century, militaries have dominated politics. Building on the foundations of the incessant warfare of the nineteenth century, the armed forces changed from rag-tag bands led by local strongmen, into professionalized, national institutions with a high degree of internal pride, often with considerable disdain for less disciplined civilian authorities. Militaries repeatedly intervened in Latin American politics in the twentieth century, supposedly to rescue their societies from disintegration. Ever more impatient with civilian regimes, particularly those that were elected and functioned democratically, militaries grew increasingly harsh until the years of terror between the mid-1960s and the early 1990s when Argentina engaged in the Dirty War and the Pinochet regime mortified Chile.

The great irony of the history of Latin American militaries is, of course, that they were never very successful in fulfilling their main mission of protecting *La Patria* (the Fatherland). In no war during the nineteenth century, even in victory, did any of the region's military branches distinguish themselves. In the Paraguayan War (1865–1870), also known as the War of the Triple Alliance, the victorious Brazil, Argentina, and Uruguay required five years to destroy a seemingly overmatched Paraguay with a fraction of the allies' population. Chile won the War of the Pacific (1879–1881) on the basis of two minor naval victories and despite a poor performance by its army. The losers of this war, Bolivia and Peru, were badly led, equipped, and supplied. Despite their disgraceful records in these wars, the militaries of Argentina, Brazil, and Chile only grew stronger and more convinced of their role as saviors of their respective nations. The two twentieth-century wars, the Chaco War (1935) and the Falklands/Malvinas War (1982), were disastrously fought. In the Chaco conflict, the armies of both antagonists, Bolivia and Paraguay, fought wretchedly. In the Falklands, the officer corps of the Argentine army fled the battlefield. With the exception of the fleeting victory by the Mexican army over the invading French forces at Puebla on May 5, 1862, there was no victory over a major foreign power throughout the entire nineteenth and twentieth centuries. In fact, the militaries were not even successful at maintaining domestic order. For example, the Mexican army was humiliated by a small number of villagers at Tomochi in 1892. The Brazilian army suffered the same fate at Canudos in 1896–1897 at the hands of a community of poor peasants. The Mexican army under Porfirio Díaz failed to halt an uprising of barely a few thousand in 1911, leading to the Great Revolution.

THE MILITARY CREDO

The sense of frustration with civilian rule came out quite clearly in the mid 1920s in Chile, when a group of young military officers took power in 1925. President Arturo Alessandri Palma (1920–1925) resigned in January of that year. He had spent the previous five years attempting without success to institute a progressive reform program, stymied by the opposition of the oligarchy and its senior military allies. A conservative military junta took over from Alessandri, but the junior officers restored Alessandri in March. He resigned a second time a few months later. Carlos Ibañez del Campo led the junior officers and eventually installed himself as dictator from 1927 until his fall in 1931. In a statement published in El Mercurio *in February 1927, Ibañez explained his position and forewarned of the military's future role.*

STATEMENT OF CARLOS IBAÑEZ OF CHILE ON THE ROLE OF THE MILITARY

The final hour—the hour for settling accounts has arrived. The malevolent propaganda of a few professional politicians and the disunifying propaganda of an audacious few who oppose all authority is not acceptable. It's necessary to apply cauterization from top to bottom. . . . The action has developed thanks to the treasonous actions of a number of professional politicians who think the Country cannot exist and progress without their concourse. . . .

I am sure that our sister the Navy supports the wishes of the Army. The two constitute the bulwark of Chile, not only in the case of external conflict but also in moments of internal gangrene. There are times when the Armed Forces must be the saviours of the people. The question stated thus, I tranquilly await developments and have faith that the sensible and patriotic portion of our country will cooperate with my work and will comprehend the motives that guide my deeds, and which are inspired by the old motto: "La Patria before all things."

Source: *El Mercurio* (Santiago), February 9, 1927. Transl. Frederick Nunn. Cited in Brian Loveman, *For La Patria: Politics and the Armed Forces in Latin America.* Wilmington: Scholarly Resources, 1999.

General Oscar Benavides (1914–1915, 1933–1939), who twice took the reins of government in Peru, expressed similar sentiments in his last will and testament. Benavides had led the first coup by the military as an institution in the history of Peru in 1914. He later took over the government after the assassination of President Luis M. Sánchez Cerro in 1933. He prevented the radical APRA movement, led by Victor Haya de la Torre, from ruling Peru, but at the same time took progressive measures to help Peru emerge from the Great Depression.

GENERAL BENAVIDES, LAST WILL AND TESTAMENT 1931

I declare that I have dedicated all my life to the service of my *patria* with the greatest abnegation and honesty, that I always sought her aggrandizement and prestige, and that it is a great stamp of pride for me to bequeath to my children a name without stain. I declare, again, that at no time in my life have I aspired to be President of the Republic and that my only ambition was to be always a good soldier of my patria. Only unexpected circumstances, against my will . . . have carried me twice to exercise the Supreme command of the Republic to save the country from anarchy and chaos. . . . In sum, I have the happy satisfaction given to my conscience that tells me that I have done whatever has been possible for the good and grandeur of *la patria.*

Source: Felipe de la Barra (General), *Objectivo: Palacio del Gobierno.* Lima: Editorial Juana Mejía, 1967 cited in Brian Loveman, *For La Patria: Politics and the Armed Forces in Latin America.* Wilmington: Scholarly Resources, 1999.

The Brazilian military has, since the overthrow of the empire in 1888, played a crucial role in politics. Not only did its officers lead the nation through the early years of the Republic during the late 1880s and 1890s, but it installed Getulio Vargas (1930–1945, 1950–1954) as president in 1930. Later the military took the reins of government again in 1964 for twenty years. A former officer in Brazil, Juracy Magalhães, had the following to say.

BRAZIL, MINISTRY OF FOREIGN RELATIONS, UNDERSTANDING THE BRAZILIAN ARMED FORCES

It is necessary to understand that the Brazilian armed forces, in comparison with the armed forces in some other countries, are far from constituting a privileged caste, but represents one of the most important and well-defined sectors of our middle class.

     . . . The armed forces, identified, as I mentioned above, with popular aspirations and loyal to them, exercise in practice a form of moderating power whenever there is manifested a strong and legitimate movement of public opinion. The armed forces intervene in the political scene supporting that manifestation and acting as instruments of transformation.

Source: Brasil, Ministério das Relacões Exteriores, Discurso do Embaixador, Juravy Magalhães em Washington, 16 de Fevereiro de 1965, *Textos e Declaraões Sobre Politica Externa: Primeiro Aniversário de Revolucão de 31 de Marco de 1964* (1965), p. 135 cited in Alfred Stepan, *The Military in Politics: Changing Patterns in Brazil.* Princeton: Princeton University Press, 1974.

THE MILITARY CONDITION

Tragically for the Latin American militaries, most of the rank and file were badly treated and minimally educated and trained. Often rank and file were draftees, quite unwilling to serve. In 1920 Captain Tobías Barros described the deplorable conditions of the Chilean military.

TOBIÁS BARROS, DESCRIPTION
OF A CHILEAN RECRUIT

Three-fourths of the recruits are illiterate, poor peasants from the countryside and workers; their spiritual nature is not much different from that of a young child . . . it is common for the peasant recruit to be unaware of the existence, and therefore, the use of undergarments, except an undershirt, . . . we even have to show them how to put on their socks and other intimate pieces of clothing . . . under the seeming air of indifference and passivity the [peasant recruit] also has a native astuteness and malice difficult to measure. This malice of the peasant is inherited from the Indian and can give us problems. [On the other hand] this is 90 percent of our recruits. The rich, with honorable exceptions, believe that the obligatory service law, noble in principle, well thought out and democratic in its objective, was not meant to apply to them . . . . [each lieutenant] should become a good educator of citizens, of soldiers, without doubt the most noble and important . . . mission of an officer.

Source: Tobás Barros (Captain), *Vigilia de armas*. Santiago: 1920. Cited in Brian Loveman, *For La Patria: Politics and the Armed forces in Latin America*. Wilmington: Scholarly Resources, 1999.

· · ·

In the case of Mexico, while the military has remained an important behind- the scenes political force, it has not received the funding for equipment and arms afforded the Brazilian and Chilean armed forces. A report on the Mexican military in 2004 clearly indicates that it has considerable capabilities for internal counterinsurgency and repression, but is badly outdated in its capacity for modern warfare.

Here are three reports on the Mexican military: the first in 1840, the second in 1910, and the third in 2004. These depict the evolution of the military over two centuries.

MILITARY BUDGET 1840, FROM MAYER,
MEXICO AS IT WAS AND AS IT IS

ARMY AND NAVY

In regard to the numbers of the Army, I am equally without information since 1840; but I may state that the forces have been considerably augmented, and in all probability amount to 40,000 men. In 1840, the Mexican army was composed of

14 Generals of Division, $500 per month
26 Generals of Brigade, $375 per month

ARTILLERY

3 brigades, (on foot,)
1 brigades, (mounted,)
5 Separate Companies

ENGINEER CORPS.

1 Director General, 3 Colonels,	$235 per month
6 Lieutenant Colonels,	$141 per month
1 Adjutant,	$104 per month
14 Captains,	$84 per month
16 Lieutenants,	$62 per month
10 Sub-lieutenants,	$39 per month

SAPPERS

1 Battalion

NAVAL AND MILITARY FORCE

Plana Mayer del Ejercito

This was composed of the General-in-Chief and a number of Colonels, Lieutenant-Colonels, Captains, &c.

PERMANENT INFANTRY

8 Regiments of 2 battalions each, each battalion of 8 companies, each company of 112 men, officers included—or in all 14,336 persons: each is paid $11 93 per month.

ACTIVE INFANTRY

9 Regiments. This body differs from the preceding, or Permanent Infantry, in being liable to service only when required by Government; or, in other words, it is a sort of national militia, well-drilled—Total number, 16,128.

PERMANENT CAVALRY

8 Regiments, each regiment composed of 2 squadrons, each squadron of 2 companies. Each regiment composed, in all, of 676 men,—or the 8 of 4,056 at $12 50 per month

35 Separate Companies in various places throughout the Republic.

ACTIVE CAVALRY

6 Regiments of 4 squadrons, each squadron of 2 companies.

NAVY

The Navy of Mexico consists at present of 3 Steam Frigates, 2 Brigs, 3 Schooners, 2 gunboats.

Source: Brantz Mayer, *Mexico As It Was and As It Is.* New York: J. Winchester, New World Press, 1844.

SOLDIERS, FROM W. R. CARSON, *MEXICO: THE WONDERLAND OF THE SOUTH*

Next to policemen, soldiers are much in evidence in Mexico, the army being an important national institution. The country is divided into several military districts, and in each of these is a certain quota of troops. Nearly every town of any size has a commandancia or barracks. As mentioned in another chapter, most of the Mexican officers are trained at Chapultepec. Over a third of the commissioned members of the army graduate from that institution. The student binds himself for seven years' service, and should he be discharged or refuse to serve, he must repay the government about ten dollars for each month he has remained in the academy. If there is a war, all retired graduates can be compelled to report for service. There is no conscription in Mexico and the soldier's pay is very small.

The Mexican standing army amounts between 25,000 and 30,000 men; but this does not represent the total forces of the Republic, which at a time of emergency could summon 86,000 reserves to the colors. Of the standing army 20,000 odd are infantry, 2000 artillery and 5000 cavalry, while there are small corps of engineers and others. Infantry and cavalry are armed with the Spanish Mauser rifles and carbines. The headquarters of the army are in Mexico city, and several battalions of infantry and regiments of cavalry are stationed there at all times.

Mexican soldiers usually wear either a blue cloth or white linen uniform, with a blue or white military cap or glazed leather Austrian-shaped kepi. One of the artillery regiments has a uniform of German appearance, blue with red facings, and a bright, spiked brass helmet. Some regiments wear the national sombrero, and in the country districts the nacionales sometimes wear a pudding-basin-shaped straw hat with a ribbon round it. All the cavalrymen have a carbine strapped to their backs, and carry revolvers as well as swords. The majority of the troops are Indians of half or whole blood.

Some of the crack regiments are presentable enough, but the average Mexican soldier looks somewhat undisciplined and sloppy. As to their fighting qualities there is a great difference of opinion, some authorities declaring them cowardly and untrustworthy, while others assert that they are brave and stubborn fighters. The truth is that there are great differences in the methods of recruiting. While the nacionales, who are equivalent to our militia, are for the most part a well-set up, loyal body of men, the regulars are quite untrustworthy and have little or no patriotism. The explanation is simple. Most of them are men who as a penalty for some crime have been sentenced to serve in the army, thus forcing them into the service, ill-drilled and with little or no knowledge of the use of firearms, so that it is scarcely to be expected that they will make good soldiers.

Source: Willam English Carson, *Mexico: The Wonderland of the South.* The Macmillan Company, 1909.

• • •

KATE DOYLE, "REPORTING ON THE MEXICAN MILITARY"

[...] The leading problems that continue to hamper the Mexican military are obsolete and heterogeneous equipment, lack of logistical control and technical maintenance, over-centralization, corruption, and inadequate training.

The Army is capable of maintaining public order, but this capability depends on how widespread civil unrest becomes. The military would not be able to control a broad-based antigovernment movement, but such an uprising is unlikely to happen in the near future.

Mexican authorities are extremely sensitive to its military associating with any foreign armed forces. Relations between US and Mexican military officers are correct, but formal. Under the current Secretary of National Defense, General Antonio Riviello Bazan, more lines of communication have been established and opportunities for exchange between the two militaries have broadened. However, relations will probably continue to expand at a slow pace because of historical antecedents, contentious bilateral immigration, and drug enforcement-related issues.

A Mexican military defense against an equal-size military force with modern weapons is not possible. Under the protection of the United States (US), and with weaker militaries to the south, Mexico has historically enjoyed the benefits of a de facto military alliance without obligations. As a result, the Mexican Armed Forces have organized and equipped primarily for internal defense. The mission of the armed forces includes the security and support of the administration, control against civil unrest, and suppression of drug trafficking.

Mexico continues to remain remarkably free of immediate security concerns from within or beyond its borders. The lack of short-term threats is particularly unique given Mexico's proximity to the sustained instability in Central America and its own significant economic difficulties. However, domestic instability could increase dramatically if the economy fails to improve despite the government's current civic and military modernization efforts. [...]

Although disciplined, the armed forces of Mexico are under-trained and antiquated. Modernization and reorganization programs are currently underway to alleviate these deficiencies, but progress will be slow because the Mexican Government has traditionally kept its armed forces organizationally divided, rendering them too weak to pose a political challenge. [...]

The organization, equipment, and training of the army are well suited for conducting counterinsurgency operations. The Mexican Army is capable of suppressing a regional insurgency, as demonstrated by its successful counterinsurgency campaign in Guerrero State in 1974. [...] Only a massive, nationwide insurrection would challenge the army's ability to maintain order.

Although Mexico is economically well developed by Third World standards, it retains much outdated and heterogeneous military equipment. Commanders from all services frequently complain of spare-parts shortages, under-qualified maintenance technicians, and lack of quality equipment.

Based on the poor condition of current Mexican weapons and equipment, it can be concluded that competent employment of any newly acquired sophisticated equipment would be highly unlikely—the Mexican military does not have a budget of sufficient size or adequate training and logistical support structures required. Although improving, this problem is not expected to be remedied in the near future.

The most significant military activity in recent years has taken place in the counter-drug arena. The army was called upon to suppress election-related civil unrest in Michoacán State in April 1990. Elements of the Airborne Brigade have provided security for some major law enforcement actions, including the arrest of a corrupt union leader and a major drug trafficking kingpin. [. . .]

Although the Mexican military has shown an ability to conduct successful counter-drug operations, the efforts have not been enough to significantly restrict or stop the trans-shipment of drugs through Mexico. [Large section deleted.]

Over the past 12 years, the Mexican Secretariats of National Defense and the Navy have significantly increased military capability, particularly in south-eastern Mexico. The buildup is part of an overall military expansion and modernization program and is also in response to perceived security threats along the borders with Guatemala and Belize. The threats include Guatemalan insurgent activity, Guatemalan army incursions, trafficking in arms and drugs, and threats to oil producing facilities. The armed forces have nearly doubled the number of combat units and aircraft assigned to south-eastern Mexico while reorganizing commands, constructing new facilities and adding new capabilities such as a radar system and special operations units.

Officers and soldiers of units with specialized missions receive appropriate training. The Group of 100 (the army's principal antiterrorist unit) and the GAFE (Special Forces Airmobile Group) train for their special operations. The personnel of the Airborne Brigade receive a grueling 11-week jump school. Units selected for Task Force Marte undergo a month of intensive training for counter-drugs before deploying.

There is no military intelligence branch; consequently, individuals from other branches attend intelligence training. There is no military intelligence school in Mexico, so officers often train in foreign schools. [. . .]

Corruption exists in the army—as in all branches of the Mexican Armed Forces—and it affects all ranks. Corruption is most notable with units participating in counter-drug operations, because drug traffickers are often able to entice some military personnel to cooperate in return for various forms of compensation.

Command and control suffers from over-centralization and a rigid command structure. Even the most minute decisions, such as requisitions for spare parts or approval of officer leave forms, must be signed at the national level. This slows routine decision-making to a crawl, although the Secretary will bypass the chain of command and communicate directly with zone commanders on important issues. Most of the Mexican Army is dispersed as garrison units controlled by military zone headquarters, with no tactical organization above battalion level. This zonal system does provide flexibility, as units can be transferred from one zone to another with little disruption. Efforts to professionalize the officer corps, coupled with operational experience in the drug war, are gradually improving the army's command and control capability.

The army's intelligence capabilities are marginal and geared mainly to collecting on domestic political groups and, more recently, on drug trafficking activity. Resources devoted to non-domestic targets are limited to surveillance of various foreign embassies and diplomats, particularly the United States and Cuba. The Secretariat of Government, responsible for internal security, runs the General Directorate of Investigations and National Security (DGISN), probably Mexico's most efficient intelligence organization. The DGISN is well organized and uses its limited resources efficiently in collecting routine, short-term intelligence.

The army's system of intelligence collection and analysis is rudimentary. Military zone commanders utilize an information platoon to collect intelligence in their area. Partidas (groups of information platoons) stationed in isolated areas and the rural defense corps also collect information. Raw intelligence is passed directly to the S-2 (intelligence) section of the National Defense Staff in Mexico City for analysis. [Deleted]

The Mexican environment is relatively favorable for the conduct of intelligence operations by the US Armed Forces. Bribery and other forms of corruption are widespread throughout Mexico, giving foreign intelligence services numerous opportunities to recruit sources. The ability of Mexican intelligence services to counter HUMINT [human intelligence gathering] operations is probably only moderate. Mexican intelligence has very little experience in combating foreign espionage operations, primarily because most of the espionage occurring inside Mexico is directed against the US; the Mexican Government has limited concern with such operations. [Deleted]

For the foreseeable future the Mexican intelligence and security establishment will face serious problems caused by corruption and inadequate funding. Effective law enforcement in Mexico faces major obstacles because of the pervasive influence of drug traffickers who have corrupted large numbers of police and intelligence personnel. Corruption is a less serious problem within the Mexican Armed Forces where greater discipline prevails. Within the PJF and the state police services, corruption is widespread and has led to large-scale dismissals. [. . .]

The January 1994 outbreak of an organized insurgency in Chiapas has presented Mexico's intelligence and security services with a serious challenge. A significant percentage of Mexican military and police forces have been diverted to Chiapas to contain the violence. Until a peace settlement is reached, this reallocation of intelligence assets is likely to remain in effect. The main consequence of this situation is a weakening of the Mexican effort against drug trafficking. At present it appears that the EZLN, the guerrilla group behind the insurgency, does not have enough resources or adherents to spread its activities to other Mexican states. If this proves true, and the government is able to reach an agreement with the EZLN, the rebellion in Chiapas will not have long-term repercussions for the stability of Mexico. On the other hand, if the EZLN and the government are unable to come to terms, there is a chance that unrest could spread to other parts of Mexico, which would threaten the overall stability of the country. [. . .]

Source: Abridged from "The Blind Man and the Elephant: Reporting on the Mexican Military" by Kate Doyle, American Program, Interhemispheric Resource Center, May 2004. Reprinted by permission of the National Security Archive.

THE END RESULT

Brazilians and other Latin Americans tried to explain what had happened. In this excerpt the Archdiocese of Rio de Janeiro looked into history.

TORTURE IN BRAZIL

"THE ORIGINS OF THE MILITARY REGIME"

What happened in Brazil to produce so many acts of grim cruelty? Were these acts of inhuman hate simply the handiwork of a few insane individuals who by chance worked in the official agencies charged with carrying out political repression?

Some historical explanation is necessary to answer this question. Torture, of course, is a very old institution throughout the world. In Brazil, as elsewhere, it has been used routinely during inquiries into the activities of political dissenters. After the 1964 military coup, however, torture was administered to members of the political opposition on a systematic basis. Moreover, the practice was an essential component of the semiautonomous repressive system that eventually grew out of all proportion even to the authoritarian state itself. Torture became a daily fact of Brazilian life because those sectors within the military that justified all measures in the maintenance of internal security held sway within the state apparatus. At the same time, the political regime closed down, eventually excluding even segments of the traditional elite from political participation. In brief, by 1968 a powerful system of repression and control was entrenched in Brazil.

This system, however, cannot be understood in isolation from the broad sweep of Brazilian history. The armed forces that assumed power by overthrowing President João Goulart in April 1964 were following a long tradition of military intervention in Brazil. This tradition goes back to the monarchist period (1822–89) and continued during the so-called Old Republic (1889–1930). Most often, the military would be called upon by the central government—whether monarchist or republican—to repress popular uprising. Indeed, the success of these repressive actions has resulted in a historically erroneous image of Brazilians as conformist, accommodating, and submissive. In reality, popular uprisings were frequent.

The monarchist period, for example, witnessed the so-called Equator Confederation, a movement for social change in the northern eastern states of Pernambuco, Paraiba, Rio Grande do Norte, and Ceará from 1824 to 1825. The Confederation was led by the Carmelite Father Joaquim do Amor Divino Rabelo Caneca, who was later executed. Other revolts occurred in Ceará in 1831 and 1832. In the northern state of Pará, the "Cabanagem," named after the huts ("cabanas") of rebels who lived on the edge of rivers, erupted from 1835 to 1840 and ended with the military killing half the state's population. From 1838 to 1841, the basket-maker Manuel Francisco dos Anjos Ferreira led cowpunchers, artisans, peasants, slaves, and ex-soldiers in a popular uprising (called the "balaiada," referring to "balaio" or "big basket") in what is today the northern state of Maranhão. In 1835, the Farrapos War began in the southern states of Santa Catarin and Rio Grande do Sul. It was settled only ten years later. The "Sabinada," named after the movement's main ideologue, medical doctor Francisco Sabino

Alvares da Rocha Vieira, took place in Salvador, bahia, Brazil's first capital, between 1837 and 1838. The Liberal Revolt, in the center-south states of São Paulo and Minas Gerais, took place in 1842; and the Praieira Revolution, in Pernambuco, in 1848.

In 1831 the National Guard was established to deal with such uprisings. It was officially an auxiliary force of the army, responsible for controlling internal opposition to the central government while the army remained in charge of defense against external aggression. In practice, the National Guard defended the interests of the rural oligarchy. Toward the end of the nineteenth century, when the influence of the rural landowners began to decline as a consequence of the growing importance of the new industrial bourgeoisie, the influence of the National Guard also declined. The war against Paraguay from 1864 to 1870 brought the regular army decisively to the fore. From that time on the army also began openly to intervene in political matters. The fact that it competed with the National Guard, which had come to be identified with the rural oligarchy, gave the army for a time a reputation for defending progressive causes.

The most important event for the army in the regard was its participation in the overthrow of Emperor Pedro II in 1889, which resulted in the establishment of a republican system in Brazil. The armed forces were in fact the main instigators of the plot, and the first two presidents of the newly established republic were military men, General Deodoro da Fonseca and general Floriano Peixoto. Nonetheless, despite its identification with progressive republicanism in Brazil and its active role in the overthrow of the monarchy, the army was also a repressive force, containing uprisings among the poorer classes when they sought to resist the authority of the republican government. These two apparently contradictory functions existed side by side.

During the first phase of republican life, the two most significant episodes involving army repression took place at Canudos, Bahia, in 1897 and in Santa Catarina in the so-called Contestado of 1912. Motivated by harsh living conditions and spurred on by messianic leaders, the peasant population in these hinterland areas rose up against the central state, only to be beaten down by the armed forces.

After 1922, the army was weakened by internal divisions. The lower military ranks, led by lieutenants, opposed the generals and other high-ranking officers implicated in the corrupt practices of big landowners. In 1924 and 1927, the lieutenants led revolts against their superiors. The epic march of the Prestes Column, a band of rebels led by Communist Party leader Luis Carlos Prestes who from 1924 to 1927 made their way through 8,000 miles of the Brazilian backlands in an effort to gain adherents for a revolt against the central government, also contributed to the agitation of the period. The common purpose of the uprisings was a call for morality in public life, universal suffrage, and greater nationalism—causes supported by the emergent urban middle classes. Although the lieutenants' movement did not seek an alliance with the workers' movement (which had grown significantly in the first two decades of the twentieth century), it did spearhead the push for political change that resulted in the 1930 revolution.

In 1930, dissident sectors of the rural oligarchy closed ranks with the rebellious lieutenants to create the Liberal Alliance. The Alliance presented Getúlio Vargas as its presidential candidate. Despite accusations of electoral fraud, and with the help of the armed forces, Vargas was inaugurated. Appearances notwithstanding, there was no deep change in the system of power. The new government was in fact formed by an alliance between old rural oligarchy and the emerging industrial sectors.

The military apparatus, now united around Getúlio Vargas, became the main instrument for consolidating the new pact between the two most powerful interests in Brazil.

The alliance between the revolutionaries who supported Vargas and the traditional oligarchy against which the revolution had ostensibly been directed caused an irreconcilable breach between Vargas and the original members of the lieutenants' movement. Their opposition to the new regime led to the formation of the National Liberation Alliance (Aliança Nacional Libertadora—ANL) in January 1935. The ANL brought together communists, whose number had grown during the 1920s, and many nationalist politicians seeking land reform and a fairer distribution of income. For a few months the ANL grew at a rapid rate, holding forth in the street and barracks. It was then banned by the Vargas government.

The army had its baptism of fire as an anticommunist force in November 1935, when the Communist Party instigated an insurrection. The rebellion was limited to army barracks and promptly suppressed, but to this day the episode is remembered by the armed forces in annual celebrations reaffirming the sacred ideals of the fight against communism. As would be the case in 1964, the violent and extended repression that followed the 1935 insurrection revealed that the objective of those in power was not simply to punish the rebels behind the so-called communist plot. Rather, the elite group represented in the cabinet felt that the time had come to strike at the democratic demands advocated by the original lieutenants' movement and legitimated, at least in part, by the 1930 revolution. The direction of the supposed "communist plot"—in reality the reassertion of these demands—provided an ideal pretext to repudiate decisively the pressures for democratization. Riding the wave of repression, the upper ranks of the armed forces united around Vargas in 1937 to introduce an undisguised dictatorship, which came to be called the "New State".

With the outbreak of World War II, the competition of the great powers for allies was intensified, and Brazil, as a strategically important part of the South Atlantic, became a focal point. The international situation was also reflected in internal Brazilian politics, with the armed forces divided in their sympathies. The early Nazi victories were celebrated by the leadership of the Brazilian armed forces, but those elements favoring the Allies gained influence as the war situation shifted.

At the same time, the nationalist gains achieved by the New State struck at American interests inside Brazil. Sectors linked to the United States began to plot Vargas' overthrow. In October 1945, soon after the end of the war, a coup d'état commanded by General Góis Monteiro deposed the former dictator.

The succeeding period in Brazilian history, 1946–64, was a time of economic development and social change that created profound modifications in the Brazilian social structure. These changes were nationalist and democratic, but also authoritarian in character. Fascist elements were strengthened within the Brazilian military.

After a brief period of democratic freedoms, President Marshal Eurico Gaspar Dutra took a sharp turn toward the political right in 1947. The Dutra government was strongly pro-American, uninterested in the needs and opinions of the people, and rigidly authoritarian in character. Particularly important in determining its course was the ideological influence of the American military on the Brazilian armed forces. Nonetheless, growing discontent with Dutra led to Vargas' reelection to the presidency in 1950 on a nationalist platform. Despite the Vargas victory, however, it proved difficult to expel American interests from Brazil. Both economically and politically, those interests were already firmly rooted.

By this time, the play of forces that would result in the April 1964 coup was beginning to take shape. The delicate balance between the interests of the foreign monopolies on which the Brazilian economy was increasingly dependant and the popular pressures for national control of development was difficult for Vargas to sustain. Once again, rightist sectors in the military planned to depose him, but their plans were preempted by Vargas' suicide on 24 August 1954. This unexpected event set off passionate popular demonstrations throughout the country directed against symbols of the presence of American capital in Brazil. Frightened by this demonstration of the popular will, the military was forced to postpone its takeover attempt.

From Vargas' suicide in 1954 to January 1956, when Juscelino Kubitschek, the newly elected president, took office, the country experienced more unrest caused by the same rightist sectors. During this period, however, the right encountered resistance from nationalist elements within the armed forces. Those officers planning a coup d'état had once again to retreat. Prevented from assuming power, they concentrated their efforts in the Superior War College and in the elaboration of the ideology that came to be known as the "National Security Doctrine."

Kubitschek finished his term in office in 1960 and was replaced by Jânio Quadros, who was elected on a wave of populist sentiment. Nonetheless, Quadros' administration was authoritarian in its approach to internal affairs, even though it maintained an open international policy. The Quadros administration was cut short by the president's resignation on 25 August 1961, a surprising gesture that historians have still not satisfactorily explained.

Quadros' vice-president, João Goulart, considered the principal heir to Vargas' nationalism of the 1950s and branded a radical by those in the higher ranks of the armed forces, was nearly impeded from succeeding Quadros by the veto of three military members of the cabinet. The veto evoked a strong popular protest, particularly in Goulart's home state, where then governor Leonel Brizola—himself Goulart's brother-in-law and political ally—led massive street demonstrations in favor of Goulart's inauguration. Fearing that the country was on the brink of civil war, the military once again withdrew. They did manage, however, to impose a parliamentary system of government that removed power from the president.

The period between 1962 and 1964 was marked by popular influence on the political system. A national plebiscite gave Goulart a landslide victory and enabled him to abolish the parliamentary system imposed by the military. This in turn allowed him to increase the pace of broad structural reforms. Goulart's program for sweeping social change, known as "basic reforms", drew on substantial support from unionized workers. In spite of the organizational weaknesses of the labor unions at the local level, they had developed an ample capacity for mobilization. The number of unions that supported Goulart's "basic reforms" increased steadily.

In addition, workers began to organize an all-encompassing structure called the General Workers' Command (CGT). Created in violation of labor legislation from the Vargas period that had been modeled on Mussolini's labor code, the CGT was seen by forces opposed to the Goulart government as a warning sign that a communist revolution was imminent in Brazil.

The period was one of high inflation, but workers generally achieved salary readjustments that kept pace with the rising cost of living. In rural areas, peasant organizations, known as Peasant Leagues, were created. By 1964, a total of 2,181 leagues had been formed in twenty states. Overt class conflicts developed in rural areas just as they had in the cities. The rural conflicts, in particular, led to panic among conservative landowners, who were determined to avoid land reform at all costs.

In the cities, students, artists, and numerous sectors of the urban middle classes joined the ranks of those committed to implementing Goulart's nationalist program, particularly a new educational structure, land reform, and legislation to control the expatriation of profits. A nationalist front was formed in the Brazilian congress, which also exerted pressure for reform.

Before this mobilization could effectively challenge the powers of the traditional elites, the proponents of a coup d'état, openly supported by representatives of the United States government, made their final preparations for a military takeover. The high inflation then manifest and the instability of the political scene favored the message of the right to the middle classes, that only a strong government could control the situation. In fact, inflation had risen from 30% in 1960 to 74% in 1963. In addition, strong opposition to Goulart's economic policies in the Brazilian congress had prevented him from implementing a three-year plan designed to spur the growth rate and reduce inflation to 10%.

Further complicating the economic situation was the problem of outflow of capital: during the first months of 1964 alone, more than two billion dollars were sent to foreign banks. The balance of payments problem was aggravated by the suspension of all U.S. government aid to Brazil, with the exception of funds sent directly to state governors opposed to Goulart, in particular those from the political and economic heart of Brazil: Carlos Lacerda from Rio de Janeiro, Adhemar de Barros from São Paolo, and Magalhães Pinto from Minas Gerais.

The readiness of the United States to collaborate in the planned coup was the final signal that spurred to action those generals interested in overthrowing President Goulart. Lieutenant Colonel Vernon Walters, at the time the military attaché to the U.S. embassy in Brazil, offered arms to General Carlos Guedes, one of the officers who would finally set the coup in motion. The United States also financed organizations such as the Brazilian Institute for Democratic Action and the Institute for Research and Social Studies, both of which were involved in massive antigovernment campaigns throughout the country.

The political crisis reached its climax during the early months of 1964, when the movement for basic reforms finally elicited support among the lower ranks of the military. In September 1963, the so-called Sergeants' Revolt had taken place in Brasília, by then the capital of the country. The Association of Navy and Marine Personnel of Brazil, also sympathetic to the reforms and to the Goulart government, had been formed in 1962. These insurgent organizations allowed the generals to invoke the need for military discipline, forcing Goulart into at least a temporary retreat. Goulart's position, like that of Getulío Vargas in 1954, became untenable. He was unable to halt the advance of the right by calling on the Brazilian people to defend the law and incapable of placating the irritated military commanders.

While the country was in the midst of these successive crisis, a huge public rally was convened. On 13 March 1964, more than 200,000 people gathered in front of

Rio's Central Brazil Railroad station. Goulart, flanked by members of his cabinet and several state governors, addressed the crowd and signed the basic reform bills then and there. The rally was intended as a demonstration of power to halt the sedition, which was already being publicly carried out. Despite the symbolic force of the act, the government and those forces sympathetic to it could not demobilize the opposition. The generals, for their part, were moved to set a date for their takeover.

Unfortunately for Goulart, practically the entire middle class as well as important sectors of the rural and urban working classes had been convinced by the anti-communist propaganda of anti-Goulart forces. They included the Social Democratic Party and the National Democratic Union, both financed by the United States. The Roman Catholic Church, particularly the hierarchy, also joined in the campaign against the Goulart government. They were supported by the major newspapers, which helped mobilize vast numbers of government critics in demonstrations that became famous as "marches of the family, with God, for freedom."

In the closing days of March 1964, marine personnel meeting in the Metalworkers' Union in Rio de Janeiro rebelled against the military authorities. This set the stage for the actual coup, which occurred on April 1. There was virtually no resistance. The nationally supported popular reform movement, based on the legal structures of a constitutionally elected government, could not resist the force of arms. With the coup, the long period of instability came to an end. Brazil entered a new phase, one which would bring about profound changes in the country's political, economic and social structure.

Source: Pp. 41-48 from Archdiocese of Sao Paulo, *Torture in Brazil: A Shocking Report on Torture by the Brazilian Military Governments,* 1964-1979 translated by Jaime Wright, ed. by Joan Dassin. Copyright © 1998. Reprinted by permission of the Teresa Lozano Long Institute of Latin American Studies, University of Texas at Austin.

We can see the most ghastly result of the century of isolation and frustration in the words of Lieutenant Commander Adolfo Francisco Scilingo, who participated in the Argentine Dirty War from 1976 to 1983.

CONFESSIONS OF AN ARGENTINE DIRTY WARRIOR

In 1977, as a lieutenant stationed at the Navy School of Mechanics (ESMA) with operative dependence on the First Corps of the army, when you were the commander-in-chief and in fulfillment of orders given by the Executive Power whose powers you then exercised, I participated in two aerial transports, the first with thirteen subversives aboard a Skyvan belonging to the coast guard, and the second with seventeen terrorists aboard an Electra belonging to naval aviation. The prisoners were told they were being taken to a prison in the south and for that reason had to receive a vaccination. They received an initial dose of anesthetic, which was reinforced by another larger dose during the flight. Finally, in both cases, they were stripped naked and thrown into the waters of the South Atlantic from the planes during the flight. Personally, I have never been able to overcome the shock that the execution of that order caused me; despite the fact that we were in the middle of the dirty war, this method of executing the enemy doesn't seem to me to be a very ethical one for military men to employ, but I believed that I would find in you the timely public acknowledgment of your responsibility for these facts.

In response to the matter of the disappeared, you said that there are subversives living under assumed names, others who died and were buried as persons unknown, and, finally, you did not reject the possibility that certain excesses might have been committed by your subordinates. Where do I fit into that? Do you believe that the weekly transporters were the result of unauthorized excesses? Let's put an end to the cynicism. Let's tell the truth. Let the list of the dead be known, even though at the time of their deaths you did not assume responsibility for having signed an order for the execution. The unjust sentence you say you carried out before the signature of the president who ordered the trial, the signature of the prosecutor who sought the conviction, the signature of the judges who established the sentence. Whether or not their action was mistaken, all of them signed. We still bear the responsibility for thousands of disappeared persons without facing the facts or speaking the truth, and you talk about vindication. Vindication is not achieved by decree.

Source: Horacio Verbitsky, *Confessions of an Argentine Dirty Warrior.* Trans. Esther Allen. New York: The New Press, pp. 7–8, 2005.

QUESTIONS

1. Does Carlos Ibañez's justification of his career ring true? Do you think he had no ambition apart from furthering the interests of La Patria?
2. According to Brazilian officer Juracy Magalhães, what differentiated the officers of the Brazilian military from those of other Latin American nations?
3. Compare the analysis of Chilean Captain Tobías Barros of his army in 1920 with that of Carson of the Mexican army a few years earlier.
4. Do you notice any imbalances in the composition of the Mexican military in 1840?
5. How do you compare the report on the Mexican military of Carson in 1912 with that of Kate Doyle in 2004?
6. How has the Mexican government, unlike any other in Latin America, except that of Costa Rica, managed to keep the military under control?
7. Why do you think that the history of the Brazilian military, as related by the report of the Archdiocese of São Paulo, led to the atrocities committed during the 1960s and 1970s?
8. Colonel Scilingo admits to the most heinous of crimes. How do you think that he could have justified his actions? Do you blame him or his superior officers?

8 EVERYDAY LIFE IN THE TWENTIETH CENTURY COUNTRYSIDE

INTRODUCTION

The countryside in Latin America during the twentieth century underwent vast changes. Millions of people, the preponderance of the population in the region, left rural areas for better economic opportunities in the cities. Agriculture shifted from subsistence to commercial crops, vast innovations in technology transformed centuries-old methods, and diets changed, confronted with relentless globalization of tastes and styles. Perhaps more than anywhere else, the contrasts and contradictions of Latin American life showed in rural areas. There remained millions of cultivators who continued as their fathers, mothers, grandfathers, and grandmothers had done to clear and burn brush, to open up new fields, to use plows pulled by oxen and pushed by the farmer with the family walking behind dropping corn seed in the furrows and kicking soil to cover them, and then to wait for erratic rain. Or in hilly terrain, farmers sowed their maize or potatoes, using the back breaking short hoe on narrow terraces that would not carry the weight of oxen and plow. At the same time, export producers employed the most modern technology in seed and equipment while watering their crops with the latest irrigation methods. They then shipped their grapes, lettuce, tomatoes, and chickpeas to burgeoning markets in the United States or Europe.

Starting with the Mexican Revolution of 1910 (see Chapter 10), agrarian reform became the cornerstone of almost every progressive movement that arose during the twentieth century. The notion was to provide landless country people with their own farms on which they could grow staple crops for their subsistence and some commercial crops for the market to provide for funds to purchase other necessities. There were three alternative programs. The first was to distribute land to individuals. Such distributions took place in the 1950s in Bolivia and the 1960s in Peru. The second was to redistribute land to collectives. The most noteworthy experiment in this was Mexico in the 1930s. The third was state ownership, a program carried out only in Cuba in the 1960s. The Bolivian, Peruvian, and Mexican (and perhaps the Cuban) worked with some degree of success for a short time, but there were inevitably long-term difficulties. Most important, land ownership, whether individual or collective, required capital for irrigation (if feasible), equipment, fertilizers, insecticides, and seed. Governments did not (or could not) provide such funds. Second, as the population grew, due to vast improvements in sanitation and disease prevention, it outpaced the amount of land available. Farms were then divided into minifundia (tiny farms) that were unsustainable.

The generally accepted views of what comprised country people and how they lived their lives, of course, were altered by the transformations of agriculture and the vast expansion of the cities. Ironically, as the traditional methods of agriculture and the ways of life that accompanied them changed and sometimes eroded or disappeared, anthropologists intensified their studies of the people who practiced them. These anthropologists were based primarily in North America during the period from the mid-1920s through the 1970s. They often portrayed indigenous peoples in Latin America in idyllic terms. Categorized by the term "peasants," Aymara, Quechua, Maya, Tarahumara, and many other indigenous peoples and mestizos supposedly lived in harmony with their neighbors, exercised grass roots democracy, and shared in their work and (albeit meager) rewards. In reality, however, indigenous and other country people lived in harsh environments. They were often enmeshed in bitter, decades-long disputes over land and water rights. Just as important, the very idea of what constituted a peasant also has changed. It is difficult nowadays to discern the difference between city and country dweller or peasant and worker or urban slum dweller and farmer.

Finally, with rapid urbanization, expansion and diversification of export agriculture, and general population growth, ecological issues have taken on crucial importance. Of particular note is the destruction of tropical jungles in the enormous drainage area of the Amazon River system in Brazil, Colombia, Ecuador, and Peru.

THE OLD WAYS: SUBSISTENCE AGRICULTURE

Small farmers all over Latin America struggled throughout the twentieth century to make ends meet in an environment disadvantageous to them. They tried to supplement their incomes in various ways, working in the cities or neighboring commercial farms. Anthropologist James D. Sexton provides us with the diary of Ignacio Bizarro Ujpán, a Tzutuhil Maya, native to southwestern Guatemala on Lake Atitlán.

SUBSISTENCE AGRICULTURE IN GUATEMALA, JOSEÑO

This year of 1987 rain was scarce. It only served to erode the land. In the month of June, it only rained a few times, but heavily. In July the *canícula* [dog days, relatively dry period, July and August, between the two periods of maximum rainfall, June to September] began soon, and in the month of August it hardly rained. Not until September did it rain again, but it was little. And then it was summer again. In the month of September we planted chickpeas on a piece of land, but because of the scarcity of rain, they didn't grow.

In the month of November began to harvest of corn, coffee, and other crops, but this year there wasn't much to harvest. The corn was very little, and there were hardly any chickpeas. There wasn't even enough for seed. Well, we who are in the highlands produced a little corn, beans, and coffee, but those who suffered more were my people of San José, San Martín, Santiago Atitlán, and other parts, who went to the coast to rent land with the *finqueros* [owners or administrators of *fincas*]. It was misery for nothing. Nothing was gained. They lost money by going to the coast, that is, the cost of the travel, food, the bad treatment of the *finqueros*, the cost of the fertilize, and, as if that weren't enough, the great sickness of malaria. They only extracted three of four arrobas of corn.

In these contracts with the *finqueros*, the renter has to pay the rent by planting grass on the cattle ranches whether he has a harvest or not. The contracts state that the *finquero* will rent part of his land to the poor people, who must pay for the two crops of corn they extract by cleaning well the land where they had planted corn and then planting it in pasture. The renters must hand the land over to the *finquero* after the second harvest, in the month of December. If the renter doesn't want to plant a second crop, he still has to go clean the area and plant the grass for the *finquero*. If the renter doesn't show up, the *finquero* demands it in court. The species of grass they plant is *Estrella Africana* [African star], which is the best pasture for the livestock.

For that reason, the poor person is always exploited by the rich. Three of my Joseño countrymen didn't want to fulfill their obligations, but they had to go by the law of the authorities. That is to say, in this year the harvest was lost. In these pueblos when coffee was planted, they had little harvest; it hardly was of any use since many owed the banks for the cost of the fertilizer. But it was due to the scarcity of rain. With regard to the big agriculturalists, they didn't lose anything because their farms are well mechanized and irrigated, and for that reason they succeed. But also it is a favor, because what they harvest is for everyone.

Source: Attached excerpt from *Joseño: Another Mayan Voice Speaks from Guatemala* ed. and trans. by James D. Sexton. Copyright © 2001. Reprinted by permission of James D. Sexton.

. . .

THE NEW WAYS: EXPORT AGRICULTURE

Growing crops for export or expanding markets in the cities was nothing new to Latin Americans. They had produced sugar, cotton, and other commodities for European markets since colonial times. During the nineteenth century and well into the twentieth, they added coffee, bananas, beef, wool, henequen, and other products. In the second half of the century, farmers began to diversify and adapt, sometimes rather quickly, to the needs of the global economy. In the following readings, we see three examples of the export economy. The first illustrates the ups and downs of the traditional crop coffee. The second reveals similar problems that confronted modern farmers in the enterprise of growing vanilla beans. And the third discusses the struggles all Latin American farmers face in competing on the world market—in this case the ramification of the North American Free Trade Agreement signed by Canada, Mexico, and the United States in 1994.

Coffee has long been a mainstay of the economies of El Salvador and Guatemala. Arthur Rule traveled through Central America during the 1920s, a period of considerable upheaval, particularly in the countryside.

EXPORT AGRICULTURE, RUHL,
THE CENTRAL AMERICANS

"On top of one of the ridges, we came to the quarters of the laborers who live permanently on the plantation instead of merely during the picking. There was a common kitchen, where the women made *tortillas* and cooked beans and rice—the raw materials were included in their wages—and several barrack-like rooms, built round a court and fitted with double-tier bunks. They were dismal, flea-ridden caves, inappropriate enough, it seemed, to a climate where fresh air and space are the cheapest things, but security is security, and as long as the permanent laborers worked on the plantation they were sure of the use of a bit of land for a garden or a roof and enough to eat.

They were just being paid off as we arrived, shuffling up rather timorously to a window, behind which a dashing *mandador*, in riding-clothes and Simon Legree mustaches, counted out the two or three colones ($1 to $1.50) which most of them seemed to have earned during a week's work. The number of "tasks" the laborer had done was written down in a ledger and 30 cents gold seemed the usual pay for the required tasks of a "day" that could be completed in from three to five hours if the workman wished to hurry a bit.

On the day down-hill, we stopped at the bungalow looking out over the valley where the son and his wife lived, went through the *beneficio* and inspected all its improved Scotch coffee-milling machinery, and so on down to the spacious house in the old-fashioned Spanish colonial style, in Santa Tecla, where the father lived. High-ceilinged *corridors*, with frescos overhead and side walls decorated with Italian and Spanish tiles, surrounded the patio, and from them opened huge rooms, five on each side the square, finished in various sorts of tropical woods.

The son-in-law, having shaken up something refreshing for his guests, gossiped of middlemen as farmers of all sorts do the world over. The roasters were great "ballyhoo" artists, he thought. They made up a blend that was profitable, sold the notion that that particular blend had something unique, and got 55 or 60 cents for what the grower received 20. What they really wanted to do, was to get in some of that "cheap, harsh-flavored Brazil coffee"—indeed, they had to do that, in order to keep up the uniformity of their blend. There wasn't enough of the mild Central American coffee grown, for uniform "mass" blending. In Brazil, they didn't need shade-trees, their trees were hardier, the pickers simply stripped the branches instead of picking the berries separately—everything was done on a more wholesale scale.

The coffee crop of "El Chitalon" was between four and six thousand quintals in a good year. On paper, the finca brought in an income of between $40,000 and $60,000 a year, but it had had a checkered life, nevertheless. One native owner had run into debt and committed suicide. The place was finally taken over by a firm of American bankers on mortgage foreclosure, and Fahr was running it in their interest.

Over behind the lazily active volcano of Santa Maria which we could see that morning from "El Chitalon" and several thousand feet higher up, lies the Old Indian town of Quezaltenango. Known in ancient days as Xelahuh, it was the second city of the Quichés as it is of the Guatemala of to-day. It is a place rather more interesting for what it was than is, and for the country through which one must go to get there. But the remoteness which long gave it a certain charm has been broken by the automobile, and in the dry season one can run up to it from Mazatenango in half a day, that is to say, leave the capital in the morning and reach Quezaltenango.

The production of vanilla in Papantla in the state of Veracruz in east central Mexico is an example of how modern day farmers respond to the global economy. The fickleness of the market, however, remains much the same as in the nineteenth century.

VANILLA FARMERS STRUGGLE WITH PRICE DROP

A price boom inspired wide-scale vanilla planting, but now farmers in Veracruz are finding it hard to make a living from the crop.

PAPANTLA, Veracruz— Vanilla farmer Salvador González hauled 25-kilogram burlap sacks stuffed with freshly-picked green pods into a processor's buying office in Gutiérrez Zamora, Veracruz, late last month, hoping his crop would fetch a profitable price.

Instead, he pocketed only 45 pesos (US $4) per kilogram, a far cry from the 500 pesos (US $45) per kilogram he received four years ago, when the world price reached dizzying heights.

"It's just not profitable," he commented after taking payment.

A drop in vanilla prices has hit farmers in northern Veracruz hard this season. For the past five years, the world price for cured vanilla hovered above US$200 per kilogram. With prices high, Veracruz farmers rediscovered the aromatic plant— which originally came from the region surrounding Papantla and was dubbed *xanath* (vanilla) by the Totonac Indians and *tlilxóchitl* (black flower) by the Aztecs.

They planted thousands of new vines; some even took out loans to finance their investment. Local and international buyers, looking to bring down prices, encouraged the planting spree, promising to purchase the future harvests.

But the world price tumbled at the same time as Mexico's new-planted vanilla vines began bearing fruit, leaving many farmers little choice but to sell their crops for a loss.

Making matters worse, a plague has diminished the size of this year's harvest, which began in early December and should continue until February.

The farmers' bitter flirtation with fickle vanilla markets has prompted second thoughts for many.

"Some of those (who started growing vanilla) will take a machete and chop down their vines," said Alfredo López, sales director at Gaya Vai-Mex, a processor in Gutiérrez Zamora that makes vanilla extract and Xanath, a vanilla liqueur.

"Why? Because they can find another way to make a living. They can plant chilies. They can plant oranges. They can pretty much grow any other type of crop."

According to Pedro Heriberto Larios Rivera, owner of Casa Larios, a Papantla-based vanilla processor, few Veracruz farmers can make money with today's market rates, saying, 80 pesos per kilogram is the break-even price.

And while farmers lose money with each sale, "The middleman still makes a lot of money," explained Larios, whose business collects raw vanilla, cures it and then sells it to a handful of large international buyers.

Vanilla prices dropped in 2005 for several reasons—virtually all of which Veracruz growers were powerless to influence. Madagascar, the world's leading vanilla producing country, bounced back after several weather-related catastrophes earlier this decade diminished its production. The island usually produces 60 percent of the world's vanilla. High vanilla prices also forced some food processors to start using cheap artificial vanilla. Craig Nielsen, CEO of Nielsen-Massey Vanillas, a family-owned Waukegan, Illinois-based vanilla processor, estimated that demand for natural vanilla has dropped by up to 40 percent since 1999, although the "correction" in prices is slowly rekindling interest. The surplus vanilla in the international market should keep prices stable for the next two to three years, he added.

Still Nielsen figured farmers in most parts of the world could turn a profit with today's market prices, but acknowledged that Mexican farmers usually have higher costs than their counterparts in Indonesia and Madagascar.

"Vanilla is very labor intensive," Nielsen explained. "It needs to be hand-picked, hand-pollinated (and) hand-cured."

AROMA AND FLAVOR

Although Madagascar supplies the majority of the world's vanilla, Mexican producers insist they produce the world's best pods, which provide a balance of aroma and flavor.

Nielsen agrees—to a certain extent—saying Mexican pods offer spicy notes like cloves and nutmeg while Madagascar's vanilla provides a rich, creamy flavor.

"(Mexican vanilla) has its special points and it is a quality vanilla," he explained, but added that when cured properly, Madagascar's vanilla can be somewhat similar.

Most of Mexico's vanilla production goes to the United States, France and Germany. Little of it is consumed domestically; most of Papantla's vendors peddle knock-off products, passing their wares off as natural vanilla.

Mexico, despite being the original vanilla heartland, now produces around 30 to 40 tons per year—approximately one percent of the world's supply, according to Nielsen. Vanilla farming fell out of favor after the advent of the oil industry in Veracruz. Cattle ranches and orange groves took over many of the old vanilla farms.

"(Mexico) is now a small percentage of the world crop," Nielsen said, explaining that vanilla production in countries like India and Uganda now far surpasses Mexico's. Only in the past 20 years have Mexican farmers returned to producing vanilla in significant quantities, but the volume still lags behind the rest of the world—a fact that bothers Gaya Vai-Mex's Alfredo López.

"It's a shame because it is a 100-percent Mexican product," he said. "Vanilla is originally from Mexico."

Source: "Vanilla Farmers Struggle with Price Drop" by David Agren, *The Herald Mexico*, El Universal, March 24, 2006. Reprinted by permission of David Agren.

The signing of the North American Free Trade Agreement opened the Mexican market for corn and other crops from the United States. Because the U.S. government subsidizes many of its farmers, U.S. growers have a competitive advantage and can undersell Mexican farmers. In this selection we see how Mexican farmers protested this unfair arrangement.

NAFTA EQUALS DEATH, SAY PEASANT FARMERS

MEXICO CITY—More than 2,000 peasant farmers from throughout Mexico staged a protest Tuesday in the capital to demand a freeze on the agricultural provisions of the North American Free Trade Agreement (NAFTA), which they blame for most of their economic and social woes.

But their demands do not appear to have much chance of winning the desired response from the government.

"I have nothing. I am here out of desperation because I am poorer than I have ever been," said Francisco Martínez, an elderly farmer who took part in Tuesday's march in Mexico City, carrying a sign that read "NAFTA Equals Death."

Under the slogan "the countryside can endure no more," farmers from 24 of Mexico's 32 states marched in Mexico City to the Congress building to present their demands and later staged protests outside the U.S. and French embassies.

UNORCA, the national union of some 30 regional peasant groups, organized the demonstrations with the aim of preventing the agricultural trade liberalization measures—agreed under NAFTA, which comprises Canada, Mexico and the United States—from taking effect in January.

The new phase of liberalization entails the complete elimination of tariffs on 21 farm products, including potatoes, wheat, apples, onions, coffee, chicken and veal.

The NAFTA mechanism, which UNORCA describes as "toxic to the Mexican countryside," establishes three steps towards liberalizing the farm and livestock sector. The first occurred in 1994 when the three-nation treaty entered into force, the second is slated for January, and the third in 2008.

In 1993, when NAFTA was still being negotiated, the government of Carlos Salinas, then president of Mexico (1988–1994), agreed to the process of a gradual elimination of agricultural tariffs with the support of the country's leading farm organizations.

Now, nearly a decade later, they are all complaining.

Recognizing the difficulties that Mexican farmers face with the deepening of trade liberalization, President Vicente Fox announced in November that the government would provide support for rural producers to the tune of 10 billion dollars in 2003, or 7.7 percent more aid than this year.

Fox stated last month that he is very concerned about how the trade liberalization process is unfolding, "in light of the U.S. subsidies to its agricultural production."

He said he would take up the matter with the George W. Bush administration, but there has not been any indication of action so far.

The Mexican president's aim would be to press the United States to eliminate its farm subsidies, which total 19 billion dollars a year, nearly double what Mexico has budgeted for its farmers in 2003.

But Washington announced that it will not alter its farm subsidy policies and that the situation of the Mexican farmers does not justify annulment of the agricultural chapter of NAFTA.

Mexico would not ask for a suspension of the trade agreement's farm provisions anyway, say Fox administration sources, because doing so would mean revoking the country's recognition of the treaty itself.

Since NAFTA took effect, Mexico's overall exports shot up from 60.9 billion dollars in 1994 to 158.4 billion dollars in 2001. In that same period, imports jumped from 79.3 billion dollars to 168.4 billion dollars annually.

More than 85 percent of Mexican trade is currently concentrated in exchange with the United States.

But for Mexico's rural areas, where 75 percent of the population living in extreme poverty is concentrated, the three–country treaty has meant the loss of more than 10 million hectares of cultivated land.

And the decline of the rural sector has pushed 15 million peasants—and mostly young people—to move to the cities, either in Mexico or in the United States, according to a study by the Autonomous National University of Mexico (UNAM).

Over the last 10 years, the participation of the farming sector in Mexico's gross domestic product (GDP) has fallen from 7.3 percent to less than 5.0 percent.

The protests Tuesday echoed similar demonstrations in November, including the blockade of a main federal highway by farmers in the state of Morelos, neighboring the Mexico City federal district, and protests by peasants from the southern states of Oaxaca and Guerrero outside government offices in the capital.

The common denominator of all of these events is the rural producers' rejection of NAFTA.

"The farmers are walking towards death because they are up against the 'disloyal' trade competition from the United States and the Mexican government's desertion of the countryside," says Alberto Gómez, UNORCA executive coordinator.

Without exception, Mexico's farmer organizations believe the new phase of NAFTA-stipulated farm trade liberalization will generate more poverty and prompt more people to leave rural areas.

They also reckon that the financial support Fox has promised will not be nearly enough.

Mariano Ruiz, an analyst with the Mexico City-based Grupo de Economistas y Asociados, says the worst blow for the Mexican farmers will come in 2008 when the agricultural tariffs on products like maize and beans are lifted.

An estimated 2.8 million Mexican farm families make their livelihood from these commodities.

"The countryside is a time-bomb that could explode very soon," commented Rosario Robles, chairwoman of the leftist Democratic Revolutionary Party (PRD), the country's third political force.

The elderly farmer Martínez, who joined his colleagues for the Mexico City march Tuesday, does not believe in anything that the Fox government is offering.

"I have heard many things in the two years since he took office. The one thing for certain is that I am getting poorer and poorer," he said.

• • •

LAND REFORM IN THE POST-MODERN REGION

Millions of Latin Americans moved from their villages and farms to the cities, because there was no land and no employment in the countryside. Nonetheless, landless people, all of them desperately poor, remain an enormous problem. Few attempted solutions have mitigated the plight of landless people in the region. Governments have tried various land reforms.

The first notable effort at land reform after World War II took place in Bolivia, where a revolution toppled the conservative regime dominated by tin-mining tycoons and large landowners in 1952. The Movimiento Nacional Revolucionario (National Revolutionary Movement), or MNR, instituted a far-reaching land redistribution.

LAND REFORM BOLIVIA

A. To distribute the arable land to the peasants who do not have enough, on condition that they work it, expropriating for this purpose the lands of the latifundists who have them in excess or receive an income without any personal work in the fields;

B. To restore to the Indian communities the lands which were taken from them and co-operate in the modernization of cultivation; respecting, and where possible making use of, collectivists traditions;

C. To free the agricultural workers from their conditions of serfdom, proscribing gratuitous personal obligations and services;

D. To stimulate increased productivity and commercialization of agriculture and grazing, aiding the investment of new capital, respecting the small and medium cultivators, encouraging agrarian co-operatives, lending technical assistance, and opening up the possibilities of credit;

E. To converse the natural resources of the country, adopting indispensable scientific and technical methods;

F. To promote currents of internal migration of the rural population, now excessively concentrated in the Inter-Andean region, with the objective of obtaining a more rational distribution of the population, strengthening national unity, and connecting the Eastern and Western parts of Bolivian territory. . . .

Article I . . . the soil, the subsoil and the waters of the territory of the Republic belong originally to the Bolivian Nation . . .

Article II. The State recognizes and guarantees private property when this fulfills a useful function for the nation; it plans, regulates, and rationalizes the use of the land and supports the equitable distribution of the land, to assure the freedom and the economic and welfare of the Bolivian population.

Source: Translated from *La Revolución Nacional a través de sus decretos más importantes—tercer año de la Victoria nacional de abril* (La Paz, 1955), pp. 46-47 in *The Quest for Change in Latin America: Sources for a Twentieth-Century Analysis* ed. by W. Raymond Duncan and James Nelson Goodsell. Copyright © 1970 by Oxford University Press, Inc. Reprinted by permission of Oxford University Press, Inc.

*The most well-known land reform, of course, occurred in Cuba in the aftermath of the
revolution in 1959. It experienced mixed results. The Cubans provide the best critique.*

THE CUBAN LAND REFORM, CHE GUEVARA

The Agrarian Reform implied such a profound institutional change that it became
immediately possible to make an effort towards the elimination of the obstacles that
had prevented the utilization of human and natural resources in the past.

Because of the predominant part which had been played by the latifundia in
agricultural production, and the enormous size of the sugar cane plantations organized along capitalistic lines, it was relatively easy to convert this type of rural property into state farms and co-operatives of considerable size. Cuba thus avoided the
slow-moving development characteristic of other agrarian revolutions: the division
of land into a fantastic number of small farms, followed by the grouping of such small
units to enable more modern techniques, feasible only on certain levels of production, to be applied.

What was the economic policy followed in agriculture after the transfer of the
large estates? As a natural part of this rural unemployment disappeared and the
main efforts were directed towards self-sufficiency as regards the greater part of
foodstuffs and raw materials of vegetable or animal origin. The trend in the development of agriculture can be defined in one word: diversification. In its agricultural
policy the Revolution represented the antithesis of what had existed during the years
of dependence on imperialism and of exploitation by the land-owning class. Diversification versus monoculture; full employment versus idle hands; these were the major transformations in the rural areas during those years.

It was well known that, nevertheless, serious agricultural problems immediately arose, and those have only begun to be solved during recent months. How can
we explain the relative scarcity of some agricultural products, and particularly the
decline in sugar production, when the Revolution began by incorporating all the
idle rural productive factors in the agricultural process, thus greatly increasing its
potentialities? We believe we committed two principal errors.

Our first error was the way in which we carried out diversification. Instead of
embarking on diversification by degrees we attempted too much at once. The sugar
cane areas were reduced and the land thus made available was used for cultivation
of new crops. But this meant a general decline in agricultural production. The entire economic history of Cuba had demonstrated that no other agricultural activity
would give such returns as those yielded by the cultivation of the sugar cane. At the
outset of the Revolution many of us were not aware of this basic economic fact, because a fetishistic idea connected sugar with our dependence on imperialism and
with the misery in the rural areas, without analyzing the real causes: the relation to
the uneven trade balance.

Unfortunately, whatever measures are taken in agriculture, the results do not become apparent until months, sometimes years, afterwards. This is particularly true as
regards sugar cane production. That is why the reduction of the sugar cane areas
made between the middle of 1960 and the end of 1961—and, let us not forget the two
years of drought—has resulted in lower sugar cane harvests during 1962 and 1963.

Diversification on a smaller scale could have been achieved by utilizing the reserves of productivity existing in the resources assigned to the various traditional types of cultivation. This would have permitted the partial use of the idle resources for a small number of new products. At the same time, we could have taken measures to introduce more modern and complex techniques requiring a longer period of assimilation. After these new technical methods had begun to bear fruit in the traditional fields, particularly in those related to exports, it would have been practicable to transfer resources from these fields to the areas of diversification without prejudice to the former.

The second mistake made was, in our opinion, that of dispersing our resources over a great number of agricultural products, all in the name of diversification. The dispersal was made, not only on a national scale but also within each of the agricultural productive units.

The change made from monoculture to the development of a great number of agricultural products implied a drastic transformation within relatively few months. Only a very solid productive organization could have resisted such rapid change. In an underdeveloped country, in particular, the foundation of agriculture remains very inflexible and its organization rests on extremely weak and subjective foundation and diversification, coming simultaneously, produced a great weakness in the agricultural productive organization.

Now that the years have passed, conditions have changed and the pressure of the class struggle has lessened, and so it is fairly easy to make a critical assessment of the analysis made during those months and years. It is for history to judge how much was our fault and how much was caused by circumstances.

At any rate, hard facts have shown us both the errors and the road towards their correction, which is the road the Cuban Revolution is at present following in the agricultural sector. Sugar now has first priority in the distribution of resources, and in the assessment of those factors which contribute to the most efficient use of those resources.

Source: Excerpted from "The Cuban Economy: Its Past and Its Present Importance" by Ernesto Che Guevara, *International Affairs* 40:4 (October 1964); 598-599. Copyright © 1964. Reprinted by permission of Wiley-Blackwell.

Brazil has the largest number of poor people and the most unequal distribution of wealth in the Americas. Recent governments have attempted to alleviate this misery. In conjunction with the World Bank, the Brazilian government began a program of land reform in 1997. Compare the report of critic Stephan Schwartzman with an earlier effort at land reform in 1952.

BRAZIL, AGRARIAN POLICY, NATIONAL COMMISSION

From the experiences of other countries that have agrarian structures similar to that of Brazil, and the new social meaning given to modern constitutions, including that of Brazil, to property rights to the land, there arise some general guide lines that should prevail in our agrarian reform. These include the following fundamental points.

I. Basic Principles:
1. The Brazilian Constitution states in Article 147 that the use of property shall be conditioned by the social well-being and that the law shall promote a just distribution of property with equal opportunity for all.
2. The fundamental objective of agrarian reform in Brazil is to offer access to property to those who work the soil, so as to prevent the proletarization of the rural masses and eliminate the effects of uneconomical and antisocial use of the land.
3. Simultaneously with the subdivision of latifundia and the consolidation of minifundia, the agrarian reform shall also take care to valorize the man and the land, so as to guarantee to all work that will make possible an honorable existence.

II. Concerning the Agrarian Regime:
1. Legislation pertaining to lands shall take into account, as much as possible, the customs and traditions of each region.
2. Agricultural legislation should provide minimal conditions that would make it possible for the small farm to carry on its social and productive functions.
3. Lands should not be subdivided indiscriminately, when, because of the nature of the crops and the type of agricultural production, this would result in the economic decline of a region.

III. Forms and Systems of Expropriation:
1. Indemnification for the expropriation of unproductive latifundia should avoid the rule of Article 141, paragraph 16 of the Federal Constitution and be used upon Article 147, even though, perhaps, a constitutional amendment may be necessary.
2. The expropriation of land in the social interest should exclude from the indemnity payments of any kind except those corresponding to the principal, the improvements, and a reasonable interest on the money invested.
3. A subdivision of lands adjacent to or near the cities is obligatory when, because of their extent and the use to which they are put, they constitute an obstacle to the development of agriculture and do not help satisfy the exigencies of supplying the urban area.
4. The following lands should be considered as most subject to expropriation:
   a. Those which remain uncultivated, despite the fact that conditions favor their permanent use;
   b. those that manifestly are poorly cultivated in a technical sense, including those which, although located favorably with respect to public irrigation projects, are not being irrigated;
   c. those which, acquired for speculative purposes, remain unused.
5. Lands whose values will be increased as a result of large public projects, which constitute latifundia whose improvement depends almost exclusively upon such projects, and which are subject to economic use by means of agricultural colonization, shall be expropriated

before the projects are undertaken. There shall be reserved for the owner whose lands have been expropriated an area equal in size to that previously maintained in permanent cultivation.

6. Areas near urban centers, the cultivation of which is essential for the supply of such centers, may not be subdivided into building lots, or if they should be, they shall be obliged to follow a plan of agricultural zoning.

IV. Colonization:
1. [There should be] unity in legislation and a central administrative agency for all colonization activities. [There should be] a careful selection of lands in accordance with the factors which guarantee a fixation of man to the land and the development of production.
2. Priority should be given to rich lands, healthful and near the centers of consumption, so that the population will give preference to natural expansion rather than to a transportation to isolated zones, irrespective of how fertile the latter may be said to be.
3. In colonization the effort should be made to maintain an equilibrium between lands suitable for grazing and those suitable for agriculture.

V. Agricultural Credit:
1. Credit by official agencies should be oriented so as actually to benefit the small farmer. For this purpose the essential condition is to decentralize credit to the maximum, eliminating the bureaucratic obstacles, and to make the guarantees demanded less harsh.
2. As a general rule, credit by official agencies should be extended in cash, as well as, under certain conditions, in machines, implements, seeds, fertilizers, and livestock, along with the necessary technical assistance.
3. Preference should be given to supplying credit through agricultural cooperatives, thus intensifying personal credit.

VI. General Dispositions:
1. The adequate imposition of taxes upon property (land tax, transmission tax, etc.) constitutes a means of discouraging the unproductive possession of the soil. When, as is the case in Brazil, these tributes are the prerogative of the states, it is essential that there be an inter-state agreement, under the auspices of the federal government, for the purpose of securing uniform provisions with respect to incidence and rates, always with due respect to the distinctive features of each unit of the Federation.
2. Provisions should be included in the agrarian reform law for stimulating, in every way possible, the proprietors of rural establishments to invest their profits in building up and improving the soil. Therefore, the estates that through exemplary management are technically and economically efficient are not to be expropriated.
3. [Efforts shall be made] to develop the small property in economically sound ways, particularly in the zones surrounding the cities, so as to establish among the agricultural enterprises the system of small horticultural farms and diversified farms.

4. There should be established, in each productive zone, the minimum size of the property, beyond which subdivision will not be permitted, even by inheritance.

5. [Programs should be developed] to promote, throughout all parts of the interior, the creation of rural cooperatives of all types, as well as organizations of proprietors and laborers of all classes, granting them favors and gifts.

6. [Measures should be taken] to eliminate or ease the taxes upon newly established rural industries.

7. [Efforts should be made] to orient our system of taxation so as to eliminate or reduce tariffs and duties on exports which increase the costs of living and production of the agriculturists.

8. The agrarian reform should set as an objective the creation of rural communities capable of progressing economically, socially, and politically within Brazilian society.

Source: Translated from *Comissão Nacional de Política Agrária, Diretrizes para una Reforma Agrária no Brasil*, (Rio de Janeiro: Comissão Nacional de Política Agrária, 1952) by T. Lynn Smith, p. 13 in *Agrarian Reform in Latin America*. Copyright © 1965. Reprinted by permission of Alfred A. Knopf, a division of Random House, Inc.

BRAZIL, LAND REFORM, STEPHAN SCHWARTZMAN

LAND REFORM IN BRAZIL AND THE LANDLESS RURAL WORKERS' MOVEMENT (MST)

Current law regulating land reform in Brazil (the *Estatuto da Terra* of 1964) was authored at the outset of Brazil's military dictatorship, based in the understanding that massive concentration of landholdings not only contributed to rural poverty but froze potentially productive assets and hindered development. The law established that the federal government could expropriate unproductive or over-large landholdings (*latifúndia*) for the purpose of land reform, and indemnify the owners with government bonds. The political power of Brazil's large landowners, however, effectively precluded significant action on land reform during the military dictatorship. When the military stepped down and were succeeded by an indirectly elected President in 1985, the civilian government announced an ambitious goal of settling 1.4 million families on 43 million hectares over four years. Only a fraction of this objective was attained—some 82,000 families were settled on 4.3 million hectares by 1989.

By the mid-1990s, however this picture would change dramatically. While World Bank descriptions of the *Cédula da Terra* belabor the need to make land reform quicker and cheaper than the Constitutionally mandated expropriation/indemnification mechanism, in reality both expropriation of unproductive areas, and settlement of landless families accelerated dramatically after 1994. The National Institute for Agrarian Reform and Colonization (INCRA) under the current government prides itself on having provided land to 372,866 families on over 8 million hectares between 1995 and

1999, over half again as many as the 218,000 families given land in the entire preceding 30 years since the promulgation of the Land Statute.

Starting in southern Brazil in the mid-1980s' Landless Rural Workers' Movement (*Movimento dos Trabalhadores Rurais Sem Terra* —MST) built a grassroots movement of the rural poor and landless, drawing on the desperation of those marginalized in the consolidation of large scale capital-intensive export agriculture and displaced by large scale infrastructure projects. The MST was able in various specific instances to contest the seemingly insurmountable political power of large landholders through the confrontational tactic of land occupation. Local groups would identify lands qualifying under the law for expropriation and dozens or hundreds of families would move in together, set up makeshift encampments and begin to farm. Growing numbers of MST adherents assembled in tent cities along roads and highways, planning new occupations. Confrontations with landowners, their hired guards, and the Military Police proliferated, as did groups identified with the MST, with varying degrees of relationship to the national coordinating body. In 1995 in Rondonia and 1996 in Pará, landless groups were massacred by military police sent to prevent or expel occupations.

The federal government was faced with a serious dilemma. On the one hand, MST direct actions generated highly visible conflicts and pressure to act on the government, and the President's, repeated commitments to social equity. On the other, the government's major parliamentary coalition partner, key to the passage of its economic reform program in the Congress, the conservative PFL (Liberal Front Party), includes most of the representatives of the landed elite. That INCRA settled more families between 1995 and 1998 than in the preceding 30 years was politically costly, controversial within the ranks of the government's parliamentary coalition, and could not have occurred without the continual, large-scale, public pressure applied by the MST strategy of land occupations.

THE CÉDULA DA TERRA IN THE CONTEXT OF LAND REFORM IN BRAZIL

When the Bank embarked upon its land reform venture, it intervened in an ongoing political conflict. Rather than taking a neutral posture that supported Land Reform as such, the Bank's project supported the government and landowners against the Landless Rural Workers' Movement and the civil society organizations aligned with it. First, the Bank planned its pilot project without consulting or informing any of the national representative organizations of the beneficiaries of land reform. While bank staff may claim that MST and other national level groups are ideologically opposed to "market-based" land reform, the fact is that no effort was made to engage these groups in dialogue at the project's inception. Second, the Bank and government refused to negotiate when rural workers' organizations made proposals (eg, the National Confederation of Agricultural Workers' (CONTAG) 1997 proposals to use *Cédula* funds for credit in areas of high concentrations of landholdings too small to support families.) Third, having bypassed the representative organizations of rural workers and the landless, the Bank designed a program, ostensibly driven by freely organized local associations of rural poor, which in fact funded and empowered state government agencies to organize or enlist associations into the program. The state government agencies are typically much more susceptible to influence and manipulation by the landed interests most intransigent in their opposition to land reform than federal agencies. The Preliminary Evaluation of the *Cédula da Terra* Report, in fact found that the *Cédula* associations typically define themselves in opposition to the MST. The evaluators state, *". . . the Cédula da Terra Program introduces a political and ideological dispute with other social movements and their mediators (principally the MST, sectors of the Catholic Church, and civil society organized in NGOs), which today have the political initiative in this area and support access to land through expropriation. "*

"MARKET-BASED" LAND REFORM—WHAT THE DATA SAY

It is of considerable importance to sort through the claims management has made for the likely prospects of this approach. If the *Cédula* approach can be shown to better the situation of the rural poor more cheaply and quickly than traditional land reform, there might be reason for concern based on participating families ability to buy land in the free market and pay off their loans.

CONCLUSION

It is puzzling, in light of the foregoing data, why the Bank would want to commit itself to a $1 billion program based in this model at this point if its goal is to construct a viable alternative approach to land reform in Brazil. Given the very serious issues raised by the official evaluation, prudence would dictate at very least that the Bank and Government wait until 1) it were possible to evaluate agricultural production on the land acquired in the pilot project over a minimally representative time period, rather than relying on projected simulations; 2) that the Bank judge the actual effects of some part of the program on beneficiaries' incomes and living standards and discuss them with governments and other actors in land reform in Brazil before deciding what course to follow. Actual effects include *inter alia* the beneficiaries' ability to repay the debts they have incurred, over a minimally representative time period, as well as the projects' effects on poverty. The Bank has produced impressive farm models, which project excellent results in virtually all scenarios. But these are models, based, as are all models, on the assumptions and presuppositions built into them. Since loan repayment only begins for the first participants in 2001, there are no actual data about the results of the program as a "market-based" land reform and poverty alleviation program. Yet management argues that this is a model pilot program. The Bank has worked in Brazil for nearly 50 years, and only supported land reform beginning in 1997. Why this sudden haste to process a $1 billion dollar, ten-year program, before any empirical results of the supposed pilot are available for review?

The Bank's approach here, intentionally or not, clearly fits well with the political agenda of the sectors of Brazil's federal and state governments that oppose the MST, CONTAG and the other representative organizations most active on land reform, as well as opponents of land reform more generally. Large scale funding would be provided through state government agencies to create or enlist rural workers associations in land purchase schemes that are subject to political manipulation by local elites at the moment of creation of the associations, selection of beneficiaries, and in the negotiation and purchase of land. In the process, part of the MST membership base can potentially be co-opted. While a $150 million pilot program may be relatively limited in its impact in a country as large as Brazil, a $2 billion, ten-year program is another matter. For the sectors of Brazilian government that seek to halt pressure for land reform, this program is an excellent tool.

Source: Abridged from "The World Bank and Land Reform in Brazil" by Steve Schwartzman, January 27, 2000. http://www.mstbrazil.org/LandReform.html. Reprinted by permission of Steven Schwartzman.

● ● ●

THERE ARE NO UTOPIAS

James D. Sexton lived in the village he names San José in Guatemala in 1970. He met a Tzutuhil Maya Indian whom he calls by the pseudonym Ignacio Bizarro Ujpán. Ignacio wrote his life story, part of which I have excerpted below. In his story of conflict between two neighboring villages, we can see how geography and class affect relations in the countryside.

SAN JOSÉ DISPUTES WITH SAN MARTIN OVER WATER RIGHTS, FROM *SON OF TECÚN UMÁN: A MAYA INDIAN TELLS HIS LIFE STORY*

When I lived in San José in 1970, Joseño told me that San José had fought with San Martin over the water supply the previous year. You did not mention this in your autobiography originally. Can you explain what happened?

Yes, I remember it well. From August to September of the year of 1969 there were heavy rains. The rain caused a landslide that in turn caused the main water tank from the source of the Kaimbal River to tumble down. With the collapse of the tank there was no potable water for either San José or San Martin. [San José and San Martin are two kilometers apart, and they get their water from the same source, which is in San José's municipal jurisdiction.]

Most of the Martineros have water faucets in their homes now, and it is a burden to carry drinking water from the lake. The water that Martineros use really belongs to the Joséños; the river from which the water flows is situated on San José's land. When the tank fell down, San José wanted to punish San Martín by not allowing them to repair it.

Friction between Joseños and Martineros goes back to the period of the mandamientos [orders for forced labor to coastal farms] during the presidency of Manuel Estrada Cabrera (1898–1920). Well, I really only now know what the old people tell me. They say that it was mainly the years of 1930 to 1936 [which places it during the vagrancy laws of President Jorge Ubico].

Because the Martineros were literate and rich, they were able to avoid the mandamientos. Perhaps they were able to become wiser by studying with the fathers in San Martin or they were more interested in going to school. Nevertheless, the poor Joseños were affected by the orders to go to the coast to work. To raise money for corn and beans they needed, they had to sell their land to Martineros. The Martineros paid them pesos during this period because that was the kind of money we had then, not quetzals [equivalent to U.S dollars]. Although I am not sure of the exact amount, martineros paid Joseños about $10 to $15 for each parcel of land, which was cheap. Because the poor little Joseños did not know how to read and write, the Martineros cheated them. That is, if a Joseño sold a Martinero one plot of land, and the Joseño actually had two plots, the Martinero bought one and stole the other. The Martinero would write on the deed that he bought two plots instead of one, and because the Joseño could not read, he was swindled.

One old man, Señor Juan Ujpan Coj, who is still alive, told me that during this period that only eight families managed to stay in San José. It was almost as if San José did not exist. They say that the Martineros even wanted to take out the image of San Juan Bautista to carry to their church in San Martin. Thus, the remaining few families carefully guarded the image of the saint from the Martineros.

Little by little, the Joseños returned from the coast, but they had no land. They had to go to the Martineros to ask for work. Since Joseños were poor, the Martineros mistreated them. The Joseños did not have anything because Martineros had bought everything. But eventually San José began to recover.

Now, there are certainly changes. This is because Joseños go to the coast to plant their corn. They bring their harvest home to San José, and thus they do not have to go to San Martín to buy corn. They plant their own beans. Because they pick cotton on the coast, Joseños earn their money in December, January, and February. Now, they no longer have to work for Martineros. For these reasons Martineros are looking now upon Joseños as equals, with the same worth as themselves. But before, this was not the case. They had to go to a rich Martinero to ask for work to sustain their families. Today, if a Joseño needs money, he goes to a farm where he can work at a regular price, or he goes to the coast to plant a patch of corn. Many Joseños are progressing. They are buying the land back from the Martineros. Now Martineros are coming to San José to ask for work or to buy corn from them. Really, what I am saying is that not long ago the Martineros wanted to act like kings toward Joseños. They can no longer do so. San José is moving up. Joseños are able to work independently. Their work experience on the coast is making them move wise, and what they earn on the coast they are not spending in San Martin but in San José.

Thus, you can see why there could be problems between Joseños and Martineros over water in 1969. But there is more to the history of this problem. Actually, Joseños believed Martineros were abusing their privilege of using water from San José. That is, when potable water came to San José on February 15, 1960, a decree of the state government of Sololá stated that San José could have 60 faucets and San Martín could have 100 since San Martín had more people living in it than San José.

San Martín built the water tank and installed the pipe, but San José provided the water. (Martineros installed the water facilities in San José as well as their own town.) What has resulted is that the Martineros, in the nine years since piped water began, have installed more than 400 faucets [about 300 more than they were allowed originally]. They have so many that the water pressure is low in San Martín, and the Martineros are always having pressure problems because they have too many faucets. In San José, there is usually enough pressure.

Because the tank that served both San José and San Martín is in the municipal district of San José, the problem of San José's not allowing San Martin to repair the tank was appealed to San José's principales [town elders who are important political figures]. San José said, "You [San Martín] may have our permission again to use the water but San Martín must pay a very high tax—$60 a month."

San Martín had not been paying a water tax before, and it did not want to agree to such a tax. The case was taken to the state court of Sololá to be settled. But since the case could not be settled in the state court, it went to Guatemala City to the Ministry of Public Works and the Ministry of Government.

When Martineros began to see they had a weak case against Joseños, they became insulting and aggressive. San José was still in conformance with the 1960 decree because it only had 38 faucets, while San Martín had 400.

Rumor arrived that Martineros were angry and were talking about killing Joseños. When Joseños discovered their reported intentions, they arose against Martineros with the same ill feelings. San José publically stated at the border between San José and San Martín, "If one Joseño dies, we are going to kill 10 or 20 Martineros because the people of San José are in their own town and are in the right. Therefore, if one Martinero kills a Joseño, know that 10 or 20 Martineros are going to die!"

It was true that some people were sincerely concerned over the need for water while others just were interested more in criminal acts. Martineros certainly had to go to San José because they had to take the harvest from the land they owned there. But they only would come to San José in groups of three or four persons. One person would not come alone because he was afraid of losing his life.

Once a man came brandishing a machete in San José. But San José gave notice, "If one Joseño dies, we are going to the boundary and wait for Martineros and kill them." Then Martineros calmed down and did not do anything until this conflict was settled.

Unlike Martineros, who needed to come to San José, Joseños did not need to go to San Martin because they had no land there. Since San José does not have its own market, Joseños usually went to San Martin to buy necessities. But during this dispute, Joseños opted to climb the mountain to Santa Ana for their market needs. Thus, the situation was less threatening to Joseños than Martineros.

The conflict sharpened when someone cut down ten coffee trees belonging to Señor Alfonso Garcia Sumosa, a rich Martinero. He thought the guilty person was Señor Bernardo Coj Mendoza, the syndic of San José. Then Señor Alfonso tried to find witnesses to prove that Señor Bernardo had cut down his coffee trees, but he could not.

Then four members of the national police arrived at San José to capture Señor Bernardo. Señor Alfonso must have paid the national policemen to punish Señor Bernardo because they struck him several times with their billy clubs, tied his hands behind his back with a rope, and marched him off to jail in San Martin. In jail they would not give him food or bedding.

The next day they took him to jail in Sololá. He was lucky since he only spent one day in jail there. The police in Sololá could not hold him because he had an alibi. When the coffee trees were cut down, he had been in the Town Hall carrying out his duties as syndic.

In February 1970, by order of the Ministry of Justice of the Government, the governor of the department of Sololá arrived in San José to execute an affidavit of reconciliation between the two towns. In effect, San Martín obtained the right to repair the tank and use the water. But in order to do this San Martín had to construct five large pilas [water basins] in the streets of San José.

By March the water was running again in San José and in San Martín. During the six months of conflict, the poor women of the two towns suffered the most. They had to carry water laboriously from the lake to prepare food for their families and to do washing. And without running water, this was a real hardship.

By the grace of God, the peace has been permanent. Since the end of the conflict, there has been peace and goodwill between the towns.

Source: Pp. 59-63 from *Son of Técun Umán: A Maya Indian Tells His Life Story* ed. by James D. Sexton. Copyright © 1981. Published by University of Arizona Press. Reprinted by permission of James D. Sexton.

• • •

AGRICULTURE AND ECOLOGY

The two contrasting sectors of agriculture, subsistence and commercial, converge in the Amazon, where they have combined to create havoc, destroying increasing amounts of tropical jungle.

DEFORESTATION IN THE AMAZON, RHETT BUTLER

Between May 2000 and August 2006, Brazil lost nearly 150,000 square kilometers of forest—an area larger than Greece—and since 1970, over 600,000 square kilometers (232,000 square miles) of Amazon rainforest have been destroyed. Why is Brazil losing so much forest? What can be done to slow deforestation?

BRAZILIAN AMAZON BEING DESTROYED?

In many tropical countries, the majority of deforestation results from the actions of poor subsistence cultivators. However, in Brazil only about one-third of recent deforestation can be linked to "shifted" cultivators. Historically a large portion of deforestation in Brazil can be attributed to land clearing for pastureland by commercial and speculative interests, misguided government policies, inappropriate World Bank projects, and commercial exploitation of forest resources. For effective action it is imperative that these issues be addressed. Focusing solely on the promotion of sustainable use by local people would neglect the most important forces behind deforestation in Brazil.

Brazilian deforestation is strongly correlated to the economic health of the country: the decline in deforestation from 1988–1991 nicely matched the economic slowdown during the same period, while the rocketing rate of deforestation from 1993–1998 paralleled Brazil's period of rapid economic growth. During lean times, ranchers and developers do not have the cash to rapidly expand their pasturelands and operations, while the government lacks funds to sponsor highways and colonization programs and grant tax breaks and subsidies to forest exploiters.

A relatively small percentage of large landowners clear vast sections of the Amazon for cattle pastureland. Large tracts of forest are cleared and sometimes planted with African savanna grasses for cattle feeding. In many cases, especially during periods of high inflation, land is simply cleared for investment purposes. When pastureland prices exceed forest land prices (a condition made possible by tax incentives that favor pastureland over natural forest), forest clearing is a good hedge against inflation.

Such favorable taxation policies, combined with government subsidized agriculture and colonization programs, encourage the destruction of the Amazon. The practice of low taxes on income derived from agriculture and tax rates that favor pasture over forest overvalues agriculture and pastureland and makes it profitable to convert natural forest for these purposes when it normally would not be so.

A CLOSER LOOK AT BRAZILIAN DEFORESTATION

Today deforestation in the Amazon is the result of several activities, the foremost of which include:

1. Clearing for cattle pasture
2. Colonization and subsequent subsistence agriculture
3. Infrastructure improvements
4. Commercial agriculture
5. Logging

CLEARING FOR CATTLE PASTURE

Cattle ranching is the leading cause of deforestation in the Brazilian Amazon. This has been the case since at least the 1970s: government figures attributed 38 percent of deforestation from 1966–1975 to large-scale cattle ranching. However, today the situation may be even worse. According to the Center for International Forestry Research (CIFOR), "between 1990 and 2001 the percentage of Europe's processed meat imports that came from Brazil rose from 40 to 74 percent" and by 2003 "for the first time ever, the growth in Brazilian cattle production—80 percent of which was in the Amazon—was largely export driven."

COLONIZATION AND SUBSEQUENT SUBSISTENCE AGRICULTURE

A significant amount of deforestation is caused by the subsistence activities of poor farmers who are encouraged to settle on forest lands by government land policies. In Brazil, each squatter acquires the right (known as a usufruct right) to continue using a piece of land by living on a plot of unclaimed public land (no matter how marginal the land) and "using" it for at least one year and a day. After five years the squatter acquires ownership and hence the right to sell the land. Up until at least the mid-1990s this system was worsened by the government policy that allowed each claimant to gain title for an amount of land up to three times the amount of forest cleared.

Poor farmers use fire for clearing land and every year satellite images pick up tens of thousands of fires burning across the Amazon.

Typically understory shrubbery is cleared and then forest trees are cut. The area is left to dry for a few months and then burned. The land is planted with crops like bananas, palms, manioc, maize, or rice. After a year or two, the productivity of the soil declines, and the transient farmers press a little deeper and clear new forest for more short-term agricultural land. The old, now infertile fields are used for small-scale cattle grazing or left for waste.

Between 1995 and 1998, the government granted land in the Amazon to roughly 150,000 families. Forty-eight percent of forest loss in 1995 was in areas under 125 acres (50 hectares) in size, suggesting that both loggers and peasants are significant contributors to deforestation.

INFRASTRUCTURE IMPROVEMENTS

Road construction in the Amazon leads to deforestation. Roads provide access to logging and mining sites while opening forest frontier land to exploitation by poor landless farmers.

Brazil's Trans-Amazonian Highway was one of the most ambitious economic development programs ever devised, and one of the most spectacular failures. In the 1970s, Brazil planned a 2,000-mile highway that would bisect the massive Amazon forest, opening rainforest lands to (1) settlement by poor farmers from the crowded, drought-plagued north and (2) development of timber and mineral resources. Colonists would be granted a 250-acre lot, six-months' salary, and easy access to agricultural loans in exchange for settling along the highway and converting the surrounding rainforest into agricultural land. The plan would grow to cost Brazil US $65,000 (1980 dollars) to settle each family, a staggering amount for Brazil, a developing country at the time.

The project was plagued from the start. The sediments of the Amazon Basin rendered the highway unstable and subject to inundation during heavy rains, blocking traffic and leaving crops to rot. Harvest yields for peasants were dismal since the forest soils were quickly exhausted, and new forest had to be cleared annually. Logging was difficult due to the widespread distribution of commercially valuable trees. Rampant erosion, up to 40 tons of soil per acre (100 tons/ha) occurred after clearing. Many colonists, unfamiliar with banking and lured by easy credit, went deep into debt.

Adding to the economic and social failures of the project, are the long-term environmental costs. After the construction of the Trans-Amazonian Highway, Brazilian deforestation accelerated to levels never before seen and vast swaths of forest were cleared for subsistence farmers and cattle-ranching schemes. The Trans-Amazonian Highway is a prime example of the environmental havoc that is caused by road construction in the rainforest.

Road construction and improvement continues in the Amazon today: Paving of roads brings change in the Amazon rainforest and the Chinese economy drives road-building and deforestation in the Amazon.

COMMERCIAL AGRICULTURE

Recently, soybeans have become one of the most important contributors to deforestation in the Brazilian Amazon. Thanks to a new variety of soybean developed by Brazilian scientists to flourish in rainforest climate, Brazil is on the verge of supplanting the United States as the world's leading exporter of soybeans. High soybean prices have also served as an impetus to expanding soybean cultivation.

Philip Fearnside, co-author of a report in *Science* [21-May-04] and member of Brazil's National Institute for Amazonian Research in Manaus, explains, "Soybean farms cause some forest clearing directly. But they have a much greater impact on deforestation by consuming cleared land, savanna, and transitional forests, thereby pushing ranchers and slash-and-burn farmers ever deeper into the forest frontier. Soybean farming also provides a key economic and political impetus for new highways and infrastructure projects, which accelerate deforestation by other actors."

Satellite data from 2004 shows a marked increase in deforestation along the BR-163 road, a highway the government has been paving in an effort to help soy farmers from Mato Grosso get their crops to export markets. Typically, roads encourage settlement by rural poor who look to the rainforest as free land for subsistence agriculture.

LOGGING

In theory, logging in the Amazon is controlled by strict licensing which allows timber to be harvested only in designated areas. However, there is significant evidence that illegal logging is quite widespread in Brazil. In recent years, Ibama—Brazil's environmental enforcement agency—has made several large seizures of illegally harvested timber including one in September 2003 when 17 people were arrested for allegedly cutting 10,000 hectares worth of timber.

Logging in the Amazon is closely linked with road building. Studies by the Environmental Defense Fund show that areas that have been selectively logged are eight times more likely to be settled and cleared by shifting cultivators than untouched rainforests because of access granted by logging roads. Logging roads give colonists access to rainforest, which they exploit for fuelwood, game, building material, and temporary agricultural lands.

OTHER CAUSES OF FOREST LOSS IN BRAZIL

Historically, hydroelectric projects have flooded vast areas of Amazon rainforest. The Balbina dam flooded some 2,400 square kilometers (920 square miles) of rainforest when it was completed. Phillip Fearnside, a leading expert on the Amazon, calculated that in the first three years of its existence, the Balbina Reservoir emitted 23,750,000 tons of carbon dioxide and 140,000 tons of methane, both potent greenhouse gases which contribute to global climate change.

Mining has impacted some parts of the Amazon Basin. During the 1980s, over 100,000 prospectors invaded the state of Para when a large gold deposit was discovered, while wildcat miners are still active in the state of Roraima near the Venezuelan border. Typically, miners clear forest for building material, fuelwood collection, and subsistence agriculture.

FIRES

Virtually all forest clearing, by small farmer and plantation owner alike, is done by fire. Though these fires are intended to burn only limited areas, they frequently escape agricultural plots and pastures and char pristine rainforest, especially in dry years like 2005. Many of the fires set for clearing forest for these purposes are set during the three-month burning season and the smoke produced creates widespread problems across the region, including airport closings and hospitalizations from smoke inhalation. These fires cover a vast area of forest. In 1987 during a four-month period (July–October), about 19,300 square miles (50,000 sq. km) of Brazilian Amazon were burned in the states of Parà, Rondonia, Mato Grosso, and Acre. The burning produced carbon dioxide containing more than 500 million tons of carbon, 44 million tons of carbon monoxide, and millions of tons of other particles and nitrogen oxides. An estimated 20 percent of fires that burn between June and October cause new deforestation, while another 10 percent is the burning of ground cover in virgin forests.

Fires and climate change are having a dramatic impact on the Amazon. Recent studies suggest that the Amazon rainforest may be losing its ability to stay green all year long as forest degradation and drought make it dangerously flammable. Scientists say that as much as 50 percent of the Amazon could go up in smoke should fires continue. Humidity levels were the lowest ever recorded in the Amazon in 2005.

SLAVERY AND VIOLENCE IN THE AMAZON

The Amazon has been a place of violence since at least the arrival of European explorers, and the present is no exception. Violent conflicts between large landowners, poor colonists, and indigenous groups over land are not unusual in the Amazon and may be worsening.

The Pastoral Land Commission, a nongovernmental group working in the region, found that land battles in Brazil's countryside reached the highest level in at least 20 years in 2004. According to the annual report by the organization, documented conflicts over land among peasants, farmers, and land speculators rose to 1,801 in 2004 from 1,690 conflicts in 2003 and 925 recorded in 2002. Tensions reached their peak earlier this year with the high-profile slaying of Dorothy Stang, an American nun who worked with rural poor, by gunmen associated with plantation owners. In response to the murder, the Brazilian government sent in the army to quell violence in the region and promised to step up environmental monitoring efforts.

The government has also stepped up efforts to end slavery in the Amazon. While Brazil officially abolished slavery in 1888, the government acknowledges that at least 25,000 Brazilians work under "conditions analogous to slavery," clearing land

and working for cattle ranches, soy farms, and other labor-intensive industries. Some groups say the true figure could be ten times that amount. In 2005, 4,133 slaves were freed after Brazilian Swat-style teams raided 183 farms.

Source: Rhett A. Butler, "Deforestation in the Amazon." http://www.mongabay.com. Reprinted by permission of Rhett A. Butler.

. . .

WHERE DOES THE COUNTRY END AND THE CITY BEGIN?

Country people were by no means isolated. As the cities expanded outward, the separation between country and city lessened. Maria Luiza Melo Carvalho, a documentary photographer, interviewed and photographed women at work in Brazil. The seven women quoted here, Jorgina, Ninice, Ana, D. Nene, Celuta, Maria, and Maria José, lived in the region around the rapidly expanding city of Belo Horizonte. None of these women fit the traditional description of a country person.

EARTH FLIES IN ALL DIRECTIONS: THE DAILY LIVES OF WOMEN IN MINAS GERAIS

JORGINA (CAMPEINO'S WIFE, MEMBER OF SÃO BENEDITO MOTHER'S CLUB)

You get up before the sun and already a child is crying. Breakfast has to be made, the beans put on, the house swept, water fetched for the garden. And it seems there's always a baby strapped to your back: When one gets a bit older, along comes another. (But, of course, the number of children depends on God's will.) On and on and on and then, you fix lunch. Sometimes there's no time to sit: You eat on the turn. After that you wash clothes and maybe steal a nap. There is always work in the fields. Really, the only holiday in the countryside is when you are asleep. Sunday we might visit friends, but there is work before we go and after we get back, just less time to do it in.

NINICE (GOLD MINER, JILL-OF-ALL-TRADES)

We only have the night to ourselves, and some of those I work straight through, making tapestry. Life here is very tight. In São Paulo it was even worse. I also had to stay up late and I was always running around doing piecework for factories. Here, it's freer, we have space, it's calm. In the city, who wasn't scared of answering the door?

Twice a week I bring clothes down to the river to wash. While they dry, I go further downstream to the spot where my sister-in-law and I always mine. My daughter is also learning. But it's not easy finding gold—some weeks it's hardly a gram. The big companies come down the river with machinery and turn over the whole bed. They can dig deeply and find a lot. For us, the currents are strong, we have to dig deep, and a shovelful of stones is backbreaking. Panning here is the hardest work there is.

ANA (POTTER)

When I got married, soon after coming here, I hated to get my hands dirty with clay. I didn't know how to make pots anyway, so we bought them. One day though, just after my first child was born, I went to see my aunt. Her neighbor was a potter, and watching this woman work, I said to myself: "I wish I could do that. I imagine the money it would save."

So I started, going off inventing, making funny shapes. Everything came out crooked, ugly, and I felt like quitting. But I kept on making them, badly finished or twisted or not. Really, I learned myself.

One market day, my husband took some pots into Capelinha and people started buying them. Then I started selling them myself. Now everyone comes here to buy them. They may be ugly, but they don't break easily and they're good for carrying water a long way.

It's hard work. It takes a whole day—and sometimes two mules—to collect the clay. Then it has to be ground, sieved, and kneaded. Next I take it outside, pound it on a rock, and start shaping pots. After they dry in the sun, they must be scraped—inside and out; the edges have to be trimmed; and the surface smoothed all over. Before the firing, they have to be coated with another thin layer of clay. Finally, they must be painted. Yes, it's hard—more than a day's work for each one, and they sell so cheaply. Sometimes I think it's better working in the fields. Still, if you want to eat, you can't stand around doing nothing. This is now my work, and suits me.

D. NENÉ (KINDERGARTEN OPERATOR)

My dream was always to be a teacher, yet it took many years. My father died, and my mother needed help raising my younger sisters. Finally I could enroll in a teacher's school. When I was hired in August 1938 to teach in the same school where I once studied, it was the happiest day of my life.

When the time finally came to retire, I didn't want to quit, so I decided to do what I liked best on my own. This little school Dom Bosco, is 22 years old now and I don't regret one minute of it. It's here for the pleasure it brings, I charge practically nothing: Each child contributes only a few cruzados per month. I stay happy because I am close to the children, I feel their affection. In their hearts, there are words of faith and hope.

CELUTA AND MARIA (MOTHER AND DAUGHTER WEAVERS)

In the morning, we always do the warping at mother's house. Then I come home, straighten up, and fix lunch while she threads the loom. When I get back to her house, we pick up where we left off. It's tough: Our lives are pretty tough. Sometimes, when we are short of cash, we'll work late into the night. We have finished two blankets in a day before, but that kills you: Your knees throb, you feel like a dishrag. With the few cruzados a blanket brings, I may buy some second-hand clothes from the priest. Buying in a store would be impossible: most of what we earn we eat.

One of the things I like doing is walking in the fields. And I enjoy talking to my friends here at home. Thankfully, the house is always full. Any night you drop by, my neighbors are here. What I know, I teach them. They come to learn, and at the same time we grow closer to one another.

MARIA JOSÉ (SECONDARY SCHOOL TEACHER)

I think you get used to being tired. Even with your head buzzing, the kids shouting, you get something done. While my children are awake, I clean the kitchen, wash clothes, straighten up. Once that's well under way, I try to distract the kids get them playing. Then I might try to prepare my lessons. Usually there are interruptions: I pick up a pen, and there's a squabble, or someone needs something. If I can't take always having to start over, I wait until I've put the kids to bed and there is a bit of peace and quiet.

That's how it is. A woman has to earn money and still be a housewife, while a man just has his job to worry about. No one sees this side of women: Housework has no value. There is so much to do and no escape. Sometimes you feel you have to get out and wind down a little. A man can go to a bar, drink a beer. When he comes home, he is relaxed: His head is lighter, only his body is tired. For women, no. We have our duty, which we are supposed to love, even when our heads and bodies are worn out entirely.

Source: Excerpted from "Earth Flies in All Directions: The Daily Lives of Women in Minas Gerais" by Maria Luiza de Melo Carvalho, *Grassroots Development* 11:2 (1987), pp. 36-40.

QUESTIONS

1. Do you think that small farms in Latin America are economically viable?
2. How did the *finqueros* exploit the country people in Guatemala?
3. Contrast the conditions on the small farms of Guatemala with those of the coffee estates described by Arthur Ruhl in the 1920s?
4. Discuss the hazards of the world market for vanilla producers?
5. What has been the overall impact of the North American Free Trade Agreement on farmers in Mexico?
6. Compare the agrarian reform programs put forth in Bolivia and Brazil? Which seemed more likely to succeed?
7. What was Che Guevara's critique of Cuban land reform?
8. According to Schwartzman, what were the disadvantages of the involvement of the World Bank in agrarian reform in Brazil?
9. In the dispute between San José and San Martín, why is water so important?
10. How did San Martín gain the upper hand in the rivalry between the two villages?
11. Who had the right on their side in the dispute?

12. Why is the clearing of the Amazon for agriculture an ecological disaster?
13. What do you think of Jorgina's statement that the number of children depends on God's will?
14. Why does Ninice prefer gold mining to piece work in the factories?
15. Why were women such as Celuta, Maria, and Ana drawn to crafts? Do you think that they received what their product was worth in the market?
16. Why is there so little mention of men in the stories of these Brazilian women?

9 LATIN AMERICAN CITIES IN THE TWENTIETH CENTURY

INTRODUCTION

Latin American cities in the twentieth century were places of extraordinary contrasts between breathtaking physical beauty and air pollution that blocked the views; between unimaginable wealth and unthinkable poverty; between manic activity and desultory idleness. After World War II, already large urban areas grew into gargantuan metropolises. They expanded exponentially in population and physical space. They grew far beyond the financial and technological means to support them.

At the turn of the twentieth century, Latin American elites looked to transform their burgeoning cities. Matters had gotten out of hand; the massive influx of people from the countryside and from abroad had overwhelmed the poorly planned, unhealthy, stinking, deteriorating metropolises. The ruling classes sought to make their cities showplaces modeled on London and Paris. They cleared the central areas of the tenements and their poor residents, creating grand boulevards in Buenos Aires and Rio de Janeiro. They also took measures to improve sanitation and health, such as vaccination campaigns and sewer construction. Discovering the origins of yellow fever and the measures to prevent epidemics vastly improved conditions in Caribbean ports, such as Veracruz and Tampico. In the decades that followed, however, the number of migrants to the cities increased manyfold, especially after 1940. It is a wonder that Mexico City, São Paulo, Lima, or Rio de Janeiro functions at all on a daily basis.

The urban geography changed, not only because of explosive population growth, but because people of all classes sought safe, healthy, reasonably priced places to live. The first to leave the downtown core were the wealthy, who, as the transportation system widened, sought refuge in suburban neighborhoods. The poor remained in the center conveniently located for access to work sites. Deteriorating tenements were cheap. Later, after 1950, the massive population increase caused the poor to seek inexpensive housing in the far reaches of the cities, sometimes beyond easy transportation. In Mexico City, for example, the barrios on the outskirts required their residents to commute as many as four or five hours a day. Often workers had to transfer two and three times from *peseros* (cheap taxis) or vans, to buses, to the Metro (subway).

As it was in the nineteenth century, the cities' main problems were water and sanitation, pollution, health, housing, noise, crime, transportation, education, and employment. There has never been enough money to solve any of these.

THE SCENE

W. J. Holland described the beauty of Rio de Janeiro at the turn of the twentieth century. He went to Buenos Aires as a representative of Andrew Carnegie, the American steel magnate and philanthropist, to establish an archeological museum. On his journey in 1912, he stopped in several port cities and in the interior of Argentina.

RIO DE JANEIRO, FROM H. J. HOLLAND,
TO THE RIVER PLATE AND BACK

The days of my stay in Rio de Janeiro, which succeeded that first day, passed so pleasantly. The impression made upon the traveler by the life of the streets in Rio de Janeiro, customs are those of southern Europe. The street-merchants and market-women, the posters and cabmen, the crowds on the side-walkers reveal by a hundred little traits in action and address that they belong to the Latin races.

Many of the public buildings of Rio de Janeiro are excellent in design and appearance. The influence of French taste is conspicuous in many of them. The Opera House, modeled after that of Paris, is as fine a building as its prototype. The Monroe Palace is recognized at once as the Brazilian Building which graced the Exposition at St. Louis, and which, transported to Rio, now adorns the Avenida. There are numerous streets which compare favorably with similar streets in any of the great European capitals. The most attractive feature of Rio is the system of boulevards intersecting the lower portion and bordering the waterfront. Nowhere in the world is there a more beautiful drive than that afforded by the Avenida Beira-Mar. The road-bed is perfection, and the exquisitely beautiful views of the bay and the mountains, which it offers at every turn.

Source: W. J. Holland, *To the River Plate and Back: The Narrative of a Scientific Mission to South America, with Observations upon Things Seen and Suggested.* New York: G. P. Putnam's Sons, 1913.

Later on Holland viewed Montevideo across the estuary of the Rio de la Plata.

MONTEVIDEO, FROM H. J. HOLLAND,
TO THE RIVER PLATE AND BACK

The older portion of Montevideo is located on a ridge which juts out westward in the form of a low promontory, north and west of which is a shallow semicircular bay, at the western extremity of which stands the Cerro, surmounted by fortifications over which rise the tall masts of the wireless signaling station. On the eastern side the promontory faces the open waters of the apparently boundless estuary, the left bank of which trends to the northeast. On this side beyond the city limits are low shelving beaches, on which in recent years have arisen numerous bathing resorts. One of the most frequented beaches is the Playa Ramirez, behind which on higher ground is a great park (Parque Urbano). Farther to the east on the low shore are Pocitos and Capurro with beautifully arranged gardens and drive-ways and a multitude of hotels, many of which compare favorably with the finest establishments of their kind in any part of the world. Montevideo is in fact not merely a great commercial port, but a seaside resort, to which the wealth and fashion of South America repair in the hot season. The municipality is growing rapidly and the numerous suburban towns and villages, which are connected with the older city by an excellent system of electric tramways, are increasing in size, as shown by the large number of new and unfinished buildings, about which workmen were swarming at the time of our visit. The population of the main city and its suburbs amounts at present to over three hundred thousand inhabitants, and it is therefore reckoned as fourth in the list of great South American municipalities, being only out-ranked by Buenos Aires, Rio de Janeiro, and São Paulo.

Source: W. J. Holland, *To the River Plate and Back: The Narrative of a Scientific Mission to South America, with Observations upon Things Seen and Suggested.* New York: G. P. Putnam's Sons, 1913.

IMMIGRANTS' VIEW OF THE CITY

In the late nineteenth and early twentieth centuries, there was a wave of immigrants from Europe into Latin America. The largest number, mostly Italians and Spaniards, poured into Argentina. Almost all settled in Buenos Aires. The following are selections from the letters of the Sola family.

IMMIGRANT BUENOS AIRES, FROM *ONE FAMILY, TWO WORLDS*

Buenos Ayres, 17 August 1901

Dearest parents,

I have been here since the 5th of this month; I am in the best of health as are my two companions. As soon as we got here, we went to the address of God-father Zocco, who then introduced us to several people from Valdengo who have been in America for some years and all are doing well more or less. The language here is Castilian, quite similar to Spanish, but you don't hear anyone speaking it. Wherever you go, whether in the hotel or at work, everyone speaks either Piedmontese or Italian, even those from other countries, and the Argentines themselves speak Italian.

This city is very beautiful. There is an enormous amount of luxury. All the streets—they call them *calle* [sic] here—are paved either with hard wood or in cement as smooth as marble, even too smooth since the horses, tram horses as well as carriage horses, which run here, keep slipping constantly. It is not un-usual to see twenty or more of them fall in one day.

There are some buildings beautiful beyond words, only five stories high, six at the most, but with ornamentation the equal of which you won't find in all of Turin. The most beautiful building is the water reservoir, built by the English, and, what is surprising, it is all marble for half its height but with certain small columns sculpted and decorated with exquisite workmanship. The other half of it is also enchanting; it occupies 10,000 square meters.

The piazza Victoria (Plaza de Mayo) is also beautiful, where all around on two sides there are only banks. They are of all nations: English, French, Italian, Spanish, North American, etc., etc. On another side is the government building where the president of Argentine Republic resides. He is Italian, Rocca by name, the third Italian president in a row who sits on the Argentine throne. There is also the railway station of the south, which is something colossal. With workshops, offices, and all the station itself it will cover one million square meters. Now they are at work on a government building for the Congress (Parliament). The architect was an Italian, as is the chief contractor, who is supervising all the work. It is a job which in the end will cost more than 700 million lire. It will occupy an area of a block which is 10,000 square meters and will be surrounded by a square, which, along with the building, will constitute an area of about 100,000 square meters. This work will be better than the first [the railway station], but perhaps I shall not be able to see it finished.

All of this is inside the city, but if you should go outside for a few hours, it's worse than a desert. You only find houses made solely out of mortar, with only a ground floor and a door you have to enter on all fours. Outside you don't see a plant; everything is desert. The plains stretch as far as the eye can see, it takes hours on the train before you come to the mountains. There are a few tracts of land, sort of green, where they may let a few horses loose to graze. Here they let the animal go out no matter what the weather might be. Here you can't find a rock, though you pay its weight in gold for it. All the ground is black like manure, thick and muddy. When it doesn't rain, it gets hard, and if you try to dig, it shoots out as if it were rock.

The food here is pretty good, but it doesn't have much flavor. This is true for all Argentina.

All the guys here are jolly as crazy men. In the evening when we get together before going to bed we split our sides laughing. They would all like to go back to Italy, but they don't ever budge. Perhaps I will do the same. Here we eat, drink, and laugh and enjoy ourselves; we are in America.

IMMIGRANT BUENOS AIRES, FROM *ONE FAMILY, TWO WORLDS*

Mendoza, 18 September 1901

Dearest Parents,

I am in still good spirits and happy that I am in America. I am now at Mendoza instead of Buenos Ayres. I didn't like Buenos Ayres too much because you don't get good wine there; and then every day the temperature changes twenty times, and I was always chilly. Otherwise it was fine.

One day I got the idea, knowing that Secondino's brother-in-law and sister were in Mendoza. Since the boss advanced me the money for the trip. I made up my mind to come here, where you see nothing but hills and mountains in the distance, like at home. You drink very well here; the wine costs half what it does in Buenos Ayres and is pure and delicious. I am living here with Carlo and his wife and a man by the name of Luigi Ferraro from Chiavazza, who has been here for seven years traveling around in America. There are few people here from Biella, but there is no shortage of Italians. I still haven't learned a word of Castilian because, everywhere you go, they speak Italian or Piedmontese.

I am better off here than in Buenos Ayres. I am only sorry to be so far from my friends—they didn't want to come—and from Godfather and the rest.

This city is ugly; it never rains even though it is close to the mountains. I have written a friend to send me the address of my schoolmate Berretta, and I might just go and see him in Peru; it takes four days or more on the train. From Buenos Ayres to Mendoza takes two nights and a day on the railroad without ever changing trains or getting off. The longest stop is a half hour. In the entire journey you don't see a plant. [There are] two or three rivers about 400 meters wide. They are all in the plain, so calm that you can't tell which way the water is going, and yet they flow on in an imperceptible way.

Throughout the journey one meets only horses, cows, and goats, none of which have stables. On the rail line you don't see a house for three hours or more, and everything is like that. The first night an ox was sleeping on the tracks; the train hit it so hard that it knocked it for a distance of more than fifty meters. It gave a long bellow and then died. There are also ostriches in great number. You find carcasses of other animals who have just died; the owners of these vast tracts don't go looking for them. They leave them there to rot as food for the vultures, which are abundant. All of Argentina is like that. From Mendoza it takes fifteen hours by mule to get to Chile. My trip cost more than thirty scudos.

Everyone, Carlo, Cichina, and Luigi, give their regards to you. Tell Secondino to come and see America, to drink and eat and travel.

Time is pressing since I have to work every evening until ten. I work at home after work.

You should write me at:

El Taller del Ferro Carril G.O.A.

Mendoza

Goodbye everybody. Kisses to Able and Narcisa. Tell Able to study hard and to learn to work. Send him to the technical schools; I imagine he has been promoted. Goodbye, Mom and Dad. Be in good spirits as I am.

Yours always,

Orestes

IMMIGRANT BUENOS AIRES, FROM *ONE FAMILY, TWO WORLDS*

Buenos Ayres, 19 July 1908

Dearest parents,

Please excuse me if since the month of this past March I have not written you at all, nor shown any life in my promise to write to you. Here is the reason.

The Argentine government is far from prompt in its salaries; they can even fall behind by years. Only this month, after many protests, which leave them cold, have they paid us for November and December. As for the months of 1908, they are not even talking about them yet. However, toward the end of the year, when they start to deal with the proposed budget of 1909, I think they will have to talk about that concerning 1908, which has remained at the mercy of the individual ministers. I have spoken with some deputies, and it looks as if they will try to intervene on my behalf.

I have delayed so much because from one day to the next one kept hoping for a solution. But now we have all resigned ourselves to the situation, and we wait. For many, almost all, who have no other resource than their government money (not everyone can hold two jobs ?!) life is a bit grim, and they are scraping by on the strength of borrowing.

The salary I get from the firm working on the Congress enables me to live with security enough, but now in part because of the increase in the cost of living, and in part because of our private affairs, and then you must realize that now I am a man with a wife to support, everything slips away without any big expenses.

Please excuse me then if so much time has gone by since I have carried out my promises. In the months to come, until I am able to get full salary from Congress, I shall send you about 100 lire a month. I know it's not much, but for now bear with me, dearest parents, and don't think badly of me in your hearts. It is not because of stinginess or carelessness; it's just that I can't come up with anything more. I'll send it to you then all at one stroke at the start of next year. In the meantime I am enclosing in this letter a check for 400 lire.

This week I have sent you two postcards which you will get a few days before this. I sent the same to Abele in Sardinia; tomorrow I'll write him a letter, giving him the news in detail. I am glad that he has found something better. I think he will be able to do what he has to and become a man. Traveling a bit from one region to another will stimulate him, and so he will gain a lot of things that will be useful to him. It is, however, necessary for him to study, to study always and hard.

Today it is five months that I've been married, and I do not regret it at all. She is sweet; she talks to me often of you and Biella (she hasn't been here long and still misses it). She takes care of the house—and all the domestic tasks—efficiently and with good taste. I am delighted with her. In the evening we enjoy a laugh together, and sometimes we go to the theater or to a concert. On Sundays, if the weather is good and not cold, we make an outing outside of town with different couples we know, and so we spend the time contentedly. She is eagerly looking forward to the Exposition of 1911 to see her own dear ones and you, for whom she makes my affection grow every day. As to any new addition, she gives no promise of one so far, but there is no hurry. Next month I'll send you our pictures, long since promised. Count on it.

Enrico Ferri landed yesterday; he came for a lecture tour. I saw him last night at about eleven at an Italian club (l'Unione e Benevolenza), which today celebrates its fiftieth anniversary. He seems to have aged a lot; perhaps the cash he will take home will rejuvenate him. I have taken a subscription for the first eight lectures. If there is anything interesting, I'll send you the newspapers. I am sending you one, in Italian, the one about his arrival.

Accept, dearest parents, so many, many kisses from your loving son and his wife, who looks upon you with the same respect as I do. One more big kiss for Mom from my wife.

Bye. Keep in good spirits.

Your dearest son,

Oreste

Source: Samuel L. Baily and Francisco Ramella, eds. *One Family, Two Worlds: An Italian Family's Correspondence across the Atlantic, 1901–1922.* New Brunswick: Rutgers University Press, 1988.

MEXICO CITY

Perhaps the greatest of the giant metropolises is Mexico City. Carlos Moncivais, Mexico's acerbic pundit, makes the following observations.

MEXICO CITY, FROM CARLOS MONCIVAIS, MEXICAN POSTCARDS

Visually, Mexico City signifies above all else the superabundance of people. In the capital, the multitude that accosts the multitude imposes itself like a permanent obsession. Intimacy is by permission only, the "poetic license" that allows you momentarily to forget those around you—never more than an inch away—who make of urban vitality a relentless grind.

Turmoil is the purpose of the city-dwellers, a whirlwind set in motion by secret harmonies and lack of public resources. How can one describe Mexico City today? Mass overcrowding and the shame at feeling no shame; the unmeasurable space, where almost everything is possible, because everything works thanks only to what we call a "miracle" – which is no more than the meeting-place of work, technology and chance. These are the most frequent images of the capital city:

- Multitudes on the Underground (where almost six million travelers a day are crammed, making space for the very idea of space);
- Multitudes taking their entrance exam in the University Football Stadium;
- The "Marías" (Mazahua peasant women) selling whatever they can in the streets, resisting police harassment while training their countless kids;
- The underground economy that overflows on to the pavements, making popular marketplaces of the streets. At traffic lights young men and women overwhelm drivers attempting to sell Kleenex, kitchenware, toys, tricks. The vulnerability is so extreme that it becomes artistic, and a young boy makes fire—swallowing it and throwing it up—the axis of his gastronomy;
- Mansions built like safes, with guard dogs and private police;
- Masked wrestlers, the tutelary gods of the new Teotihuacan of the ring;
- The *Templo Mayor*, Indian grandeur;

- *'piñatas'* containing all the most important traditional figures: the Devil, the Nahual, Ninja Turtles, Batman, Penguin. . . ;
- the Basilica of Guadalupe;
- the swarm of cars. Suddenly it feels as if all the cars on earth were held up right here, traffic jam having now become second nature to the species hoping to arrive late at the Late Judgment. Between four and six o'clock in the morning there is some respite, the species seems drowsy . . . but suddenly everything moves on again, the advance cannot be stopped. And in the traffic jam, the automobile becomes a prison on wheels, the cubicle where you can study Radio in the University of Tranquility;
- the flat rooftops, which are the continuation of agrarian life by other means, the natural extension of the farm, the redoubt of Agrarian Reform. Evocations and needs are concentrated on the rooftops. There are goats and hens, and people shout at the helicopters because they frighten cows and the farmers milking them. Clothes hang there like harvested maize. There are rooms containing families who reproduce and never quite seem to fit. Sons and grandsons come and go, while grandparents stay for months, and the room grows, so to speak, eventually to contain the whole village from which its first migrant came;
- the contrasts between rich and poor, the constant antagonism between the shadow of opulence and the formalities of misery;
- the street gangs, less violent than elsewhere, seduced by their own appearance, but somewhat uncomfortable because no one really notices them in the crowd. The street gangs use an international alphabet picked up in the streets of Los Angeles, fence off their territories with graffiti, and show off the aerial prowess of punk hairstyles secure in the knowledge that they are also ancestral, because they really copied them off Emperor Cuauhtemoc. They listen to heavy metal, use drugs, thinner and cement, destroy themselves, let themselves be photographed in poses they wish were menacing, accept parts as extras in apocalyptic films, feel regret for their street-gang life, and spend the rest of their lives evoking it with secret and public pleasure.

The images are few. One should add the Museum of Anthropology, the Zócalo at anytime (day or night), the Cathedral.

Mexico: another great Latin American city, with its seemingly uncontrollable growth, its irresponsible love of modernity made visible in skyscrapers, malls, fashion shows, spectacles, exclusive restaurants, motorways, cellular phones. Chaos displays its aesthetic offerings, and next to the pyramids of Teotihuacán, the baroque altars, and the more wealthy and elegant districts, the popular city offers its rituals.

I will now enumerate the points of pride (psychological compensation):

- Mexico City is the most populated city in the world (the Super-Calcutta!);
- Mexico City is the most polluted city on the planet, whose population, however, does not seem to want to move (the laboratory of the extinction of the species);
- Mexico City is the place where it would be impossible for anything to fail due to a lack of audience. There is public aplenty. In the Capital, to counterbalance the lack of clear skies, there are more than enough inhabitants, spectators, car-owners, pedestrians;

The National Museum of Anthropology in Mexico City. © Mexican National Tourist Council

- Mexico City is the place where the unlivable has its rewards, the first of which has been to endow survival with a new status.

And how do we reconcile this sense of having reached a limit with the medium- and long-term plans of every city-dweller?

Despite the disaster twenty million people *cannot leave Mexico City or the Valley of Mexico, because there is nowhere else they want to go; there is nowhere else, really, that they can go.*

To stay in Mexico City is to confront the risks of pollution, thermic inversion, lead poisoning, violence, the rat race, and the lack of individual meaning. To leave it is to lose the formative and informative advantages of extreme concentration, the experiences of modernity (or post-modernity) that growth and the ungovernability of certain zones due to massification bring. The majority of people, although they may deny it with their complaints and promises to flee, are happy to stay, and stand by the only reasons offered them by hope: 'It will get better somehow.' The worst never comes.

Source: "Identity Hour or, What Photos Would You Take of the Endless City? (From a Guide to Mexico City," in Carlos Moncivais, *Mexican Postcards*. Ed. and trans. John Kraniauskas. New York: Verso, 1997.

MAP, MEXICO CITY 1910

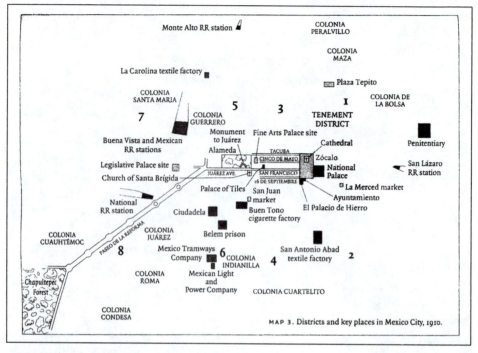

Districts and key places in Mexico City, 1910. (John Lear, *Workers, Neighbors, and Citizens: The Revolution in Mexico City.* Lincoln: University of Nebraska Press, 2001)

DAILY LIFE

In the 1950s, anthropologist Oscar Lewis wrote a series of studies about poor Mexicans suggesting that people fell into a culture of poverty that elicited generalized behaviors that exacerbated their plight and spilled over into the next generations. In the 1980s, writer Louis Werner explored the newer poor neighborhoods of the capital to see if Lewis's ideas held any validity three decades later. Werner found that the newer communities were far from the center of the city and were comprised of residents who had moved from other barrios seeking cheaper housing. He also discovered that there was a degree of community activism not present in the earlier studies. One typical inhabitant of the Nueva Casa Blanca barrio was Macedio Rosas Garrido. An excerpt from his interview follows.

THE SÁNCHEZ FAMILY REVISITED

I'm thirty three years old and was born in Mexico City. I've got about 10 brothers and sisters living all over the city. One sister lives next to me here in Nueva Casa Blanca. My father died about 17 years ago, but my mother is still living in a little village called Tecama in the colonia 5 de Mayo. I've been married 11 years and have three children, two girls and a boy. I'm an eight-wheel truck driver, but it's been more than a year since I had regular work.

We ended up living here four years ago because we heard that the ejidatorios were selling land. We were interested because we were living in a tenement of about 10 families. We were renting there, and twice a year the owners would raise our rent. We started off paying 230 pesos a month and by the time we left, it was up to 1,500. So with a lot of sacrifice, we bought this lot there and built the house, little by little. The cement floor just went down last year.

In the center of the city, life in a tenement is crowded, sad, but here it's sadder still. Over there we had water, sewers, electricity—all the services. Maybe not one or two blocks away, but we had everything we needed, like markets and schools. Out here we have to fight to get an education for our kids, and it's dangerous because the schools are so far away. We even battle for water to drink.

Friendships and sense of solidarity are the same here as there. I left a lot of compadres in the tenement, a lot of friends. I'm very sincere when I make a friend, and I think that when someone is my friend, they're sincere too. When I first got here I didn't know anyone, but then—little by little—I got to know people.

The earthquake didn't do much damage here. We were getting up and the house shook, that was all. Something happened afterwards, though. About a year ago during the windy season between January and March, there were really strong gusts, and wind devils. We didn't have any problems with the earthquake, but with the high winds, yes, we did. On one case a mother was washing clothes outside her house and had left her baby hanging inside in a cradle. A gust came up and took the roof off her house and everything inside it—including the baby.

We have to fight for everything. Sometimes it can be dangerous. I really don't know much about the man who got killed because when I moved here it had already happened. My neighbors told me about it. They said he was killed because he was putting up electrical wires for people. You know, illegal hookups to get electricity to the houses. They say nobody had killed him. The men he was working with just killed him because they thought they could charge money for what this guy was doing for free to help the community. Some say the killers got caught and others say they didn't.

Some people are afraid to do too much because of this killing. It's an example. That guy was a government employee, a bodyguard for the ex-president's brother, and he still got killed. What can his neighbors think, who don't have any protection like he had?

In Nueva Casa Blanca there aren't any official organizers . . . any politics of any kind. It's simply a battle we're all fighting together—all the neighbors—for the benefit of the colonia. And by the way, we aren't afraid of the authorities as much as of each other. Afraid that somebody among us might propose some dirty business like those killers did. Those guys didn't have any political connections, nothing to do with the authorities, just personal ambition.

There are various groups that maintain the electrical hookups. Each group is in effect the owner of its own transformer box. Some boxes have 10 or 20 families hooked up—ours has 50—and everyone has to mark their own cable so they know which is theirs. But there's one person in charge of the box, and when he needs money to buy a new fuse or a new main cable, we all pitch in. With our box we've always had cooperation from everybody. Some other guys run their box like a business, and call meetings every week just to ask for more money. That's what happened to us at first. One guy appointed himself in charge, and he exploited us whenever he could. Finally we got tired, and chose someone else who does a good job.

I've got this big cistern, but not for any special reason because I want to make money out of it. In the rainy season the water trucks can't get through the muddy streets, so they don't come. Not everyone has the luxury of having a cistern. Some get their water in 50-gallon barrels, while others, with less money, get theirs in buckets. When it's wet and the people with buckets run out, I give a little to whoever needs it. You know, some people charge 400 pesos for 200 liters and 100 pesos for a bucket. It's robbery because really water shouldn't even cost half that much.

The primary school we're building came from the idea of one person, who told someone else, who told another person, and that's how the idea started taking shape until the moment came that it became a reality. It wasn't anything political. We're all cooperating in the construction. It's work for men, but to finish the school, the mothers do some heavy work too. They work side by side with the men.

We have plenty of labor but no capital to buy materials. We give what we can— 100, 200, 500, 1,000 pesos—but you must realize, it's a real sacrifice. We're using pieces of old wood and used cardboard. We've already got seven temporary classrooms, but I hope to God that the winds don't come up early; because then we'd lose these rooms and everything. By the time the windy season starts, we've got to have the classrooms more secure.

You see, we're humble people here. We've barely got money to eat so it's impossible to finish the school right. Maybe over the long term, if we build two classrooms a year. We still hope the government steps in. But if the government says no, we've only got our own resources to work with, which are very low. Yet little by little, maybe one classroom a year. . . .

The owners are still a threat. We're afraid they might come by, not to take back the lot, because that's impossible now that we've petitioned the authorities, nor to steal our building material. What we're really afraid of is that they'll come for revenge and burn all the laminated panels we put up as a temporary roof. They'd go up in a second. But we won't have to worry once the real roof is in place.

Source: Pp. 23-32 from "The Children of Sanchez Revisited" by Louis Sanchez, (1988), *Grassroots Development*, 12:1. Copyright © 1988. Reprinted by permission of Louis Werner.

QUESTIONS FOR DISCUSSION

1. To the American W. J. Holland, what was the most striking attribute of Rio de Janeiro?
2. What impressed W. J. Holland about Montevideo?
3. Was Holland's favorable opinion of Buenos Aires and Montevideo due to their similarities to European cities?
4. In Oreste's first letter to his parents, does he present a true picture of his new home?
5. Why did Oreste move to Mendoza?

6. Once Orestes settles in, what happens to his obligation to his parents?
7. In reading Carlos Moncivais's description of Mexico City, what is the most overwhelming feeling you have? Do you feel closed in? Would you want to live in Mexico City?
8. Was Macedonio Rosas Garrido a typical dweller of an urban barrio?
9. What do you think is the key element in organizing urban barrios?
10. How do urban dwellers survive on a daily basis?
11. Are city dwellers optimistic? If so, why? Why not?

10 THE MEXICAN REVOLUTION

INTRODUCTION

The Mexican Revolution (1910–1920), along with the Chinese (1911) and Russian (1917) revolutions, was one of the first of the twentieth century. Lasting nearly ten years, it cost the lives of two million Mexicans and caused widespread damages. The Mexican economy did not recover to its 1910 levels for perhaps two decades.

The Revolution ended the long rule of dictator-president Porfirio Díaz, who had taken power in 1876 and ruled until 1911. The revolutionaries comprised a rare multi-class coalition that included workers rendered unemployed by the depression of 1907, village peasants whose communal lands had been stolen by landed estate owners and politicians, discontented middle class citizens excluded from access to political office and treated unfairly by governments at all levels, and disaffected upper class members dislodged from political power in their regions by Díaz and his henchmen. In 1910 Francisco I. Madero emerged as a charismatic leader in opposition to Díaz and unified the various discontented groups. Díaz went into exile in May 1911, when his army was unable to quell the scattered rebellions that had broken out, most notably in Chihuahua and Morelos. Madero subsequently became president. The coalition soon broke apart, however, with the first defection led by Emiliano Zapata, whose followers sought land reform that Madero was unwilling to rush. In 1913 Victoriano Huerta, then serving as Madero's commanding general, overthrew and assassinated him. Former adherents to Madero, headed by Venustiano Carranza, the governor of the state of Coahuila, opposed Huerta, and civil war ensued. Carranza defeated Huerta through the efforts of two generals, Pancho Villa and Alvaro Obregón. Villa, joining with Zapata, then broke with Carranza and the civil war resumed. Ultimately, Carranza and Obregón prevailed. Obregón and Carranza fought in 1920 with the former winning out. By 1923 Zapata, Villa, and Carranza had died at the hands of their enemies. In 1917 the revolutionaries adopted a new constitution that incorporated the most radical provisions of any such document anywhere.

The decade-long civil wars took an enormous toll. It was a wonder how the combatants continued on through their disappointments and disillusionment and the enormous destruction. Mexico would never be the same as a result. The excerpts that follow illustrate the reasons men and women rebelled, why they continued to fight on in the long struggle, and what life was like in this terrible war.

WHY DID MEXICANS REBEL?

A broad cross-class coalition ousted Porfirio Díaz in 1911. The Liberal Party, led by the Flores Magón brothers, was one of the first organized protest groups. The three brothers, Jesús (1871–1930), Ricardo (1874–1922), and Enrique (1877–1954), began their political activities against the dictatorship in 1900, when Ricardo founded the newspaper Regeneración. *Exiled in the United States for a number of years, they continued their agitation. The Liberal Party had an underground following among middle and working class Mexicans, particularly along the northern border. The Program of the Liberal Party was published in 1906.*

PROGRAM OF THE LIBERAL PARTY 1906

Every political party that struggles to acquire effective influence in the direction of the public affairs of its country is obliged to declare to the people, in a clear and precise form, the ideals for which it fights and the program that it proposes to put into practice if it is favored by victory. This duty might even be considered an advantage to honorable parties, for their objectives, being just and beneficent, will undoubtedly win the sympathy of many citizens, who will adhere to the party inspired by such objectives in order to attain them.

The Liberal Party, dispersed by the persecution of the Dictatorship, weak, and nearly moribund for a long time, has succeeded in healing its wounds and is now in the process of organizing itself. The Liberal Party is struggling against the despotism that today rules our country and, sure as it is of finally triumphing over the Dictatorship, believes that it is time solemnly to declare to the Mexican people in detail the desires it proposes to realize once it obtains the influence it seeks in the orientation of our national destinies. . . .

Since all the amendments that have been made to the constitution of 1857 by the Government of Porfirio Díaz are considered illegal, it may seem unnecessary to call for the reduction of the presidental term to four years and a ban on re-election. However, these points are so important and were proposed with such unanimity and forcefulness that it has been deemed fitting to include them explicitly in the Program. The advantages of the alternation of power and of not surrendering it to one man for an excessively long time do not have to be proven. . . .

Compulsory military service is one of the most odious of tyrannies, incompatible with the rights of the citizen of a free country. This tyranny will be suppressed. In the future, when the national Government will not sustain it, all those who are forced to bear arms today will be free, and only those who wish to will remain in the army. . . .

The education of children ought to receive very special attention from a Government which truly desires the advancement of the country. The basis of the greatness of a people lies in the primary school, and the best institutions are of little value and run the risk of being destroyed if alongside them there do not exist thousands of well-equipped schools where the citizens who will safeguard those institutions may be formed. . . . The need to create as many new schools as are required by the country's school-age population will be immediately acknowledged by everyone who is not an enemy of progress. . . .

It is pointless to declare in the Program that the Mexican should be given preference over the foreigner, other conditions being equal, for this is already part of our constitution. As a means of effectively avoiding foreign domination and guaranteeing our territorial integrity, no measure seems more fitting than to consider all foreigners who acquire real estate as Mexican citizens. . . .

The Catholic clergy, exceeding the bounds of its religious mission, has always attempted to make itself a political power and has brought great evils upon the country, either as co-ruler of the state with conservative governments or as a rebel against liberal governments. This attitude of the clergy, inspired by its savage hatred of democratic institutions, produces a similar attitude in honorable governments which will not permit religious encroachments on civil power nor patiently tolerate the continuous rebelliousness of clericalism. If the Mexican clergy would emulate the conduct of its counterparts in other countries, such as England and the United States . . . no government would disturb it or take the trouble to keep it under surveillance. . . . The aggressive attitude of the clergy toward the liberal state compels the state to make itself respected energetically. If the Mexican clergy, like that of other countries, always remained within the religious sphere, political changes would not affect it. But since it is at the head of a militant party—the conservative party—it must resign itself to suffer the consequences of its conduct. . . .

A government that is interested in the effective welfare of the entire people cannot remain indifferent toward the very important question of labor. Thanks to the Dictatorship of Porfirio Díaz, which puts its power at the service of all the exploiters of the people, the Mexican worker has been reduced to the most wretched conditions; wherever he lends his services, he is obliged to work long and hard for a daily wage of a few cents. The sovereign capitalist imposes, without appeal, the conditions of labor, which are always disastrous for the worker, who has to accept them for two reasons: because poverty forces him to work at any price or because the bayonets of the Dictatorship take care of subduing him if he rebels against the abuses of the rich. Therefore, the Mexican worker accepts jobs of twelve or more hours a day for salaries of less than seventy-five cents, and finds himself obliged to endure discounts from his miserable wage for medical services, religion, civil or religious holidays, and other things, in addition to the fines that are imposed on any pretext.

The rural worker is in an even more deplorable situation than the industrial worker, for he is a veritable serf of the modern feudal lords. In general, these workers are supposedly given a daily wage of twenty-five cents or less, but they do not even receive this meager sum in cash. Since the masters have taken pains to burden the peons with more or less nebulous debts, the former collect the latters' wages as interest and provide them with some corn and beans only to keep them from dying of hunger. . . .

A work day of eight hours and a minimum daily wage of one *peso* is the least that can be sought so that the worker will at least be rescued from poverty, so that fatigue will not drain him of all his energy, and so that he may have the time and desire to seek education and diversion after his work. . . . What is being sought now is to uproot the abuses of which the worker is a victim and to put him in a position to struggle against capital. . . . If the worker were left in his present situation, he would barely manage to improve, for the black poverty in which he lives would continue to oblige him to accept all the conditions of the exploiter. On the other hand, if he is guaranteed fewer hours of work and a higher salary . . .his yoke will be lightened, and he will be able to fight for greater gains, to unite and organize and strengthen himself in order to wrest new and better concessions from capital. . . .

The improvement of working conditions on the one hand and, on the other, the equitable distribution of land, with facilities for cultivating and developing it without restrictions, would produce inestimable advance for the nation. Not only would the classes, directly benefitted be saved from destitution and acquire certain comforts, but there would be great development of our agriculture and industry and all the sources of public wealth, which are today stagnant because of our widespread poverty. In effect, when the people are too poor, when their resources are enough only to eat badly, they consume only articles of prime necessity, and on a small scale at that. How can industries be established, how can textiles, furniture, and similar objects be produced in a country in which the majority of the people cannot obtain any of the comforts of life? . . . But if these starvelings get enough to eat, if they are in a position to satisfy their normal needs, in a word, if their labor is well or at least adequately remunerated, they will consume an infinity of articles of which they are today deprived, and large-scale production of these articles will become necessary. When the millions of pariahs that today vegetate in hunger and nakedness eat less badly, use clothing and shoes, and no longer have mats as their sole furniture, the now insignificant demand for thousands of objects will increase in colossal proportions, and industry, agriculture, and commerce will all be impelled to develop on a scale which will never be reached so long as the present conditions of general poverty continue. . . .

Mexicans: Make a choice between what despotism offers you and what the Program of the Liberal Party offers! If you prefer shackles, poverty, humiliation before the foreigner, the gray life of the debased pariah, support the Dictatorship that gives you all this. If you prefer liberty, economic betterment, the dignity of Mexican citizenship, the proud life of the man who is his own master, come to the Liberal Party, which fraternizes with all worthy and virile men. Unite your efforts with those of all who fight for justice, in order to hasten that glorious day on which the tyranny shall fall forever and the long awaited democracy shall rise with all the splendors of a star that shall never cease to shine in the serene horizon of the fatherland.

Source: From Jesús Silva Herzog, *Breve Historia de la Revolución Mexicana* (Mexico: Fondo de Cultura Económica, 1960. Transl. in Lewis Hanke, ed. *History of Latin American Civilization*, Vol. 2. Boston: Little, Brown, 1973.

Just having obtained release from prison after his unsuccessful run for president against Díaz in 1910, Francisco I. Madero went briefly into exile in the United States and issued his Plan de San Luis Potosí, *explaining why he was taking up arms. He appealed to Mexicans shut out of the Díaz system. Madero wanted to restore democratic government.*

PLAN DE SAN LUIS POTOSÍ

Abusing the law of vacant lands, numerous small property owners, in the majority Indian, have been dispossessed of their lands by acts of the Ministry of Development or by judgments of the courts of the Republic. It being totally just to restitute arbitrarily dispossessed lands to their former owners, such acts and judgments are declared subject to revision, and those that acquired land by such immoral methods, or their heirs, will be required to return those lands . . . and also to pay an indemnity for damages incurred.

In addition to the Constitution [of 1857] and laws in force, the principle of NO RE-ELECCIÓN . . . is declared the Supreme Law of the Republic.

I assume the character of provisional President of the United Mexican States with all necessary powers to fight the usurper government of General Díaz.

Fellow Citizens: If I call upon you to take arms and to overthrow the government of General Díaz, it is not only as a consequence of the excesses that he committed during the last elections, but also in order to save the nation from the somber future that awaits it if it continues under his dictatorship and under the government of the nefarious oligarchy of *científicos* who are unscrupulously absorbing and destroying the national wealth at that speed. If we allow them to remain in power, they will carry out their plans within a very short term: they will lead the people into ignominy and debasement; they will suck out all their wealth and leave them in the most absolute misery; they will cause the bankruptcy of our weak, impoverished, and handcuffed nation, which will be incapable of defending its borders, its honor, and its institutions.

As far as I am concerned, I have a clear conscience and no one can accuse me of promoting the Revolution for personal gains, for the nation is aware that I did everything possible to arrive at a peaceful settlement, and I was determined even to withdraw my candidacy, provided that general Díaz had let the nation choose at least the Vice President of the Republic. But, dominated by enigmatic pride and incredible arrogance, he refused to listen to the voice of the nation, and he preferred to precipitate Revolution rather than to give an inch, rather than to return to the people a particle of their rights.

He himself justified the present Revolution when he said [in 1876]: "That citizens may not impose and perpetuate themselves in the exercise of power, and this shall be the last revolution."

If the interests of the nation had weighed more in general Díaz's spirit than his own sordid interests and those of his advisers, he would have prevented this Revolution by making a few concessions to the people.

But, because he did not do so, so much the better! Change will come faster and shall be more radical, because the Mexican people, instead of lamenting like cowards, will accept the challenge like brave men. And because General Díaz intends to rely on brute force to impose an ignominious yoke on the people, they will have to resort to this same force in order to get rid of that yoke, to overthrow that doleful man from power, and to re-conquer their liberty.

Source: Pp. 37–39, "Plan de San Luis Postal" from *Revolution in Mexico: Years of Upheaval, 1910–1940* ed. by James W. Wilkie and Albert L. Michaels. Copyright © 1984 by The Arizona Board of Regents. Reprinted by permission of the University of Arizona Press.

In the south central state of Morelos, peasants despoiled of their lands by the expansion of the sugar plantations rose up in rebellion at the same time Madero led his revolt in the north. Emiliano Zapata, a village leader from Anencuilco, emerged as the head of the movement. The Plan de Ayala reflected the desire of country people to own their own land, and their discontent about the unfairness of the dictatorship. Zapata proclaimed the Plan on November 28, 1911, just days after Madero took office as president. It was a warning that the country people in the south would continue to fight until they recovered their lost lands.

PLAN DE AYALA

We, the undersigned, constituted as a Revolutionary Junta, in order to support and fulfill the promises made by the Revolution of November 20, 1910, solemnly proclaim in the face of the civilized world that is judging us . . . the following plan:

. . . we declare the said Francisco I. Madero unfit to realize the promises of the Revolution of which he is the author, because he is a traitor to the principles . . . which enabled him to climb to power . . . and because, in order to please the *científicos, hacendados,* and *caciques* who enslave us, he has crushed with fire and blood those Mexicans who seek liberties.

The Revolutionary Junta of the State of Morelos will not sanction any transactions or compromises until it secures the downfall of the dictatorial elements of Porfirio Díaz and Francisco I. Madero, because the nation is tired of traitors and false liberators who make promises and forget them when they rise to power . . . as tyrants.

As an additional part of the plan that we proclaim, be it known: that the lands, woods, and water usurped by the hacendados, científicos, or caciques, under the cover of tyranny and venal justice, henceforth belong to the towns or citizens in possession of the deeds concerning these properties of which they were despoiled through the devious action of our oppressors. The possession of said properties shall be kept at all costs, arms in hand. The usurpers who think they have a right to said goods may state their claims before special tribunals to be established upon the triumph of the Revolution.

. . . the immense majority of Mexico's villages and citizens own only the ground on which they stand. They suffer the horrors of poverty without being able to better their social status in any respect, or without being able to dedicate themselves to industry or agriculture due to the fact that the lands, woods, and water are monopolized by a few. For this reason, through prior compensation, one-third of such monopolies will be expropriated from their powerful owners in order that the villages and citizens of Mexico may obtain *ejidos*, colonies, town sites, and rural properties for sowing or tilling, and in order that the welfare and prosperity of the Mexican people will be promoted in every way.

The property of those hacendados, científicos, or caciques who directly or indirectly oppose the present plan shall be nationalized, and two-thirds of their remaining property shall be designated for war indemnities—pensions for the widows and orphans of the victims that succumb in the struggle for this plan.

Source: Pp. 45–46, "Plan de Ayala" from *Revolution in Mexico: Years of Upheaval, 1910–1940* ed. by James W. Wilkie and Albert L. Michaels. Copyright © 1984 by The Arizona Board of Regents. Reprinted by permission of the University of Arizona Press.

Francisco "Pancho" Villa was the most controversial leader of the Revolution. Historians once dismissed him as a bandit who had a meteoric career as a military leader and who lacked any social agenda. Thanks to the research of Friedrich Katz, however, we have learned that Villa was a complex man who had deep feelings about everyday Mexicans. The excerpt that follows comes from an unpublished portion of his memoirs. Villa, like Zapata, had a vision of land for the people.

VILLA'S MEMOIRS

And I see that orderly grouping of little houses in which soldiers/farmers live: clean and white, smiling and hygienic, the homes for which one really fights with courage and for whose defense one would die.

I see these luxurious fruit orchards, these abundant vegetable gardens, these sown fields, these corn fields, these alfalfa fields which not only a large *landowner harvests* and *accrues* benefits from but rather an entire family *cultivates* and *gathers, cares for,* and *harvests.*

And I see that the school is the tallest building in the hamlet and the teacher is the most respected man; and that the one who studies and knows the most is the most appreciated youth; and that the happiest father is he who will leave his land, animals, and house to his learned, good, and honest child, so that new, healthy, learned, good, hard-working children will arise from this sanctified home, who will dignify the country and honor the race.

Oh, if life will only permit me to live long enough to see this dream realized! . . . The true army of the people, which I loved so much, dispersed through the entire land, plowing the soil, making it respectable and respected! Fifteen years! twenty years, perhaps! And the sons of my soldiers, who will bring this ideal to fruition will know with what tenderness I caressed this dream of my soul. And they will not suffer, they will not have the threat of suffering, which I endured in the fullest years of my life, which formed my youth and my entire maturity.

Source: The passage comes from Villa's memoirs discovered by Guadalupe Villa Guerrero, "Francisco Villa, Historia, Leyenda y Mito" (Thesis, University of Mexico, 1976) quoted in Friedrich Katz, *The Secret War in Mexico.* Chicago: University of Chicago Press, 1981, pp. 280–281.

The Mexican Revolution spawned musical ballads, sometimes humorous, often melancholy, that related the people's history of the Revolution. Although at times the corridos, as they were called, mixed fact and fiction, we learn much about why people fought by listening to the words.

CORRIDOS

Bitter Times

"Tiempos Amargos" (Bitter Times)

Oh, how pleasant it is to live
during these times of today.
We are the agraristas,
though some people still doubt it.

These are no longer the times of Porfirio (Díaz),
when they cried for the master
when they'd meet him, they'd shake his hand,
and button his pants.

If one day the steward
became angry with a worker
it was because there was another one
closer to the snaps of his pants.

If someone had pretty daughters
he'd get a job as a night watchman,
or else he'd land a good job,
at least as a payroll clerk.

If someone had a pretty wife
they didn't let him rest,
they'd get them up very early
to work just like the oxen.

I bid you farewell, friends,
you'll forgive my frankness.
I've sung about the bitter times
under the Porfiristas.

"Corrido Historia Y Muerte del Gral. Francisco Villa"

Part I

In a hacienda in my country,
marvelous México,
from a worker of the land
the great General Villa was born.

He worked to support
his mother and sister,
and aspired to be known
as a good worker.

But the son of the boss,
with money and power,
seduced the peon's sister,
who, as a woman, was helpless.

But Pancho was truly a man
and, proving his courage,
cleared his name with blood,
badly wounding the seducer.

He joined Madero's forces
with a strong hand,
and the once lowly farmworker
became an undefeated rebel.

Due to his extraordinary bravery
and unsurpassed fierceness,
at Rellano Don Pancho (Madero)
promoted him to the rank of general.

His most courageous soldiers
were his elite guard:
the indefectible dorados
of the Northern Division.

Yet an unforeseen incident,
or the treachery of a scoundrel,
caused him to lose his brilliant campaign
in the battle of Celaya.

Part II

He was fearless and courageous
and of noble heart,
and accepted into his ranks
President Obregón's men.

In payment for his deeds
they gave him "El Canutillo,"
the hacienda he administered
with his aide, Trillo.

But envy and treachery
lurked nearby
waiting for the opportunity
to take his life.

Near Parral,
the motive has yet to be discovered,
they killed the General
as he was driving his automobile.

But they did not have the courage
to face the leader,
they fired treacherously
and also killed Trillo.

His soldiers grieved for him
because he was their hope,
and the brave Dorados
swore to avenge his death.

That is how they defeated
such a fearless leader
who was respectfully known
as the gentleman of "El Canutillo."

May you rest in peace, because your name
shines like a star in history:
immortal will be the fame
of General Pancho Villa.

"El Cuartelazo" (The Coup d'Etat) (Part I)

Nineteen hundred and eleven,
twenty second of February,
in Mexico's capital
they killed Madero.

At five in the morning
was the first cannon blast,
that was the signal
for the coup d'etat.

As the clock struck
seven that morning
into México City arrived
Mondragon and his armed troops.

Félix Díaz arrived
with a military order:
"Either you resign
or I'll have you killed."

Madero answered
from his presidential chair:
"You'll have to kill me first
before you make me resign."

Madero in the presidential palace
said: "How unfortunate is my fate!
I give my life for the people,
I do not fear death!"

Madero answered then:
"I will not resign!
I'm not a self-appointed president,
I was chosen by the people."

Gentleman, let me tell you
what happened in México:
a bunch of murderers
killed Madero.

Madero is dead now
and buried down below,
only Carranza is left
as Minister of War.

The artillery arrived
transported by train,
they were going to attack
the jail of Belen.

The bugles were calling
and the drums were playing and the
canon niño
was placed nearby.

Source: Lyrics of "Tiempos Amargos" by an unknown composer. Reprinted from the CD *The Mexican Revolution: Corridos about the Heroes and Events 1910-1920 and Beyond*! (CD 7041–7044). Translation courtesy of Arhoolie Records (http://www.arhoolie.com).

WHY DID THEY CONTINUE TO FIGHT?

The civil wars went on for nearly a decade, with the heaviest fighting taking place in 1914 and 1915 as the rebel factions, Villa and Zapata on one side and Carranza and Obregón on the other side, tore each other apart. Carranza and Obregón defeated Villa in a series of bloody battles in 1915 that forced him eventually to return to guerrilla warfare.

The Carrancista armies pushed the Zapatistas into guerrilla operations at the same time. Villa made it very difficult for the victors to control the northern states, until he agreed to peace in 1920 after Carranza's death. Zapata fell victim to an ambush in 1919. Throughout these years, combatants struggled on and on. They became hardened and cynical, but they continued to fight.

John Reed was a North American radical journalist who traveled with Pancho Villa during the heaviest fighting of the Revolution. Reed reported in detail the feelings of the common soldiers.

JOHN REED, INSURGENT MEXICO

Captain Fernando leaned over and patted my arm. "Now you are with the men (*los hombres*). When we win the Revolution it will be a government by the men—not by the rich. We are riding over the lands of the men. They used to belong to the rich, but now they belong to me and to the *compañeros*."

"And you will be the army?" I asked.

"When the Revolutión is won," was the astonishing reply, "there will be no more army. The men are sick of armies. It is by armies that Don Porfirio robbed us."

"But if the United States should invade Mexico?"

A perfect storm broke everywhere. "We are more *valiente* than the Americanos— The cursed gringos would get no further south than Juarez—Let's see them try it—We'd drive them back over the Border on the run, and burn their capital the next day . . . !"

"No," said Fernando, "you have more money and more soldiers. But the men would protect us. We need no army. The men would be fighting for their houses and their women."

"What are you fighting for?" I asked Juan Sanchez, the color-bearer, looked at me curiously. "Why, it is good, fighting. You don't have to work in the mines . . . !" Manuel Paredes said: "We are fighting to restore Francisco I. Madero to the Presidency."

By the time he was halfway through, the entire Tropa was humming the tune, and when he finished there was a moment of jingling silence.

"We are fighting," said Isidoro Amayo "for Libertad."

"What do you mean by Libertad?"

"Libertad is when I can *do what I want*!"

"But suppose it hurts somebody else?"

He shot back at me Benito Juarez's great sentence:

"Peace is the respect for the rights of others!"

I wasn't prepared for that. It startled me, this barefooted *mestizo's* conception of Liberty. It is only correct definition Liberty—*to do what I want to*! Americans quote it to me triumphantly as an instance of Mexican irresponsibility. But I think it is a better definition than ours— Liberty is the right to do what the Courts want. Every Mexican schoolboy knows the definition of peace and seems to understand pretty well what it means, too. But, they say: Mexicans don't want peace. That is a lie, and a foolish one. Let Americans take the trouble to go through the Maderista army, asking whether they want peace or not! The people are sick of war. But just to be square, I'll have to report Juan Sanchez's remark: "Is there war in the United States now?" he asked.

"No," I said untruthfully.

"No war at all?" He meditated for a moment. "How do you pass the time then . . . ?"

And there was a sullen, Indian-faced woman, riding sidesaddle, who wore two cartridge belts. She rode with the *hombres*—slept with them in the cuartels.

"Why are you fighting?" I asked her.

She jerked her head toward the fierce figure of Julian Reyes.

"Because he is", she answered. "He who stands under a good tree is sheltered by a good shade."

"A good rooster will crow in any chicken coop," capped Isidro.

"A parrot is green all over," chimed in someone else.

"Faces we see, but hearts we do not comprehend," said José sentimentally.

At noon we roped a steer, and cut his throat. And because there was no time to build a fire, we ripped the meat from the carcass and ate it raw.

"*Oiga*, Meester," shouted José, "Do the United States soldiers eat raw meat?"

I said I didn't think they did.

"It is good for the *hombres*. In the campaign we have no time for anything but *carne crudo*. It makes us brave."

By the late afternoon we had caught up with the coach, and galloped with it down through the dry arroyo and up through the other side, past the great *ribota* court that flanks the Hacienda of La Zarca. Unlike La Mimbrera, the Casa Grande here stands on a level place, with the peons' houses in long rows at its flanks, and a flat desert barren of chaparral for twenty miles in front. Che Che Campa also paid a visit to La Zarca. The big house is a black and gaping ruin.

Old Güereca was a white-haired peon in sandals. He had been born a slave on one of the great haciendas; but years of toil, too appalling to realize, had made him that rare being in Mexico, the independent owner of a small property. He had ten children—soft, dark-skinned girls, and sons that looked like New England farmhands—and a daughter in the grave.

The Güerecas were proud, ambitious, warm-hearted folk. Longinos said: "This is my dearly loved friend, Juan Reed, and my brother." And the old man and his wife put both their arms around me and patted me on the back, in the affectionate way Mexicans embrace.

"My family owes nothing to the Revolución," said Gino, proudly. "Others have taken money and horses and wagons. The *jefes* of the army have become rich from the property of the great haciendas. The Güerecas have given all to the Maderistas and have taken nothing but my rank. . . ."

The old man, however, was a little bitter. Holding up a horsehair rope, he said: "Three years ago I had four *riatas* like this. Now I have only one. One the *colorados* took and the other Urbina's people took, and the last one José Bravo. . . . What difference does it make which side robs you?" But he didn't mean it all. He was immensely proud of his youngest son, the bravest officer in all the army.

We sat in the long adobe room, eating the most exquisite cheese, and *tortillas* with fresh goat-butter—the deaf old mother apologizing in a loud voice for the poverty of the food, and her warlike son reciting his personal Iliad of the nine-days' fight around Torreon.

"We got so close," he was saying, "that the hot air and burning powder stung us in the face. We got too close to shoot, so we clubbed our rifles—" Just then all the dogs began to bark at once. We jumped from our seats. One didn't know what to expect in the Cadena those days. It was a small boy on horseback, shouting that the *colorados* were entering the Puerta—and off he galloped.

Longinos roared to put the mules in the coach. The entire family fell to work with a fury, and in five minutes Longinos dropped on one knee and kissed his father's hand, and we were tearing down the road. "Don't be killed! Don't be killed! Don't be killed!" we could hear the Señora wailing.

We passed a wagon loaded with cornstalks, with a whole family of women and children, two tin trunks, and an iron bed, perched on top. The man of the family rode a burro. Yes, the *colorados* were coming—thousands of them pouring through the Puerta. The last time the *colorados* had come they had killed his daughter. For three years there had been war in this valley, and he had not complained. Because it was for the Patria. Now they would go to the United States where But Juan lashed the mules cruelly, and we heard no more. Farther along was an old man without shoes, placidly driving some goats. Had he heard about the *colorados*? Well, there *had* been some gossip about *colorados*. Were they coming through the Puerta, and how many?

"Pues, quien sabe, Señor!"

At last, yelling at the staggering mules, we came into camp just in time to see the victorious Tropa straggle in across the desert, firing off many more rounds of ammunition than they had used in the fight. They moved low along the ground, scarcely higher on their broncos than the drab mesquite through which they flashed, all big sombreros and flapping gay serapes, the last sunshine on their lifted rifles.

The room was full of smoke from the fire on the floor. Through it I dimly made out some thirty or forty troopers squatting or sprawled at full length—perfectly silent as Silveyra read aloud a proclamation from the Governor of Durango forever condemning the lands of the great haciendas to be divided among the poor. He read:

Considering: that the principal cause of discontent among the people in our State, which forced them to spring to arms in the year 1910, was the absolute lack of individual property; and that the rural classes have no means of subsistence in the present, nor any hope for the future, except to serve as peons on the haciendas of the great landowners, who have monopolized the soil of the State;

Considering: that the principal branch of our national riches is agriculture, and that there can be no true progress in agriculture without that the majority of farmers have a personal interest in making the earth produce. . . .

Considering, finally: that the rural towns have been reduced to the deepest misery, because the common lands which they once owned have gone to augment the property of the nearest hacienda, especially under the Dictatorship of Diaz; with which the inhabitants of the State lost their economic, political, and social independence, then passed from the rank of citizens to that of slaves, without the Government being able to lift the moral level through education, because the hacienda where they lived is private property. . . .

Therefore, the Government of the State of Durango declares it a public necessity that the inhabitants of the towns and villages be the owners of agricultural lands. . . .

When the paymaster had painfully waded through all the provisions that followed, telling how the land was to be applied for, etc., there was a silence.

"That," said Martinez, "is the Mexican Revolución."

"It's just what Villa's doing in Chihuahua," I said. "It's great. All you fellows can have a farm now."

An amused chuckle ran around the circle. Then a little, bald-headed man, with yellow, stained whiskers, sat up and spoke.

"Not us," he said, "not the soldiers. After a revolución is done it wants no more soldiers. It is the *pacificos* who will get the land—those who did not fight. And the next generation . . . " He paused and spread his torn sleeves to the fire. "I was a schoolteacher," he explained, "so I know that Revoluciones, like Republics, are ungrateful. I have fought three years. At the end of the first Revolución that great man, Father Madero, invited his soldiers to the Capital. He gave us clothes, and food, and bullfights. We returned to our homes and found the greedy again in power."

"I ended the war with forty-five pesos," said a man.

"You were lucky," continued the schoolmaster. "No, it is not the troopers, the starved, unfed, common soldiers who profit by the Revolución. Officers, yes—some—for they get fat on the blood of the Patria. But we—no."

"What on earth are you fighting for?" I cried.

"I have two little sons," he answered. "And *they* will get their land. And they will have other little sons. They too, will never want for food . . . " The little man grinned. "We have a proverb in Guadalahara: 'Do not wear a shirt of eleven yards, for he who wants to be a Redeemer will be crucified.'"

"*I've* got no little son," said fourteen-year-old Gil Tomas, amid shouts of laughter. "I'm fighting so I can get a thirty-thirty rifle from some dead Federal, and a good horse that belonged to a millionaire."

Just for fun I asked a trooper with a photo button of Madero pinned to his coat who that was.

"*Pues, quien sabe, Señor?*" he replied. "My captain told me he was a great saint. I fight because it is not so hard as to work."

"How often are you fellows paid?"

"We were paid three pesos just nine months ago tonight," said the schoolmaster, and they all nodded. "We are real volunteers. The *gente* of Villa are professionals."

Then Luis Martinez got a guitar and sang a beautiful little love song, which he said a prostitute had made up one night in a *bordel.*

The last thing I remember of that memorable night was Gino Güereca lying near me in the dark, talking.

"Tomorrow," he said, "I shall take you to the lost gold mines of the Spaniards. They are hidden in a canon in the western mountains. Only the Indians know of them—and I. The Indians go there sometimes with knives and dig the raw gold out of the ground. We'll be rich. . . . "

Source: John Reed, *Insurgent Mexico.* New York: Penguin Books, 1983, pp. 38–45. First published in 1914.

QUESTIONS FOR DISCUSSION

1. To whom did the Liberal Party appeal in its program of 1906? Do you think it effective?
2. Madero appealed to a broad range of the population. Do you think that his Plan de San Luis Potosí was meant to maintain the cross-class alliance of his supporters? What was he trying to justify?
3. What do you see as the differences between the Plan de San Luis Potosí and the Plan de Ayala?
4. How does the Plan de Ayala compare with Pancho Villa's "dream" of a new Mexico? Which sounds more sincere?
5. Why did the rebels continue to fight the long, hard Revolution?

11 THE TIME OF TERROR

INTRODUCTION

From the mid-1960s, when the Brazilian military overthrew the mildly left government of João Goulart, to the 1990s, several nations in Latin America endured a series of brutal right-wing, military-led regimes that conducted widespread violations of their citizens' human rights. At the same time, others experienced decades-long guerrilla insurgencies that resulted in protracted civil wars. The result was thirty years of terror. Tens of thousands perished either in actual warfare or in so-called collateral damage. Hundreds of thousands fled their homes. The physical destruction was enormous. The psychological impact of the terror and warfare is incalculable. The selections that follow present a sense of the everyday terror experienced by Latin Americans during these desperate years.

THE DICTATORSHIPS

A military coup, led by General Agustín Pinochet, then the Commander of the Chilean armed forces, violently overthrew the presidency of Dr. Salvador Allende, the first socialist elected head of state in the Americas, on September 10, 1973. Allende had struggled after his election in 1970 to build a coalition between left and center. But a decline in the world market price for copper, Chile's main export; the opposition of the United States; and blunders by the socialist government led to a downturn in the economy, which undermined Allende's efforts. His failures to meet the economic needs of all classes were manifested in street protests by women, who famously leaned out the windows and banged their pots in protest against Allende's policies.

On December 1, 1971, thousands of women came together in the Plaza Italia in Santiago—Chile's largest city—to protest against the Unidad Popular, Allende's coalition political party. Chanting the slogans from the following selection, they directed their anger at the fact that the Allende government's policies had led to food shortages. The angry women particularly aimed their ire at Allende's close relationship with Fidel Castro, who had led a communist revolution in Cuba in 1959 and continued to rule that island until 2006.

STREET SONG V. ALLENDE

Allende, listen, we women are many!
Chile si! Cuba no!
Dungeon, dungeon, Fidel go home!
There's no meat—smoke a Havana!
The left has left us without food?
There's no meat in the pot, and the government looks the other way!

Source: Chanted slogans translated by Margaret Power in *Right-Wing Women in Chile: Feminine Power and the Struggle Against Allende, 1964–1973* by Margaret Power. Copyright © 2002. Published by Penn State University Press. Reprinted by permission of Penn State University Press.

After the restoration of democracy in Argentina in 1983, new president Raul Alfonsín established the National Commission on the Disappearance of Persons, to look into the fates of those thousands whom the dictatorship (1976–1983) had kidnapped, tortured, and murdered. The commission elected Ernesto Sabato, the internationally known novelist, as its president. With 50,000 documents the commission published its findings in 1984 in Spanish and later in English under the title Nunca Más (Never Again). *The following are excerpts from some of the cases the commission uncovered.*

ARGENTINA, NEVER AGAIN

In file No. 3860, Alberto Santiago Burnichon's disappearance is described by his wife as follows:

At 12.30 A.M. on 24 March 1976, our house in Villa Rivera Indarte in Córdoba province was broken into by men in uniform carrying rifles. They identified themselves as belonging to the Army, and were accompanied by a number of youths in casual dress. They trained their guns on us while they stole books, objets d'art, bottles of wine, etc., which the uniformed men carried outside. They did not talk to each other, but communicated by snapping their fingers. The looting of our house lasted for over two hours; before the raid there had been a blackout in all the neighbouring streets. My husband, a trade union official, my son, David, and myself were abducted. I was freed the next day. My son was freed some time later, after being held in the La Ribera camp. Our house was completely destroyed. My husband's body was found with seven bullet wounds in the throat.

ARGENTINA, NEVER AGAIN

Lucio Ramon Perez, of Temperley in, Buenos Aires province (file No. 1919), describes his brother's abduction in the following way:

My brother was kidnapped on 9 November 1976. He was asleep with his wife and five-year-old son when they were wakened at about 2 a.m. by a loud explosion. My brother got out of bed, opened the front door, and saw four people jumping over the fence.

They were in civilian clothes; one of them had a moustache and a jersey wrapped round his head like a turban; they all carried rifles. Three of them burst into the flat and ordered my sister-in-law and the boy not to look. The neighbours say that two of them dragged out my brother and forced him into a Ford Falcon. That's the last we heard of him. They also say there were several cars and a truck on the scene, and there were a lot of men with rifles behind the trees. The traffic had been halted, and a helicopter was circling over the house.

These gangs did not bother to conceal their faces when carrying out the abductions. In the capital and the other large urban centres, their anonymity was guaranteed by the number of inhabitants. In the provinces, where they might have been identified, some attempt was made at disguise. They often used balaclavas, hoods, wigs, false moustaches, glasses, and so on. The only region in which this was not always the case was Tucumán province, where the repressive forces acted with even greater impunity, and the inhabitants were even more defenceless.

The story of Carlos Godoy was indicative of the madness that gripped Chile. He was a "do-gooder." But to try to alleviate the suffering of the poor or unfortunate meant that, to the thugs of Pinochet, he was an enemy of La Patria. Remember Chile was a group initiated in the United Kingdom when former dictator Pinochet was arrested in Britain for crimes committed when he ruled Chile.

CARLOS GODOY

I left Chile with my young family on 21st September 1976. My friend Carlos was not at the airport for a farewell—he had been detained seven weeks before. We had discussed, on a couple of occasions, exile as an option, but it was never the right time. As doctors, each of us had a job, Carlos in a small peripheral hospital administered by the Roman Catholic Church, myself in an independent institution. It seemed possible to survive and resist, and we would kid ourselves about the apparent randomness of the actions of the secret police.

Denial is a well-known psychological defence-mechanism, particularly when both reality and facing reality are unbearable propositions. However, when Carlos was caught on the same day as our common friend Iván Inzunza, also a medical doctor, I knew that this time the blow was well-aimed, and that my family and I should leave Chile as soon as possible. When our plane was flying over the Atlantic Ocean my wife and I gave a sigh of relief and drank a toast for our freedom. We allowed ourselves to forget for a minute our friends left in Chile, thinking that our children were not any longer in danger of suffering the fate of Carlos' children. It was a short-lived comfort. We took one of the papers brought on board during a fuelling stop in Rio, gave a glance to the first page and freeze. There, big-lettered Portuguese titles hit us with the news that a car-bomb explosion had dismembered the body Orlando Letelier, Allende's last Defence Minister, in Washington!

It was August 4, 1976, at four o'clock in the afternoon, when Carlos Godoy Lagarrigue, aged 39, left the San Bernardo Hospital by car. He had just finished his daily ward round and was as usual on his way to his outpatient clinic in La Granja. It is only 15 minutes by car from the hospital to the clinic, although the road passes through the densely populated outskirts of Santiago. He never arrived. Somewhere along the way, he vanished and has not been seen or heard of since. His wife and children waited at home that evening, and continued to wait for years and years.

Needless to say, Carlos' wife and family did their utmost to trace him, appealing to the police, the courts and government ministries. Social and family contacts gave them access to national figures of the highest rank, but all was in vain. Nobody knew or was willing to say where he was. International organisations, including medical ones, took up his case and interceded on his behalf.

I had known Carlos for over twenty years. He has many personal qualities of which I could write. I would like to single out just one, his passionate devotion to the underprivileged. When he first qualified in 1964, he went immediately to the rural district of Melipilla. The hard life of the poor peasants of the region was a challenge to him, their poor social and economic standards constituting insurmountable disadvantages in their struggle against illness and disease. In six years, by combining medical care and a crusade for improved social conditions for the impoverished inhabitants, he achieved remarkable success. He managed to reach more than one hundred thousand peasants with a basic health care program based on free medical and dental care delivered from many new rural posts. The program was based more on organisation and enthusiasm than on better resources, and largely depended on Carlos' personal charisma. During that time he was also head of the Obstetric Department in the District Hospital, and gave himself time to write a book on his experience in the organisation of rural medical services.

In 1970 another doctor and social leader, Salvador Allende, was elected President of Chile and in the following year introduced an extensive range of social reforms, including a progressive National Health Programme. The new government enlisted the help of many doctors, among them Drs Godoy and Inzunza, the former in the Department of Rural Medicine of the NHS, the latter in the Directorate of Public Employees Medical Service. From that position, Dr Godoy was able to secure new funds to bring about improvement in health care for rural areas. He launched a comprehensive national health plan for those regions, promoted a more efficient use of medical resources, emphasised preventative health measures and created posts for paramedical staff where only doctors had been employed before. Hundreds of young midwives, nurses, dentists, health visitors, social workers and others were appointed to form professional teams led by young doctors who began to put into practice his ambitious scheme. I recall the efforts of Carlos to ensure fair selection procedures, which he achieved by establishing a standard assessment that took into account, above all else, the qualifications and professional experience of candidates. He was scrupulously fastidious in defending the rights of right-wing professionals that other less even-handed officials may have been tempted to pass over. For the first time ever, full employment for all those qualified in medical and related fields was achieved.

In September 1973, general Pinochet's coup d'état resulted in the prohibition of political parties, trade unions and community organisations; Parliament and town councils were closed down; military vice-chancellors were appointed to the country's universities and the Ministry of Health was taken over by the Air Force. All bodies dealing with social programmes were dissolved—in the eyes of the military, they were mere instruments for the dissemination of communism. The world was shocked by the tragic killings that took place throughout the country and the medical services were decimated by the terrible fate suffered by those doctors sympathetic towards the deposed government. Twenty-one medical doctors were killed by the dictatorship between 1973 and 1976[1]; of the country 6,000 doctors, more than 500 were imprisoned, most of them without trial or even the bringing of charges.

Immediately after the military take-over, Carlos was expelled from the NHS and prohibited from practising professionally in state hospitals. His house was forcibly entered and its contents searched. But he never showed any sign of panic or despair. Carlos decided to stay in Chile, and believing that he could not be allowed to work as a medical doctor any longer, he bought a loom, installed it in his garage and started to experiment in producing textiles. Carlos was proud of his ever-improving craftsmanship, and would not stop talking about his experiments with textures and colour combinations. Unfortunately, he was not a very good business-man, and gave away his products at a ridiculous price.

But a doctor is a doctor is a doctor. When in 1974 the Archbishop of Santiago offered him a modest position as a medical assistant in the parish hospital of San Bernardo, a southern district of the capital, he took the offer with alacrity. Within months we came to see in Carlos the same dedicated and compassionate clinician we had known before, earning the love and admiration both of the hospital staff and of the whole community.

However, the situation was far from rosy. In a conversation we had probably in March 1976, Carlos told me that certain sources had intimated to him that secret po-lice agents were at work within his hospital and that he had received a friendly warn-ing to be careful. His popularity and sociability were interpreted equivocally and he was considered politically suspect. The situation in the country was extremely inse-cure for such people. Disappearances were frequent and the denunciations of grave violations of human rights in Chile at the American States Organisation and the United Nations were backed up by well grounded and widening documented evi-dence. The weeks before his disappearance he was worried by threatening phone calls he had had at home. He thought he was followed, had seen strangers near his house, and the rumours in the hospital continued. One day, all of a sudden, every-thing ceased, and two days later he was kidnapped.

The detention of Carlos was never officially admitted. The sole response of the authorities was to deny all knowledge of his whereabouts. The family applied for a writ of habeas corpus, but the Home Ministry and the Police responded they did not have any detained person with that name. The case reached the Supreme Court that confirmed there was no case to consider. His wife learned that she could not have access to his current account—it had been frozen due to "superior orders," and even today, more then twenty years later the situation has not changed. Even his old Cit-roen 2CV vanished for good.

Carlos wife's ordeal is typical of the experience of so many others. She turned to the Law, the Courts, the Police, influential people, the Roman Catholic Church, medical organisations, international bodies, finding always a wall of silence, denials, false information, mockery and betrayal. In 1976 the Military Junta itself responded to the United Nations that both Carlos Godoy and Iván Insunza had requested visas to travel to Canada, which was promptly denied by the Canadian Embassy in Santiago.

Carlos' family was connected with Mrs Alicia Godoy, the wife of one of the four generals who formed the ruling military Junta. She informed them that Car-los had been in the secret camp of Four Alamos since August 1976, and that soon the situation would be clarified. On the basis of that information, the family initi-ated criminal procedures against the secret police DINA. The Court officially sum-moned DINA agents, but they never attended and the trial was officially dismissed years later.

I do not know what happened to Carlos in captivity, but from the well-known patterns of operation documented about DINA's methods, it is not difficult to imag-ine his ordeal and his death. Carlos Godoy, and his colleagues Iván Insunza, Ed-uardo González, Carlos Lorca, Enrique Paris, Jorge Klein, and so many others belonged to a generation of medical doctors attempting to bring the benefits of modern medicine justly and equally to all social sectors. As many other Chilean victims, they paid with their lives for their loyalty to the oppressed and the under-privileged, and for their commitment to social reform and justice. It is disturbing to think that today.

Source: Reprinted from *http://www.remember-chile.org.uk.*

Although Argentina, Chile, and Brazil were notorious for their times of terror, recent investigations in previously inaccessible archives in Mexico have revealed that country's horrors in the government's campaign against the Left during the 1970s.

BORNEMANN, SURVIVING MEXICO'S DIRTY WAR

That Sunday morning, time threatened to slide by even more slowly than usual. One more week of my captivity had been completed, and nothing had happened during those even days to undo the tedium produced by my inactive confinement in my small cell. I thought I'd observed a pattern of bureaucratic behavior as I registered the coming and going of prisoners around the middle of the week, especially Wednesdays. Perhaps the apparent pattern had derived from previous agreements among high level government functionaries. Whatever the case, it had not held true this week. Still, I was lying down on the floor of the cell, wrapped in my quilt, trying to sleep as long as possible before dinner. As was usual, the radio sounded at full blast. Trying to isolate myself from the noise by using balls of bread in my ears had proven a resounding failure. Close to sixty days after my forced disappearance into the Campo Militar Número Uno, my life seemed to hang in suspense. That very morning, however, in a short while I would see that I was wrong. My life was not in suspense—I was still being tested. That Sunday morning, I'd barely begun to slide into unconsciousness when a metallic rat-a-tat shook me out of my lethargy. I suspected that someone had reached the gate of my cell and was coming for me. Even before I saw him, I knew who it was: yes, the same dark-skinned individual, the gun-bearing, irascible thug who'd appeared in the June 10, 1971 picture; the same one who'd plucked out my eyelashes and eyebrows as he removed the adhesive over my eyelids when I was interrogated the first time after my arrival at Campo Militar Número Uno. While he addressed me, looking at me coldly and disdainfully, the man repeatedly hit one of the bars in the grill of my cell with a small metallic object held in his right hand, perhaps a key. He was trying to wake me up with that nervous, repetitive movement and get my attention. He did immediately. As I rose, a shiver traveled through my whole body, putting it in a state of alert. In fractions of a second, the lassitude that I constantly felt in those days transformed into fear and irritation. It was a situation that I absolutely hadn't expected to face that morning. It may be silly, but after weeks had gone by, I had absurdly expected that I wouldn't be removed from my cell for interrogation and torture again. That was, or so I wanted to believe, a completed stage of my detention.

The dark-skinned, somber and stern guy was accompanied by the blond, karate-practicing Halcón who opened the door of my cell and took me out gruffly. He then placed himself behind be and grabbed me by the shoulders with his small but strong and coarse hands. He took me to the fearsome room located in front of the water basin. There a short man waited for me. He had a big belly, yellow skin, and bulging big eyes; his demeanor was impatient and unfriendly; and he looked as if he were completely bored. His hair was cut to standard military fashion; his mustache was scarce and uneven; he had fetid breath, and altogether the look of a butcher. When I appeared in front of him, very thin and pale with a two-month-old beard and long and massy hair, he glanced at me from head to toe as if contemplating what he could apply to my body from his sadistic experience. The dark one ordered the other two to place me in the school chair that sat in the middle of the room. Immediately, they proceeded to tie my arms tightly behind the back of the chair with a dirty rag, while the first one supervised the maneuver very attentively. The fat one, drenched in sweat, burped acid air on my face, while without any compunction, he tightened the porous fabric around my compressed wrists. Standing before me with an air of severity, the one in charge declared that this was the last opportunity I had to give them concrete and relevant information about the principal members of the Organization to which I claimed to belong. Right after the warning, the fat man intervened. He leaned the trunk of his body and his hostile face toward me, fixing his bulging, rat-like eyes on mine, all the while exhaling his stinking breath on me. He described in abundant detail what he was going to do with me. He would start, he said, by disfiguring my face and breaking my body with blows and kicks; next, he would use a knife to remove my teeth, one by one, then the fingers of my hands, and the soles of my feet. He would crush all of these in a coffee grinder so that my dental pieces would disappear along with my finger and footprints. Then he would throw me into a ditch where my remains would be covered with lime and other chemical substances. Quickly I would turn into bare bones. My relatives would never know what happened to me or ever have the consolation of burying me in the family plot.

The threats and savage descriptions of the fat man finished off my fragile will to resist, rather like a programmed sequence in which plastic explosives are used to demolish urban structures step by step that have been damaged by time, fire, or earthquake. The first great blow to the structure of my morale and will had been the revelation of the old Indian man from the Huasteca of Hidalgo. A month after my arrival in the clandestine military jail, he reported that he had already "been disappeared" for two years into different prison installations within the military gulag. That story had commenced the collapse of any hope that I might be freed someday from the inhumane situation in which I found myself.

From that night on, never a moment passed in which I ceased to imagine with ever greater anguish and despair the sorts of painful situations that my disappearance must have given rise to for my wife and daughter as well as for my parents. So the dread of being destroyed and physically disappeared in the atrocious manner announced by the fat man generated my total moral and physical breakdown. In my demoralization, I mentioned three possible locations in which some members of the Organization might be found. I cannot deny that I did this out of cowardice, of course, but I also calculated that the compañeros would surely have abandoned those locales by now, possibly even the very night of September 4th. After all, two months had gone from the day of my capture. Moreover, in the case of Dionisio and Olivia, I only knew the spot where I had picked them or left them, not the precise place where they lived. Faced with growing physical and moral pressure, in a desperate wish to make the information seem credible. I mentioned that the couple used to travel in a current model year red Volkswagen with Jalisco plates. I assumed that they'd gotten rid of the vehicle, the only intelligent move they could make. But to their ill-fate and my sorrow, they never did. When the feds arrived at a spot near the Ayotla textile factory, there set a red 1974 VW with Jalisco registration, possibly right in front of the couple's abode. The federal security police only had to wait for Dionisio to appear on the street to detain him. Olivia was apprehended moments later, apparently in the house or apartment where they lived together.

A few hours later, having been taken back to the basement of the Campo Militar Número Uno, I spent the most bitter and painful moments of my life. I had to listen to Dionisio's interrogation and torture from my current cell—the first one of the back corridor, adjacent to that dreadful room. I felt horribly culpable at having facilitated his detention. Yet, at the same time, I was very angry with him for not having changed either vehicle or dwelling two months after my capture. Each time Dionisio screamed or moaned under torture, I felt his pain in my heart and in the pit of my stomach. I wanted to let him know what I had declared, so as to let him avoid unnecessary suffering. I did that very late at night, raising my voice as high as I could, almost yelling from one corridor to another. The likelihood that one of the Halcones could be listening while sitting on the stairway didn't matter to me.

To my shame, these were not the only detentions that I furthered. There were three other arrests that happened in a circumstantial way similar to the previous one as well as a result of my reference to a rented house in the town of Oacalco, Morelos, where months before Susana and Francisco had taken refuge. The police couldn't find them there, and they decided to pressure the landlady, who informed them that the couple had moved nearby—something that I already knew—about five hundred meters away, to an old, unused train station where they were immediately apprehended. The last person detained was Luis, the neurologist who attempted to cure Lucio. His arrest produced a mobilization and protests from members of the medical world. Together with the political influence of illustrious relatives, this may have helped make possible our departure from the Campo Militar Número Uno and a formal juridical consignment.

I know that none of the events that I am now recounting honors me. The fear of pain and of dying without my loved ones knowing became stronger than my will to resist. The time that had elapsed since then, and the experiences that I lived through in the three public prisons of Lecumberri, Reclusorio Oriente, and Santa Martha Acatitla have allowed me to understand how difficult it is for us human beings to acknowledge our mistakes and trespasses in an open and honest manner. Instead, we commonly blame others before questioning ourselves, even if we know deep inside us that we also share responsibility for the mistakes of others. If I can say something in my own defense, it is that I gave my compañeros a considerable time advantage, some sixty days, during which they could have taken pertinent security measures. I would like to say that I could have identified many more compañeros, both in the leadership and the base of the Organization, most of them peasants or urban workers. But I didn't, so none of them was apprehended. Those whose imprisonment I was responsible for also bear some responsibility—they did not take into account the fact that I was in the hands of the government, that I possessed vital information, and that they could be affected. In those days of heroic dreams, I fashioned myself invariably as a valiant social fighter, ever ready to face the pain of torture and death itself before bending to the power of imperialism and the bourgeoisie. But in my real confrontation with the ferocious political repression of the state and with myself, the basic instinct of self-preservation nullified all else. I believe that this is what happens most frequently, although I accept, of course, that there are honorable exceptions. I'm not trying to boast of cynicism, but I believe that there are not too many other explanations to the fact that so many political prisoners did not die under torture, but ended up like I did in the preventive jail of Lecumberri, in the Santa Martha penitentiary, in the Chilpancingo prison, in the municipal jail of Acapulco, in the penal facilities of Oblatos in Guadalajara and Topo Chico in Monterrey.

Source: Pp. 119–123 from *Surviving Mexico's Dirty War: A Political Prisoner's Memoir* by Alberto Ulloa Bornemann, trans. & ed. by Arthur Schmidt and Aurora Camacho Schmidt. Copyright © 2007 by Temple University. Used by permission of Temple University Press. All Rights Reserved.

THE CIVIL WARS

From the late 1960s through the mid 1990s, civil wars and repressive governments tore Latin America asunder. Revolutionary movements erupted in Colombia, El Salvador, Guatemala, Nicaragua, and Peru that led to prolonged guerrilla insurgencies. In Nicaragua, the Sandinista National Liberation Front (FSLN, Frente Sandinista de Liberación Nacional) defeated the longstanding dictatorship of the Somoza family, while in El Salvador the Farabundo Martí Front for National Liberation (FMLN, Frente Farabundo Martí de Liberación Nacional) and in Peru the Shining Path (Sendero Luminoso) nearly toppled the governments of their nations. The FMLN eventually negotiated peace with the Salvadoran government in 1991. The Peruvian government captured Sendero leader Aníbal Guzmán in 1992, and the movement lost its force thereafter. Guatemalans achieved peace only in 1996 after two decades of warfare that killed 200,000 people. The Colombian upheavals have continued to the present. (See Chapter 12.)

During the same era, starting with the military coup in Brazil in 1964 and extending through the mid-1980s, right wing regimes carried out vicious campaigns of terror against the center and left, targeting especially rural organizers, union leaders, school teachers, priests and nuns, university professors, and young people in general.

The Shining Path (Sendero Luminoso) began its insurgency in 1980. Coupled with another rebel group, the Túpac Amaru Revolutionary Movement (Moviemiento Revolucionario Túpac Amaru), the Sendero brought the Peruvian government under Presidents Alan García and Alberto Fujomori (1990–2000) to its knees. In retaliation, the government declared a state of emergency in many parts of the country and embarked on a fierce counterinsurgency program. Amnesty International investigated the human rights violations during this desperate civil war.

AMNESTY INTERNATIONAL: SUMMARY OF CONCERNS 1980–1995.

PERU: SUMMARY OF AMNESTY INTERNATIONAL'S CONCERNS 1980–1995

Since 1980 Amnesty International has reported on human rights violations committed by Peru's security forces in the context of the counter-insurgency policies of four successive governments. The organization has also reported on human rights abuses by the *Partido Comunista del Perú (Sendero Luminoso)*, PCP, Communist Party of Peru (Shining

Path), and the *Movimiento Revolucionario Túpac Amaru,* MRTA, Túpac Amaru Revolutionary Movement (see Endnote 1). The PCP and the MRTA initiated their armed campaigns in May 1980 and June 1984 respectively. The pattern of human rights abuses by government and armed opposition forces were confined for a number of years, almost exclusively, to zones declared under a state of emergency. However, between 1988 and 1992 the pattern of abuses spread to areas not declared under a state of emergency.

Since 1980 Amnesty International has also appealed to the Peruvian authorities to bring to a halt the pattern of systematic human rights violations which have persisted in Peru up to the present. The organization has on several occasions made recommendations to the Government designed to uphold international and regional human rights standards ratified by Peru.

The pattern of systematic human rights violations summarized below spans a period of 16 years. This period consists of three distinct phases:

   a. May 1980 to December 1982, during which Amnesty International documented cases of torture by members of the Peruvian National Police;
   b. January 1983 to December 1992, during which Amnesty International documented thousands of cases of "disappearance" extrajudicial execution and torture by members of the armed forces and the police;
   c. May 1992 to December 1995, during which Amnesty International documented thousands of cases of unfair trial. The organization also documented during this period hundreds of cases of prisoners of conscience and possible prisoners of conscience, and of torture and ill-treatment.

In addition, throughout these 16 years Amnesty International has documented thousands of cases of human rights abuses by members of the PCP and the MRTA.

ENFORCED DISAPPEARANCES

Between May 1980 and December 1982 the *Policía Nacional del Perú,* PNP, Peruvian National Police, had operational responsibility for counter-insurgency operations directed against members of the PCP, and activists in political, trade union and community organizations whom the authorities perceived as bearing responsibility for PCP attacks. During this period Amnesty International did not document any complaints of enforced disappearances. However, the organization did document numerous cases of torture and arbitrary detention by the police. The victims, detained in zones declared under a state of emergency, were held on suspicion of committing terrorism-related offences.

At the end of December 1982 the government transferred operational responsibility for combatting the PCP from the PNP to the *Fuerzas Armadas del Perú,* Peruvian Armed Forces. With the exception of the region in and around Lima, the capital, zones declared under a state of emergency were placed under the political-military command of the Peruvian Armed Forces. In the wake of this transfer Amnesty International began to receive reports of hundreds of cases of enforced disappearance.

Between January 1983 and December 1993—a span of 11 years—Amnesty International documented at least 4,200 cases of enforced disappearance. During the same period the UN Working Group on Enforced or Involuntary Disappearances documented 2,847 cases under the terms of its mandate, of which 2,240 remained outstanding by the end of December 1993. Amnesty International has received official documents from the Peruvian *Ministerio Público*, Public Ministry, showing that between 1983 and 1990 it received at least 5,000 complaints of enforced disappearance.

Relatives of the victims and Peruvian human rights organizations attributed responsibility for these violations mainly to members of the *Ejército del Perú*, Peruvian Army, although members of the *Marina de Guerra del Perú*, Peruvian Navy, and the PNP were also held accountable.

Between January 1993 and December 1995—a span of three years—Amnesty International documented 123 cases of enforced disappearance. Although Amnesty International has not yet had access to statistics compiled by the UN Working Group on Enforced or Involuntary Disappearances for the years 1993 to 1995, the figure is expected to reflect a marked reduction in "disappearances." This reduction follows the implementation by the Government of Peru of policies and measures designed to tackle the country's long-standing pattern of enforced disappearances.

EXTRAJUDICIAL EXECUTIONS AND DEATH THREATS

Amnesty International did not document any extrajudicial executions between May 1980 and December 1982 when the PNP were responsible for counter-insurgency operations.

Between January 1983 and December 1992 Amnesty International documented at least 1,000 reported extrajudicial executions, including the cases of at least 500 victims killed in 18 separate massacres. In the vast majority of these cases members of the Peruvian Army were held responsible, although a significant number were attributed to members of the National Police and the Navy.

Between January 1993 and December 1995 Amnesty International documented a sharp decline in the number of reported extrajudicial executions, although the organization received compelling evidence that members of the Peruvian Army had extrajudicially executed at least 30 peasants in April 1994, during a single counter-insurgency operation on the left bank of the Alto Huallaga river, in the department of Huánuco.

Throughout the years 1983 to 1995 the organization also documented hundreds of cases of attempted killings and acts of intimidation, including death threats.

No precise statistics on reported extrajudicial executions, attempted killings and acts of intimidation are known to have been kept by the Peruvian Public Ministry, or by international and regional government organizations monitoring Peru's human rights record.

Again, it was the implementation by the Government of Peru of policies and measures designed to tackle Peru's long-standing pattern of human rights violations that resulted in a significant reduction in the number of reported extrajudicial executions from 1993 onwards.

TORTURE AND ILL-TREATMENT

The welcome reduction in enforced disappearances and extrajudicial executions over the past three years has not been matched by a parallel reduction in the cases of reported torture. Indeed, reports of the torture and ill-treatment of prisoners accused of having links to the PCP and the MRTA have persisted between 1980 and 1995.

Amnesty International has no precise statistics on complaints of torture and ill-treatment over these years. Similarly, no precise figures on cases of torture and ill-treatment are known to exist on the files of the Peruvian Public Ministry, or those of international and regional government organizations.

However, torture is reported to be routinely practised on detainees suspected by the security forces of having links to the PCP and the MRTA. In many of the cases of extrajudicial execution referred to above, the victims showed signs consistent with torture. In addition, since May 1992, when the Government of Peru brought into force a new set of anti-terrorism laws, Peruvian human rights organization documenting cases of arbitrary detention began to receive hundreds of testimonies that detainees had been tortured and ill-treated following detention by members of the Armed Forces or National Police, or during interrogation, when the suspect was under the custody of the *Dirección Nacional Contra el Terrorismo*, National Anti-terrorism Directorate, a branch of the Peruvian National Police.

Indeed, in the initial report sent by the Government of Peru to the UN Committee against Torture (CAT) in February 1994, the Government of Peru informed the CAT "that agents of the State still resort to [torture]". The CAT concluded, after having examined Peru's initial report in November 1994, that there exists a widespread practice of torture during the interrogation phase in terrorism-related cases, and that impunity is enjoyed by the perpetrators.

IMPUNITY

The vast majority of the cases of enforced disappearance, extrajudicial execution, and torture and ill-treatment, filed before the Public Ministry and other authorities during the years 1980 through to 1995, have never been effectively investigated, the perpetrators have not been brought to justice, and the victims and their relatives have received no compensation. The impunity surrounding widespread and systematic human rights violations in Peru led the UN Special Rapporteur on extrajudicial, summary or arbitrary executions to state, in his report following a visit to Peru in 1993, that "the institutionalization of impunity in Peru [is one of] the main problems with regards to [a lack of respect for] the right to life".

That "institutionalized impunity" to which the UN expert referred was made legal in June 1995, when the Government of Peru promulgated two amnesty laws. These laws effectively closed all unresolved cases of human rights violations committed by the military, the police and other authorities, between May 1980 and mid-June 1995. In addition, the first of the two laws rendered void the few prison sentences handed down by the military and civil courts to members of the Armed Forces and the National Police convicted of human rights-related crimes.

THE DEATH PENALTY

The 1979 Constitution of Peru made provision for the death penalty for the crime of treason committed during times of war with a foreign power. Acts of treason committed in this context remain included in Peru's Code of Military Justice and carry the death penalty.

In 1993 the Peruvian Congress approved a new Constitution which widened the scope of the death penalty. Under the 1993 Constitution the death penalty was extended to include "the crime of terrorism". However, by the end of December 1995 no article has been incorporated into Peru's Criminal Code which makes provision for what effectively remains a constitutional law.

The article on the death penalty remains enshrined in the 1993 Constitution despite a Consultative Opinion issued by the Inter-American Court of Human Rights (IACHR) in December 1994, in which the IACHR ruled that: "the promulgation of a law in manifest conflict with the obligations assumed by a State upon ratifying or acceding to the [American] Convention [on Human Rights] is a violation of that treaty." (See Inter-American Court of Human rights (IACHR), Consultative Opinion OC-14/94 of 9 December 1994.)

Amnesty International opposes the death penalty in all cases without exception. The organization believes the death penalty to be the ultimate denial of human rights. It violates the right to life as proclaimed in the Universal Declaration of Human Rights and other international and regional human rights instruments. Amnesty International opposes the death penalty totally and unconditionally and demands the worldwide abolition of this form of punishment.

UNFAIR TRIALS

Amnesty International is also concerned about the thousands of prisoners in Peru charged with terrorism-related offences who have been denied the fundamental right to a fair trial. Almost coincidental with the significant reduction in widespread enforced disappearances and extrajudicial executions referred to above, a new "model" of extensive and systematic human rights violations appeared in 1992.

Anti-terrorism laws passed in that year have resulted in the detention, between May 1992 and December 1995, of at least 5000 prisoners accused of terrorism-related offences who have been tried or are awaiting trial under procedures which fall far short of international fair trial standards. Hundreds of these prisoners—all of them civilians—have been charged with the terrorism-related crime of treason and tried by military courts which are neither competent, impartial nor independent, when hearing cases in which civilians face such a charge.

Congress passed positive amendments to these laws in November 1993, November 1994 and April 1995. However, by the end of December 1995 the laws had not yet been brought fully into line with international fair trial standards.

PRISONERS OF CONSCIENCE AND ARBITRARY DETENTIONS

The present anti-terrorism laws have also given rise to the detention of prisoners of conscience and possible prisoners of conscience. Since the anti-terrorism legislation came into effect in May 1992 the organization has adopted 86 prisoners of conscience. These prisoners have all been falsely accused of terrorism-related offences. Amnesty International believes there is no credible evidence to link them to the political beliefs and actions with which they have been imputed, and the charges they face appear to be politically motivated. Amnesty International considers all prisoners of conscience to be arbitrarily detained.

The organization has also documented the cases of at least 1,000 possible prisoners of conscience, 600 of whom remained in prison at the end of December 1995.

ABUSES BY THE ARMED OPPOSITION

The pattern of gross human rights violations by the security forces described in this report has occurred against a background of widespread abuses by the PCP, and to a lesser scale by the MRTA. Over the past 16 years Amnesty International has received regular reports of human rights abuses attributed to the PCP. Most of the victims have been members of peasant communities who were either suspected of collaboration with the military or else refused to join or support the PCP. They have often been killed after mock trials conducted before forcibly assembled villagers. The victims have included hundreds of mayors and other local state authorities, community leaders, agronomists, engineers, and administrators working on government and independent development projects. Political and trade union activists who do not support the ideology and practices of the PCP have also been systematically threatened and killed.

Amnesty International has repeatedly and unequivocally condemned the grave human rights abuses by the PCP and the MRTA. The organization's condemnation of such abuses is based on principles derived from international humanitarian law, in particular humanitarian standards enshrined in Common Article 3 of the Geneva Conventions of 1949. The organization has consistently urged the PCP and MRTA to fully respect and abide by Common Article 3, paragraph 1(a), (b), and (c), of the Geneva Conventions which protect people taking no part in the conflict from "violence to life and person", being taken hostage, and "outrages on personal dignity, in particular humiliating and degrading treatment".

Amnesty International believes that the type of abuses committed by the PCP and the MRTA can never justify the violation by the authorities of fundamental human rights. In the words of the UN Human Rights Committee: "Recognizing that the Government has a duty to combat terrorism, the Committee considers that the measures taken to do so should not prejudice the enjoyment of fundamental rights enshrined in the [International] Covenant [on Civil and Political Rights]. . . ." (UN Doc. CCPR/C/79/Add.23, paragraph 8.)

Source: As reported on *http://www.amnesty.org.*

The more human side of the terror emerges from the testimony of "Lupe." Like the Nobel Peace Prize winner Rigoberta Menchú, she witnessed a terror thankfully unknown to most of us.

"LUPE" IN *THE HOUR OF THE POOR, THE HOUR OF WOMEN: SALVADORAN WOMEN SPEAK*

> *We are the blood of the earth*
> *the seed that fell into the furrow.*
> Chan, *"Love Poem II"*

Lupe's story is the story of her family's escape from the purges in the Aguilares area following Father Rutilio Grande's assassination. But it is a story of danger that seems without end. When I took this interview, Lupe spoke of her town as the town of her deliverance. Yet, three months after this interview her town was bombarded by the Salvadoran Air Force in an attempt to dislodge FMLN guerrillas who held the town during the November 1989 offensive.

Amid chickens and children, Lupe had explained to me that she would have to continue making atol (a liquid corn drink) with her daughter during our interview. When the taping session began her husband left the room but listened in a side room. When he saw that Lupe was distracted by squeezing the thick maize through cloth, he quietly took over her task and worked with his daughter making atol for the next two hours.

In the past fifteen years, during the death purges, Lupe has seen her brother, a delegate of the word, murdered; her husband and brothers fled to the hills where they slept every night for five years; her sister was captured; her home was surrounded by soldiers; she was interrogated by a member of ORDEN; her daughter's godmother was assassinated; her husband's cousin was killed with machetes—by "chopping off parts of her body, starting with her nose." Yet Lupe remained in the village with her husband, five children, her mother, and her sister-in-law, refusing to quit her clandestine Bible study meetings with the base community.

I was born in Tres Ceibas near Suchitoto. That's where I grew up. My husband lived in a valley very far from me. For the feast of Flores de Mayo [a May celebration of the rosary] I went to the home of my husband's grandmother. I was fourteen, very young. I saw him and he saw me. My aunt said to me, "I think he likes you," but as I was young, I gave it no importance. But I felt something in my heart that set very well with me.

He didn't speak to me directly, nor I to him. But when I was fifteen, he began to speak to me. He was older and had other girlfriends. But I was afraid to accept him as my *novio* [boyfriend] because I was young. My parents said, "Maybe he won't marry you but just leave you pregnant. He may not respect you!"

But when I was eighteen we married, and we've been married twenty-one years. My husband had one and a half *colones* [$.30] in his pocket when we married.

We were married at the time we began to work for the base Christian communities in the mid-1970s. We formed these communities with Father Rutilio Grande. All of us, mother, father, brother, and sisters, worked in the base communities. My brother was killed. My brother worked as a delegate of the word. After they killed Rutilio they came after my brother. September 22 is the anniversary of my brother's death.

My mother still feels his death, and we try to encourage her so she doesn't feel so sad. My mother's brother was a delegate of the word. He was killed when he went to the burial of a friend. They killed him in a cemetery in Guazapa.

The National Guard attacked many of us. I was pregnant with my youngest child when we had to flee. The men took the body of my uncle amid flying bullets back to Tres Ceibas. My grandmother, who is eighty-four years old, was seventy-two then. We were afraid she'd have a heart attack seeing her son carried away. She saw this tragedy, but had great faith in God and was able to live through it. The reason she survived this well was that people told her that her son had served the community generously. He had never made excuses not to serve.

But the situation became more and more terrible. It got to a point where our young people would be taken by the military. So our people began to say to our youths, "They're coming, they're coming! Flee to the hills!" My brothers, sisters, and husband did not sleep in our house but in the hills instead. For five years they slept in the hills. All of our people began to flee but I stayed behind because I had five children.

One of my sisters was captured in 1979 and I couldn't leave. I participated in the base Christian communities and I also worked in Aguilares with three-day Bible study conferences. Once I was a participant in a conference where a man arrived along with some religious women. He was an informer for the death squads. During this time of persecution he knew me and I knew him. He followed me to my house and said,

"Listen, give me your husband's weapons." "He doesn't have any," I said.

"Yes, he does. Where is he now?"

"He's taking our sick child to the hospital right now." But I only said this as an excuse. Actually he was in the house all the time playing with a top with the children. He'd just arrived back from two months in the hills. Some people came by and warned my husband to get out.

Then a group arrived at my house and said, "Hand over the weapons. Hand over your *cédula* [an identification card]."

"There it is on the table," I said.

We had been warned that they would send the women into houses and surround them. That's when I told them to go into the house and get the *cédula*. "So you're the one who meets with your uncle who has taken courses in medicine," they said.

"It's true my uncle can give injections and deliver babies. He is at the service of the whole community."

"So you're going to be meeting," they said. They meant our Bible meetings. I said no, that I had no time for such involvement because of my small children. I denied this involvement. We had to bury our songbooks and Bibles because if they found them it meant death for you.

They killed many people. They killed my husband's cousin, who had a small child. My husband's cousin thought she would not be taken because of her child. But they took her and left her child at a house. Then they killed her with a machete by chopping off parts of her body, starting with her nose.

Our houses were made of grass and clay tiles; They set fire to our house. Everything was burned. We had put our clothes on the clay roof to dry and they were all burned also. Seeing our houses burning, we gave thanks to God that we were not burned ourselves.

Then we heard reports of friends who had been killed. They came to kill my daughter's godmother. The death squads came and demanded to be fed and my daughter's godmother was fixing them dinner. Then they took her away to kill her, leaving her little daughter crying and crying in the house.

I haven't told you about threats to me yet. I don't know how I felt when they insisted I was meeting with subversive groups. I denied it, but inside I prayed, "God help me to defend my children." I felt my body didn't exist, that I didn't exist. I felt great pain in my stomach.

They kept demanding and I denied everything, especially when the informer accused me. He had a toupee and a special sport coat and a cowboy string tie. He had some wool things on his arms. The people knew he was an informer.

I denied I was involved in these meetings. I kept asking God to free me, to free me. Nearby I heard shooting; perhaps it was those soldiers. When the informer heard shots he left. I felt great anxiousness. The same day they put a rifle in my mother's stomach. They accused my brothers of also being involved in these meetings. My mother denied this saying, "My children aren't involved in anything." Then they said, "The next time we come through, if you don't hand over your children we will kill you."

Just three of us, my mother, my sister-in-law, and I, stayed in the house that night. The others were in the hills. I didn't have courage to go to the hills, to leave my children. I said if they kill me at least it will be in the house. My mother said, "Isn't it better to go to another town?" She knew a neighbor called Trinidad, who had a brother who lived here as a catechist, a good person who would not refuse us.

So we left with my children, my mother, and my sister-in-law, but my husband wouldn't come. He said, "No, I won't be a coward. I won't leave my people." My brothers and father and husband stayed behind. So we came here but always with the thought of them up there. While living here I went back two or three times to bring them things, sugar, food, knowing they couldn't go into town to buy food or they'd be captured and killed. When we went the first time there was no problem. We left at night. But the second time people told us not to return to the city because an army battalion was active. All night long we heard the shooting. I decided not to go back.

Finally in 1983 my mother-in-law and others left. They were the ones we were bringing food to. My family members, brothers, father-in-law, and sisters left one by one until all returned here. My father-in-law died here as an old man.

To walk through the hills, especially with children, is impossible. But when we came here we felt sad because we didn't know anyone. We thought people would say, "Those people are from up there," and they would kill us.

And so I was afraid. I don't know how to express this. I had participated in the church and now I could not. I felt ... I don't know what.

In the year we came, we saw a group of helicopters shooting close to here. We felt isolated, without our normal surroundings. But little by little we met people and began to form communities here. That's how we came to participate in the Christian communities. They asked me if I wanted to become a missionary. At first I felt like saying no, but then I said yes. I kept wondering, Will the same thing happen here that happened there? With a bit of fear we began little by little. Now I feel strengthened. I feel that all this community is mine. We know all the communities. I feel very, well, happy. The profound fear I'd felt is gone. The Gospel of St. Matthew says to us, "Happy are those who are persecuted, who are spoken evil against, happy are those who are killed because of my cause. They will be given the kingdom."

St. Matthew gives us great strength. If we die for this cause I feel at peace. This fear I felt before has left me now. We have so many people we know right now. Everyone in the community is my family, like my own, as if all of us were a family without fear.

I want my children to stay involved with church, not to follow another ideology. We have a daughter twenty years old. We advised her not to continue her relationship with someone involved with the army. This boyfriend didn't ask about her family. He came here and I asked about his family and he said they were involved with the National Police. This young man had been in a military operation in Chalatenango where many were killed. He said they took three young men who denied they were involved. He said the *muchachos* [guerrillas] died with their fists raised. That doesn't surprise me because the *muchachos* have their own promise to keep just as the soldiers have their promise to keep. They didn't die by selling out.

I told this young man if they die because of their commitment, it is the same commitment that you make. He said he saw all those demonstrations of UNTS [a coalition of the popular organizations]. I told him they were demanding justice, even though people told not to speak so frankly because it's dangerous. I told him that UNTS was demanding good prices for grains for basic living. But he said "These people always have weapons." My daughter was listening, sitting there, and she shook her head. After he left she called him a *pendejo* [son of a bitch]. I said to her, "Think this over carefully, daughter. Remember what we suffered. Don't you remember how we trembled up there? How your father, brothers, and aunts were not at peace?"

"That's right, mother. I hadn't thought of all that and also he had not told me all this." My daughter stopped her relationship with him. Later she had another boyfriend. His father worked for the police.

I told her, "Look, his father works for the police." She said, "Yes, but that's his father, not him."

It could be true; the son doesn't necessarily follow the path of the father. But I keep praying to God that she finds a man not involved in the military, or whose family is not involved with the police.

She broke up with this man. Now she is with a man whose parents were both killed. They were in the teachers' union called ANDES. They lived in Chalatenango and then they transferred to Apopa, where the father taught classes. Informers accused him and he was killed. I told her to marry when she's ready to, but to someone who has suffered as we have suffered. This boy is very conscientious.

What worries me the most right now is the forced recruitment, because I have two sons and a brother. They recruited my brother, but a nurse in the parish with connections with the air force was able to get him out. I'm always worried when my boys don't come home. I go out looking for them.

When I know they are recruiting I'm afraid. With the new government, ARENA, there's no way to bribe them. I don't want my children to kill our own people. If they go to kill, what are they defending? This is what is affecting me the most right now.

My family was Catholic. My grandmother was a *rezadora*, one of the official prayer persons. Six of us grandchildren would go travel with her all day. I felt a great desire to follow her example. During the two-week missions, we'd reflect on the gospel I felt my faith being formed. But when they killed Rutilio, that's when I felt a desire to go out and do this work even more. One time when we went to meetings in Aguilares, I thought, Why do they kill people for going to meetings to struggle for justice? The struggle inspired me, and now I hope to continue. My job in the mission now is to go visit communities. We go to neighborhoods where there is no base Christian community to help people form one.

The faith I feel is that through our communication the people will become conscious of the situation in our country. Many people don't understand the sin and injustice we live in, and we hope to help them become aware.

To coordinate the mission we meet every Wednesday to discuss the Saturday meeting. We discuss questions of the gospel and our objectives in the communities we will visit. We consider whether a community is losing its spirit. If it is, we want to go to give it life.

We haven't yet reached a point where we can discuss women's issues. But in the meetings we always show that women's roles are as important as men's. Women were stepped on, marginated the most. If women saw their value they would be involved in the work of the church rather than with advertising, which does not respect their dignity but uses their bodies to sell more. I think all us women should get together and refuse to buy products from companies that use women.

Source: Pp. 84–88, "Lupe" from *The Hour of the Poor, The Hour of Women: Salvadoran Women Speak* by Renny Golden. Copyright © 1991. Published by Crossroads Publishing Company, 1991. Reprinted by permission of Dr. Renny Golden.

One revolution succeeded in taking power. The Sandinista National Liberation Front or FSLN defeated the three-decade-long dictatorship of the Somoza family in 1979 and controlled the government for a decade thereafter. It eventually succumbed to electoral defeat in 1990, when the effects of a prolonged civil war, economic blunders, and generally poor leadership alienated the Nicaraguan people. One of the Sandinistas major failures was in gender relations. The testimony of Doris Tijerino helps explain the Sandinista defeat.

DORIS TIJERINO, IN *SANDINO'S DAUGHTERS REVISITED*

It's clear that the revolution made a great many concrete changes, positive changes, in women's lives. Yet women voted overwhelmingly against the revolutionary project in the 1992 elections. Why?

It's true: people say women voted against the revolution, against the FSLN. But I don't know. I don't know if that's not a bit too simplistic. Maybe just because women are in the majority here.... But votes don't have gender. I mean, there's no way to know for sure if a particular vote is male or female. You can go by the polls, but I'm not convinced. Women may have voted against the FSLN, but I don't really think they voted against the revolutionary project. It just wouldn't make sense.

What I believe is that among the many things the revolution wasn't able to finish was the profound and necessary change in human consciousness. We weren't really able to get people to understand what the literacy crusade meant, what the improvement in public health meant, what our educational programs meant. Ideologically, the revolution wasn't what it should have been. Tomas Borge once said, "The war isn't going to be won by those who fire the most rounds, but by those who raise the most consciousness." And I think that has a lot to do with what happened in the elections.

After the United States invaded Grenada, and even more so after Panama, we literally saw an "invasion psychosis" here. People were terrified that the U.S was going to invade Nicaragua. And it wasn't as if this was farfetched there, were enough signs; the message was quite international. And people opted for the simplest route: elect a government the United States wants. As simple as that.

Because people's lives had improved; there's no question about it. The Sandinista government initiated an agrarian reform program; people were given ownership of the land they worked. If you couldn't pay your electric bill, we never cut off the power like Somoza did. You just went and explained your problem: there was a new level of understanding of people's needs. And extended electrical power to remote mountain areas where people had never seen a light bulb before. We opened child-care centers where they'd new existed; before the revolution we didn't even have those in the *cities!*

But in spite of all these improvements, the United States kept on funding and supporting the counterrevolution. It was clear all along that they were going to keep on doing everything possible to undermine the revolutionary process to defeat Sandinism. We were in the midst of a terrible economic crisis here, and it wasn't only a result of the U.S blockade; it was a part of the global recession. Plus there were extensive areas of the country where you couldn't ever travel because of the war. So this was the situation; I don't blame people for voting for a government favored by the United States, although their naiveté may be painful. The UNO vote was a vote for peace. How else can you explain the fact that people continue to demand the very same things the revolution had begun to provide?

It reminds me of the situation among a fair percentage of Cuban exiles in Miami and elsewhere, people who fled to the United States, who detest the Cuban Revolution. Yet they are astonished that there's no health care available to them, that drugs and crime are such problems, that there's such a high unemployment rate. . . . The social services they'd come to expect from the revolution are suddenly not available in the country of their dreams. They've been victims of some very convincing propaganda. . . .

But I know you want me to talk about women, specifically. Women did benefit under our revolutionary program. Peasant women, for example, got titles to the land along with peasant men—although it's true there were problems with the application of agrarian reform; it never really worked as it was supposed to, as it was conceived. I remember we frequently had to protest the fact that women weren't benefiting as they should have from the land reform.

Nevertheless, don't think sexism alone is to blame, on the part of the institutions, the policies, or the men themselves. The problem is, the women who complained or protested were always a small minority: leadership women, or some small group of women who saw things more clearly, who were more ideologically advanced than the majority of the female population. A minority of women were organized here. And this is where I believe our greatest political failure lies. We never did the ideological work we should have done.

An example: up in Matagalpa, over near Sébaco, you'll find communities—somewhat off the beaten path, it's true, but accessible to anyone who wants to go there—where the situation of women is truly dramatic. The role assigned to them during the decade of revolution, and which they themselves assumed, was an absolutely subordinate one. And I'm not blaming the women. It was up to our leadership to have made sure they understood that there were other possibilities. We had the organization and we didn't use it. And in barely two years of UNO government to see how those women have retreated, without so much as a protest, back into the most traditional roles. . . .

Doris, you were the national head of AMNLAE just before and just after the elections. That's a period which has elicited a great deal of discussion, particularly among women. How do you see what happened?

I have a great many complaints about the Party from that period. . . .

That's precisely the question I'm getting at. Because it's not only an issue that's relevant here in Nicaragua; it's something that's being debated in many parts of the world. Should a mass women's organization or movement be subject to a political party—almost always controlled be men—or must it be autonomous to really function?

I know the consensus today is that an autonomous movement is necessary. But I think there's an initial period in which the Party has to keep control of the different mass organizations. The problem here was that we let that initial period go on too long. During the Somoza years there were no serious organizations of any kind: just a bunch of bourgeois parties that played the dictator's. . . .

Source: Margaret Randall, *Sandino's Daughters Revisited: Feminism in Nicaragua.* New Brunswick: Rutgers University Press, 1994.

LIBERATION THEOLOGY

Liberation theology emerged out of the Roman Catholic Church's need to struggle with social injustice that had caused revolutionary movements to spring up all over the world. It had particular urgency in Latin America where the model of the Cuban Revolution in 1959 posed a poignant threat to the status quo. Dom Hélder Camara was one of the leaders of the movement. He was archbishop of Recife, one of the largest cities in Brazil during the 1960s, and located in the impoverished northeast.

DOM HÉLDER CAMARA, *REVOLUTION THROUGH PEACE*

The Church is present in the world. The Church is present in the building of the world. The Church is present in man's effort to humanize the world. No one should be startled at the expression "humanize"; if man is linked to God through the Man-God, humanizing the world means cleansing Creation of every mark of sin, so that man may attain the fullest measure of development.

> *You therefore are to be perfect, even as your heavenly Father is perfect.*

Which is more difficult and more exciting: to humanize subhuman men made wretched by misery, or to humanize supermen dehumanized by luxury? The two tasks complement each other in such a way that the realization of each is dependent on that of the other.

It is time for God's people in the underdeveloped world to throw themselves heart and soul into the struggle to develop the sons of God who have been reduced to subhuman dimensions by a subhuman life. The Latin American bishops who met in Mar del Plata decided there that the Church must assume an active role in the development and integration of the Latin American continent.

. . . If religion has no role at just those moments which . . . peoples see as decisive and in efforts which seem sacred to them, we will lose an exceptional opportunity of being useful and will be deprived of the necessary moral ascendancy to enable us to keep today's peaceful effort from being tomorrow's violent struggle. . . .

Source: Dom Hélder Camara, *Revolution through Peace*. Translated by Amparo McLean. New York: Harper Colophon Books, 1972, p. 9, 11.

QUESTIONS FOR DISCUSSION

1. What accounts for the terrible brutality of the dictatorships in Chile, Argentina, and Brazil?
2. Do you believe that the tactics employed by the government of Peru were justified in its struggles against the Shining Path guerrillas?
3. Why were women particularly hard hit by the terror? Why were they treated so badly?
4. Why did rightist death squads target people like Carlos Godoy? Why was Godoy a threat?
5. Why do you think that the right wing dictatorships eventually abdicated? Why did the leftist insurgencies ultimately fail?
6. Why was liberation theology, Camara's peaceful path, not able to make a difference?

12 THE NEW LATIN AMERICA

INTRODUCTION

The new millennium has brought revived hope and optimism to Latin America, despite some harsh realities. Four broad trends have marked Latin American politics since the beginning of the twenty-first century. First, Colombia and Mexico, governments of relatively longstanding stability, have still not been able to resolve conflicts with armed guerrilla movements that have widespread public support but insufficient military power to overthrow the existing regime. At times, the stalemate in Colombia has threatened the viability of the government, but with the presidency of Álvaro Uribe (2002–) the contestants have established at least a seemingly workable equilibrium. The uprising and continued protests in Chiapas, Mexico, which may have initially helped end the seven-decade rule of the Institutionalized Revolutionary Party, have evolved into a protracted, fruitless series of negotiations. Second, beginning with the election of Hugo Chávez in Venezuela in 1998, several nations have elected left-of-center governments. This so-called "pink tide" has elected socialist, populist, or worker presidents in Argentina, Bolivia, Brazil, Chile, Ecuador, Nicaragua, Uruguay, and Venezuela. These governments have struggled, sometimes successfully, to mitigate the inequities of the free market policies that predominate in the world economy. Third, in direct contradiction to the ongoing civil strife and the "pink tide," a number of Latin American nations have elected conservatives to lead them. Finally, throughout Latin America, regardless of whether the regime is conservative or liberal, popular participation has expanded notably. Repressed people, such as the indigenous of the Ecuadorian highlands and Amazon rainforests, have organized and successfully protested against and contested with governments and transnational corporations.

Economically, Latin American governments have gone in one of two directions. Some have completely adopted neo-liberal policies that open domestic markets to international competition and shrink the size of government by eliminating public ownership of corporations. Others, as in the case of the "pink tide" nations, have chosen to continue the neo-liberal policies of previous regimes, while attempting to mitigate severe inequities in income through new anti-poverty programs. The turn of the century brought somewhat improved conditions for many Latin Americans, because the economies of most nations in the regions began to grow again after a decade of stagnation or shrinkage. In addition, governments largely have brought inflation, the most damaging economic phenomenon, under control. Nonetheless, severe inequities in income distribution and widespread poverty continued to undermine the region's economy and politics. In response to the inability of their home nations to create opportunities in employment, Latin Americans have continued to seek better lives in neighboring countries.

GUERRILLA WARS WITHOUT RESOLUTION

The Revolutionary Armed Forces of Colombia

The Revolutionary Armed Forces of Colombia (Fuerzas Armadas Revolucionarias de Colombia), *known by the acronym FARC, is the oldest guerrilla movement anywhere in the world. It has fought for nearly a half century against the Colombian government. The FARC had its origins in an earlier, communist insurgency of the 1950s. It has controlled considerable territory in the countryside. Since the early 1990s, FARC has filled the void created when the government reached a series of agreements with the leaders of cocaine cartels that ended the so-called "drug wars." The guerrillas provide protection for the production and transportation of cocaine in return for payment of hundreds of millions of dollars in "taxes." The government has tried at various times to reach a peace agreement with the FARC, but the rebels have proven unwilling to enter into any lasting ceasefire. The document excerpted here, "Forty years of struggle for peace, sovereignty, and social justice," is the FARC's justification for its existence.*

FORTY YEARS OF STRUGGLE FOR PEACE, SOVEREIGNTY, AND SOCIAL JUSTICE

Forty years ago in Marquetalia in the Department of Tolima 16,000 soldiers began their offensive against 48 campesinos, who were forced to take up arms in their own defense, providing the origins of the Fuerzas Armadas Revolucionarias of Colombia which has become today the Army of the People that has made itself into a true popular alternative power.

Since May 27, 1964 FARC-EP has not left the battle ... in defense of the most heartfelt interests of our people in search of . . . an exit from confrontation with the military. . . .

Just 20 years ago . . . there was a ceasefire but because of the myopic view of the oligarchy which did not change the fundamental economic and social structure of the nation or the rules of the political game. . . .

On account of the oligarchy the nation is run for the benefit of North American capital with resulting misery for millions. . . . Land is concentrated in the hands of a few while peasants are despoiled and displaced . . . communications and other of our patrimony have been shredded and tossed into savage competition with transnational corporations. . . . turned over our subsoil rights to huge international companies . . . privatized crucial services leaving them to speculators. . . .

The causes of the conflict have remained the same for 40 years with the recent Treaty of Extradition with the United States. . . .

Source: Translated by Mark Wasserman from "Forty years of struggle for peace, sovereignty, and social justice," *The Revolutionary Armed Forces of Colombia,* 2005.

THE ZAPATISTAS

The long rule of the Party of the Institutionalized Revolution began to crumble during the early 1990s, when the first of a series of notorious murders occurred. In May 1993, narcotics gangsters assassinated Mexico's most important Roman Catholic cardinal. Then, on January 1, 1994, the Ejercito Zapatista de Liberación Nacional (the Zapatista National Liberation Army) or EZLN, rose in rebellion in the impoverished state of Chiapas in southern Mexico. In March 1994, Donaldo Colosio, the PRI candidate for president in the 1994 election, fell victim to an assassin's bullets. The PRI collected itself to triumph in one more election before yielding the presidency in 2000 to Vicente Fox (2000–2006), the candidate from the Partido Acción Nacional or PAN (National Action Party). The EZLN's search for social justice continued, however, and like the FARC, it reached a series of uneasy agreements with successive governments that yielded little in the way of reforms. Unlike in the Colombian case, the EZLN did not expand violent resistance. Instead the EZLN became adept at modern communications. The document below, "Today we say 'enough is enough!'" is its call to arms. It has been widely disseminated over the Internet.

"TODAY WE SAY 'ENOUGH IS ENOUGH!'"

First Declaration from the Lacandon Jungle
EZLN's Declaration of War
"Today we say 'enough is enough!'
(Ya Basta!)"

TO THE PEOPLE OF MEXICO: MEXICAN BROTHERS AND SISTERS

We are a product of 500 years of struggle: first against slavery, then during the War of Independence against Spain led by insurgents, then to avoid being absorbed by North American imperialism, then to promulgate our constitution and expel the French empire from our soil, and later the dictatorship of Porfirio Diaz denied us the just application of the Reform laws and the people rebelled and leaders like Villa and Zapata emerged, poor men just like us. We have been denied the most elemental preparation so they can use us as cannon fodder and pillage the wealth of our country. They don't care that we have nothing, absolutely nothing, not even a roof over our heads, no land, no work, no health care, no food nor education. Nor are we able to freely and democratically elect our political representatives, nor is there independence from foreigners, nor is there peace nor justice for ourselves and our children.

But today, we say ENOUGH IS ENOUGH.

We are the inheritors of the true builders of our nation. The dispossessed, we are millions and we thereby call upon our brothers and sisters to join this struggle as the only path, so that we will not die of hunger due to the insatiable ambition of a 70 year dictatorship led by a clique of traitors that represent the most conservative and sell-out groups. They are the same ones that opposed Hidalgo and Morelos, the same ones that betrayed Vicente Guerrero, the same ones that sold half our country to the foreign invader, the same ones that imported a European prince to rule our country, the same ones that formed the "scientific" Porfirsta dictatorship, the same ones that opposed the Petroleum Expropriation, the same ones that massacred the railroad workers in 1958 and the students in 1968, the same ones that today take everything from us, absolutely everything.

To prevent the continuation of the above and as our last hope, after having tried to utilize all legal means based on our Constitution, we go to our Constitution, to apply Article 39 which says:

"National Sovereignty essentially and originally resides in the people. All political power emanates from the people and its purpose is to help the people. The people have, at all times, the inalienable right to alter or modify their form of government."

Therefore, according to our constitution, we declare the following to the Mexican federal army, the pillar of the Mexican dictatorship that we suffer from, monopolized by a one-party system and led by Carlos Salinas de Gortari, the maximum and illegitimate federal executive that today holds power.

According to this Declaration of War, we ask that other powers of the nation advocate to restore the legitimacy and the stability of the nation by overthrowing the dictator.

We also ask that international organizations and the International Red Cross watch over and regulate our battles, so that our efforts are carried out while still protecting our civilian population. We declare now and always that we are subject to the Geneva Accord, forming the EZLN as our fighting arm of our liberation struggle. We have the Mexican people on our side, we have the beloved tri-colored flag highly respected by our insurgent fighters. We use black and red in our uniform as our symbol of our working people on strike. Our flag carries the following letters, "EZLN," Zapatista National Liberation Army, and we always carry our flag into combat.

Beforehand, we refuse any effort to disgrace our just cause by accusing us of being drug traffickers, drug guerrillas, thieves, or other names that might be used by our enemies. Our struggle follows the constitution which is held high by its call for justice and equality.

Therefore, according to this declaration of war, we give our military forces, the EZLN, the following orders:

First: Advance to the capital of the country, overcoming the Mexican federal army, protecting in our advance the civilian population and permitting the people in the liberated area the right to freely and democratically elect their own administrative authorities.

Second: Respect the lives of our prisoners and turn over all wounded to the International Red Cross.

Third: Initiate summary judgments against all soldiers of the Mexican federal army and the political police that have received training or have been paid by foreigners, accused of being traitors to our country, and against all those that have repressed and treated badly the civil population and robbed or stolen from or attempted crimes against the good of the people.

Fourth: Form new troops with all those Mexicans that show their interest in joining our struggle, including those that, being enemy soldiers, turn themselves in without having fought against us, and promise to take orders from the General Command of the Zapatista National Liberation Army.

Fifth: We ask for the unconditional surrender of the enemy's headquarters before we begin any combat to avoid any loss of lives.

Sixth: Suspend the robbery of our natural resources in the areas controlled by the EZLN.

To the People of Mexico: We, the men and women, full and free, are conscious that the war that we have declared is our last resort, but also a just one. The dictators are applying an undeclared genocidal war against our people for many years. Therefore we ask for your participation, your decision to support this plan that struggles for work, land, housing, food, health care, education, independence, freedom, democracy, justice and peace. We declare that we will not stop fighting until the basic demands of our people have been met by forming a government of our country that is free and democratic.

JOIN THE INSURGENT FORCES OF THE ZAPATISTA NATIONAL LIBERATION ARMY.

General Command of the EZLN 1993

Source: "Today we say 'Enough is Enough,'" Ejercito Zapatista de Liberación Nacional.

THE "PINK TIDE"

Nestor Kirchner (1950–) won election to the presidency of Argentina in 2003, after having served three terms (1991–2003) as governor of the southern state of Santa Cruz. His success in improving the economy of his state, at a time when the national economy was collapsing, skyrocketed him to prominence. As president, he had to pick up the pieces of Argentina's shattered politics and economy. Of his two predecessors, one had resigned from office in 2001 after riots had erupted and the second had adopted policies that had led Argentina into recession. In December 2001, Argentina had defaulted on $132 billion in loans. Kirchner gained popularity by vowing to end the policies that had resulted in the collapse. He negotiated an agreement with the hated International Monetary Fund (IMF) and within three years paid off the nation's $84 billion debt to that institution. Strict fiscal and monetary policies brought economic growth averaging about nine percent per annum. Argentina thus has prospered. Critics asserted that Kirchner has relied too heavily on his charisma and has tended to adopt authoritarian methods. In the speech that follows, he defended his controversial aggressive negotiations with the IMF and expounded on his considerable accomplishments.

SPEECH TO THE COUNCIL OF THE AMERICAS, SEPTEMBER 21, 2006

PRESIDENT NESTOR KIRCHNER'S SPEECH FROM THE DINNER WITH THE COUNCIL OF THE AMERICAS IN NEW YORK 09/21/2006—UNITED STATES, NEW YORK

They were certainly difficult times the first time that we gathered here, during which Argentina was going through the most profound crisis in its history.

I had to be here after a short time of an asymmetric devaluation, the also traumatic halt of the convertibility plan, and during a time when Argentina was not complying with all of its internal and external commitments. The external commitments are broadly known; internally, the country and its citizen were being condemned to becoming indigent and poor.

These were the circumstances, reality had to be confronted, and the credibility of the country had to be rebuilt.

The fact that the region was also experiencing different kinds of problems, with critical implications in the majority of the cases, with some exceptions, created a very difficult framework to work from and find solutions.

Argentina overcame these moments and is in an important and permanent rebuilding process. To give you an idea, when I began to lead Argentina, the collection system collapsed, our country was facing a significant social crisis. After the government had passed the fifty laws dictating the intangibility of bank deposits, savers suffered the "corralito" effect, by which all the financial obligations towards those citizens that had saved, and that had trusted in the system, were violated. We were also experiencing a very difficult social situation; our "Casa Rosada" (Government House), had permanent visitors in the "Plaza de Mayo" and we had friends who, with a great deal of justice, complained about the terrible situation they were forced to go through.

We began to be on the path; we started to grow and to announce as fundamental factors that we want to be a balanced and just country. We said that indigence and poverty are stains that Argentina could not afford. We had substantial differences with regards to how the International Monetary Fund would view the process of economic recovery. With all due respect, I myself tell you that if I had followed the suggestions of my friends at the International Monetary Fund, the crisis would surely be considerably more severe. This is why some have recently asked me, "Are you heterodox with regards to the economy?" Yes, I believe in economic heterodoxy; I believe fundamentally that if a juncture is agreed upon within a strategic project framework, there can be different answers that can work and that in many cases, it is necessary to respond to the situation of each particular country.

We did not find the answers in the International Monetary Fund and we had to recreate our own ideas and actions, leading to the restructuring of the private external debt process, through which we were able to obtain 70,000 million dollars in national savings. For the first time, Argentina had its negotiation leverage up to the standards of the circumstances.

We also decided to cancel the obligations with the International Monetary Fund because it was impossible to lead the economy with the intervention of the Fund's public bureaucrats, which had no real understanding of the country. We credited them with 10,800 million dollars and ended an important problem. Which was necessary to carry out the actions lying ahead of us.

Likewise, we took decisions that were central and fundamental. We had to promote trust in the financial system and recreate the trust of Argentineans themselves in order to rebuild investor's trust. To this end, I believe that it is fundamental to avoid altering and changing the economy everyday. Instead, we should promote predictability not only on the juncture, but also, with regards to the strategic framework. An investor should know that when he goes to the country, he has the certainty that the government will not be constantly passing special provisions that lead to an inverse power relationship. Because what has happened in Argentina is that the fervent supporters of the neoliberal theories like to dictate much more than I, even though they have accused me of liking to govern in an authoritarian fashion.

We are trying to generate a two-way deal that allows investors to have clear, certain and concrete rules that predetermine and determine security to those who come to invest in our country.

To give you a clear idea, Argentina went from an indigence level of 27.7 percent, when I began my government, to 11.2 percent, and from a 20 percent of homes living in indigence to 8 percent today. Poverty in my country decreased from 54 percent to 31.4 percent; during the first semester of 2005 this figure was 38.8 percent, and during the first semester of 2006, it is 31.4 percent. In a year, we reduced poverty by 7.5 percent and since we began governing, poverty has been reduced by 23 points. Indigence was decreased by 16.5 points since the beginning of my government and went down by 2.8 percent when compared with the 2005 and 2006 semesters. Unemployment during the past month of July was 10 percent—it was 24.1 percent the day I assumed the presidency of the republic.

We expect that growth in Argentina will certainly surpass or be around 8 percent for this year. Regardless of the exact number, the information is that have exceeded our own optimistic framework, as growth from July 2005 to July 2006 was 9.4 percent, a considerably high number. With inflation, growth was 9.1 percent and the accumulated growth rate for this year is 8.6 percent.

Industrial growth last year was 7.7 percent; this year, from August, it was 7.2 and we have a 7.6 percent of accumulated growth. We expect, of course, to be in the same, or higher, industrial growth range as last year. What is the industrial growth based on?

Logically, a country growing with the same strength as Argentina will need to invest sturdily in order to continue consolidating the necessary infrastructure for the country's development. Also, we believe that this process of economic transformation, economic reconstruction, the country's economic growth, ending indigence, putting a definite brake to stop poverty, having a strong level of employment, and eliminating the framework of global unemployment that so strongly hit Argentina, require deep educational reforms. Because in determining moments in Argentina, the situation led to the closing of those technical schools that prepared our children and youth, and in many cases—you know this—firms demand people, and we do not have a prepared and trained workforce, typical of this kind of situation. We have decided to undertake two fundamental educational projects. Six points of the Argentinean Gross Product will go towards investing and financing education. We call it the Law of Education Finance, and this year we are discussing the education law with the entire society, so that the economic growth is definitely accompanied by high quality standards of the education system that allow us to have economic growth with human resources.

To give you an idea of what it means to have lowered poverty and indigence from semester to semester, we have taken 1,562,000 people out of poverty in one year and 562,000 have been lifted from indigence. Minimum salary in Argentina went from 200 pesos to 830, in other words, it experienced a 400 percent increase and the economy did not suffer at all.

It is fundamental for us to strike a balance between economic growth and equity and justice. The environment must be good for those of us who govern, for those who invest, for the businessmen, who are part of the growth and make the reality in Argentina for the people, for society, for the different sectors of society in order to rebuild a national entrepreneurial force and a middle class, which is the engine that permanently allows for the Argentinean growth, developing the potential of their own human resource capabilities and the definitive consolidation of a qualified middle class, with employment, that can be integrated into the growth.

In the region, we are working strongly to build MERCOSUR. We believe in the task that we are able to achieve with MERCOSUR; there was an integration process in Latin America. It is very important; we believe that the construction of the countries of South America will serve as a prevailing instrument; we firmly believe that the economic recovery of our countries will enable us to build a sound MERCOSUR. When these countries were in crisis, it was impossible to create as a bloc the necessary space within the countries of South America since there was no response, fundamentally, when the two largest countries were going through a deep crisis, like was the case with Brazil and Argentina.

We are very interested in having businessmen come and make a lot of money, because if businessmen make a lot of money, Argentineans will also have the possibility of striking a deal, so we can also be part of that growth, of those good results obtained from those that come to invest in Argentina, and that we are able to provide the national businessmen with the policies and with a country experiencing growth, so that you know that Argentina is beginning to take the place that history had reserved for it, and some Argentineans have had to wait a long time and we are trying to recover the time lost.

Gentlemen, Argentina wants to thank all of those who have collaborated with us; we thank those that got upset because at the end, they were able to understand us; and to those who are still angry, we will continue to wait for you with opened arms. But always know that we are a country that has its destiny in our own hands; and like this country, the United States, which has shown how to build a capitalist system with national decisiveness, Argentineans too, want to do the same. Thank you very much.

Source: President Nesto Kirchner's Speech, September 21, 2006, New York, U.S.

THE GREAT MIGRATIONS

Latin Americans have been on the move within the Western Hemisphere for a century or more in search of better lives in the form of employment and political asylum. For example, migrants have come from Mexico to the United States seeking jobs since the beginning of the twentieth century. They have formed the labor force for much of the agricultural sector in the United States. As economic conditions worsened in Mexico during the last quarter of the previous century, the tide of legal and illegal immigrants overwhelmed the U.S. border. More than 3 million illegal immigrants from Mexico have come since 1990. Between 2000 and 2004 alone, almost a half million illegal workers crossed the border. In an attempt to look after the well-being of its (former) citizens, the Mexican government published a pamphlet titled, "Guide for the Mexican Migrant." It proved to be quite controversial, because critics thought it inappropriate for the Mexican government to facilitate illegal activities.

GUIDE FOR THE MEXICAN MIGRANT

GUIDE FOR THE MEXICAN MIGRANT

Distributed by the Mexican Ministry of Foreign Relations

INTRODUCTION

Esteemed Countryman:

The purpose of this guide is to provide you with practical advice that may prove useful to you in case you have made the difficult decision to search for employment opportunities outside of your country.

The sure way to enter another country is by getting your passport from the Ministry of Foreign Affairs, and the visa, which you may apply for at the embassy or consulate of the country you wish to travel to.

However, in practice we see many Mexicans who try to cross the Northern Border without the necessary documents, through high risk zones that involve grave dangers, particularly in desert areas or rivers with strong, and not always obvious, currents.

Reading this guide will make you aware of some basic questions about the legal consequences of your stay in the United States of America without the appropriate migratory documents, as well as about the rights you have in that country, once you are there, independent of your migratory status.

Keep in mind always that there exist legal mechanisms to enter the United States of America legally.

In any case, if you encounter problems or run into difficulties, remember that Mexico has 45 consulates in that country whose locations you can find listed in this publication.

Familiarize yourself with the closest consulate and make use of it.

DANGERS IN CROSSING HIGH RISK ZONES

To cross the river can be very risky, above all if you cross alone and at night.

Heavy clothing increases in weight when wet and this makes swimming and floating difficult.

If you cross by desert, try to walk at times when the heat will not be too intense.

Highways and population centers are far apart, which means you will spend several days looking for roads, and you will not be able to carry foodstuffs or water for long periods of time. Also, you can get lost.

Salt water helps keep liquids in your body. Although you may feel more thirst if you drink salt water, the risk of dehydration is much less.

The symptoms of dehydration are:

—Little or no sweat.
—Dryness in the eyes and in the mouth.
—Headache.
—Tiredness and excessive exhaustion.
—Difficulty in walking and thinking.
—Hallucinations and visions.

If you get lost, guide yourself by lightposts, train tracks, or dirt roads.

BEWARE OF HUMAN TRAFFICKERS (COYOTES, POLLEROS)

They can deceive you with assurances of crossing in a few hours through the mountains and deserts. This is simply not so!

They can risk your life taking you across rivers, drainage canals, desert areas, train tracks, or highways. This has caused the death of hundreds of persons.

If you decide to hire people traffickers to cross the border, consider the following precautions:

Do not let them out of your sight. Remember that they are the only ones who know the lay of the land, and therefore the only ones who can get you out of that place.

Do not trust those who offer to take you to "the other side" and ask you to drive a car or to take or carry a package for them. Normally, those packages contain drugs or other prohibited substances. For this reason, many people have ended up in jail.

If you transport other persons, you can be confused with a human trafficker, and they can accuse you of the crime of trafficking or auto theft.

Do not entrust your minor children to strangers who offer to take them across to the United States.

DO NOT USE FALSE DOCUMENTS

DO NOT USE FALSE DOCUMENTS OR THOSE THAT DO NOT BELONG TO YOU, NOR DECLARE A FALSE NATIONALITY.

If you try to cross with false documents or those of another person, take into account the following:

To use false documents or those of another person is a federal crime in the United States, for which you can be tried in a criminal proceeding and end up in jail; likewise if you use a false name or say that you are a citizen of the United States when you are not one.

Do not lie to officials of the United States at ports and points of entry.

Source: As published by the Mexican Ministry of Foreign Relations.

POPULAR PARTICIPATION

Democratization and most recently the "pink tide" has facilitated the rise of popular organizations such as the Confederation of Indigenous Nationalities of Ecuador (Confederación de Nacionalidades Indigenas de Ecuadoror) or CONAIE. Founded in 1986 it has sponsored and led popular uprisings in 1992, 1994, 1997, 2000, and 2005 favoring land reform and protesting against neo-liberal economic policies that have, for example, allowed transnational mining companies to ruin the ecology. It used roadblocks as its most effective tools. CONAIE's efforts resulted in the adoption of changes to the constitution that called for a multiethnic and multicultural state, expanded the rights of indigenous people, and allowed for self-determination for indigenous lands. Its 2005 uprising led to the ouster of Ecuadorian President Lucio Gutiérrez (2003–2005). CONAIE was one of the most important supporters of Rafael Correa, who won election as president in 2007. CONAIE has also campaigned against the activities of foreign oil companies in the Amazon, which have had deleterious effects on the lands of indigenous peoples in the region. The accompanying documents lay out CONAIE's program.

CONAIE'S "SIXTEEN POINTS" "SIXTEEN DEMANDS" "CONVOKING AN UPRISING"

CONAIE'S SIXTEEN DEMANDS

1. Return of lands and territories taken from indigenous communities, without costly legal fees.
2. Sufficient water for human consumption and irrigation in indigenous communities, and a plan to prevent pollution of water supplies.
3. No municipal taxes on small properties owned by indigenous farmers.
4. Long-term financing for bilingual education programs in the communities.
5. Creation of provincial and regional credit agencies to be controlled by CONAIE.
6. Forgiveness of all debts to government ministries and banks incurred by indigenous communities.
7. Amendment of the first article of the constitution to proclaim Ecuador as a multi-national state.
8. Immediate delivery of funds and credits currently budgeted for indigenous nationalities.
9. Minimum two-year price freeze on all raw materials and manufactured goods used by the communities in agricultural production, and reasonable price increase on all agricultural goods sold by them, using free-market mechanisms.
10. Initiation and completion of all priority construction on basic infrastructure for indigenous communities.
11. Unrestricted import and export privileges for indigenous artisans and handicraft merchants.
12. National legislation and enforcement to provide for strict protection and controlled exploration of archaeological sites, under the supervision of CONAIE.
13. Expulsion of the Summer Institute of Linguistics, in accordance with Executive Decree 1159 of 1981.
14. Respect for the rights of children and greater government awareness of their current plight.
15. National support for indigenous medicine.
16. Immediate dismantling of political party organizations that parallel government institutions at the municipal and provincial levels, and which manipulate political consciousness and elections in indigenous communities.

Source: p. 41, "CONAIE's Sixteen Demands" from "Ecuador's Pan Indian Program" by Les Field, *NACLA Report on the Americas, 25*:3 (December 1991). Copyright © 1991 by NACLA. Reprinted by permission of Les Field and NACLA.

LOS 16 PUNTOS

1. Declaration of Ecuador as a "plurinational state."
2. Grants of land and legalization of territories for the nationalities.
3. Solutions to the problems of water and irrigation.
4. Absolution of debts to FODERUMA and the National Development Bank.
5. Freezing of consumer prices.
6. Conclusion of priority projects in the communities.
7. Non-payment of rural land taxes.
8. Expulsion of the Summer Language Institute, in accordance with the 1981 decree.
9. Free importation and exportation of commercial and artisan products for CONAIE members.
10. Control, protection, and development of archeological sites under the supervision of CONAIE.
11. Legal recognition and funding by the state of Indigenous medicine.
12. Cancellation of decrees that created parallel institutions to local governments.
13. Immediate granting of budgeted funds for Indigenous nationalities.
14. Permanent funding of bilingual education.
15. Real respect for the rights of the child, without demagoguery.
16. The fixing of fair prices for farm products and free access to markets.

Source: Translated by Dr. Marc Becker from "Gobierno contestópor punto los pedidos indígenas" *Hoy* (Quito), June 29, 1990, 5ª. Translation reprinted by permission of Dr. Marc Becker, http://www.yachana.org

Quito, March 12, 1999

CONAIE CONVOKES INDIAN LEVANTAMIENTO (UPRISING)

Facing the authoritarian attitude demonstrated by the State of Emergency and the announcement of economic measures, the Indigenous Peoples and Nationalities of Ecuador express the following:

- President Mahuad, in his nationally televised address, lied to the country and demonstrated that he does not believe in consultation and deliberation (concertación). Taking an extreme and unilateral position, he has taken measures that destroy the popular economy.
- The President hid the origins of the crisis that was generated in the national financial system, and neither penalized those responsible nor recuperated the millions of dollars that were given under the pretext of saving the banks.
- We totally and unequivocally reject the economic measures taken by the government that are a clear demonstration of its lack of initiative in using the same models that have for many years failed to produce results and only exacerbated the divide between rich and poor.
- Raising the IVA (Value Added Tax) from 10 to 15% means generating a tax in addition to the increase in prices provoked by the 100% devaluation of the sucre.
- The 200% increase in gasoline prices directly affects the prices of all articles of mass consumption. This increase in prices will provide the government with 1 trillion

500 billion sucres, while the increase allocated for the "poverty bond" (bono de la pobreza) is only 50 billion, 3% of the total, not counting the amount collected in the tax on luxury vehicles.

- We hold the National Congress responsible for the viability they give to the projects presented by the President that are violent attacks against the national patrimony.
- The only measures with which we agree are the punishment of tax-evasion and the obstruction of related credits which can prevent the irresponsible actions of corporate bankers. We also favor the re-structuring of the foreign debt, something not part of the President's initiative.

We hold the government responsible for the death of our *compañero* Luis Alberto Cabascango Cobacango, who fleeing from the leveling actions of the police and military in the community of San Pablito de Agualongo, fell in a hidden well and died.

We hold the government responsible for and denounce the illegal detention of *compañero* José Maria Cabascango, Official *(Vocal)* of the Supreme Electoral Tribunal. In violation of his immunity as a member of this state body, he was arrested by police for interceding on the behalf of imprisoned compañeros detained in the sector of Cayambe y Tabacundo.

For the aforementioned reasons, we ratify the resolutions of the Peoples' Congress held yesterday, March 11, 1999. We call upon our base communities and organizations to hold Community Assemblies and an emergency National Assembly on March 15 in order to define mandates and actions that will launch the next LEVANTAMIENTO INDIGENA

We demand the lifting of the State of Emergency that with the economic plan has brought us to a state of social unrest.

We suspend our participation in the Forum of Concertation of the Government and Indigenous Peoples.

Antonio Vargas President

Source: The Indigenous Peoples and Nationalities of Ecuador.

INFLATION

Perhaps the greatest danger to the political stability in Latin America during the twentieth century was inflation. Its impact was always harshest on the middle and lower classes. The members of the middle class often reacted with fear to the possibility of downward mobility and joined with the extreme right in an effort to retain their status.

Workers and peasants usually sought solutions to economic malaise on the left, thereby creating bitter conflicts.

LATIN AMERICAN INFLATION

Latin American inflation is going down, with Argentina and Venezuela as the exceptions.

LATIN AMERICAN INFLATION

Annual percent change

	1980	1990	2000	2003	2004	2005	2006	2007
Argentina	100.8%	2,314%	−0.9%	13.4%	4.4%	9.6%	12.9%	15.0%
Bolivia	47.1%	17.1%	4.6%	3.3%	4.4%	5.4%	3.4%	3.1%
Brazil	132.6%	2,947%	7.1%	14.8%	6.6%	6.8%	4.9%	4.4%
Chile	35.1%	26.0%	3.8%	2.8%	1.1%	3.1%	3.8%	3.0%
Colombia	25.9%	29.1%	9.2%	7.1%	5.9%	5.0%	4.7%	4.2%
Costa Rica	18.1%	19.0%	11.0%	9.4%	11.5%	13.6%	13.1%	11.0%
Dom. Rep.	21.7%	50.5%	7.7%	27.4%	51.5%	4.2%	8.5%	5.0%
Ecuador	13.0%	48.5%	96.1%	7.9%	2.7%	2.4%	3.4%	3.0%
El Salvador	17.4%	24.0%	4.3%	2.5%	5.4%	4.0%	4.0%	2.5%
Guatemala	10.7%	41.0%	6.0%	5.6%	7.6%	9.1%	6.9%	5.4%
Haiti	18.0%	20.4%	11.0%	26.7%	28.3%	16.8%	13.1%	8.9%
Honduras	18.1%	23.3%	11.0%	7.7%	8.1%	8.8%	6.8%	5.7%
Mexico	26.5%	26.7%	9.5%	4.5%	4.7%	4.0%	3.5%	3.0%
Nicaragua	35.1%	3004.1%	9.9%	5.2%	8.5%	9.6%	8.8%	6.1%
Panama	13.8%	0.8%	1.4%	0.6%	0.5%	2.9%	2.2%	1.5%
Paraguay	22.4%	38.2%	9.0%	14.2%	4.3%	6.8%	7.4%	4.4%
Peru	59.1%	7,481.7%	3.8%	2.3%	3.7%	1.6%	2.7%	2.2%
Uruguay	63.5%	112.5%	4.8%	10.2%	7.6%	5.9%	5.5%	4.9%
Venezuela	21.4%	40.7%	16.2%	31.1%	21.7%	15.9%	11.7%	17.3%
Total	69.2%	567.6%	7.6%	10.5%	6.5%	6.3%	5.8%	5.6%

Source: World Economic Outlook, April 2006, International Monetary Fund. Copyright © 2006. Reprinted by permission of Copyright Clearance Center on behalf of International Monetary Fund.

QUESTIONS FOR DISCUSSION

1. What justification does FARC have for staying in the field at war for forty years? Do you think its reasons are sufficient for all the years of bloodshed?
2. Why do you think that the EZLN asks that international organizations "watch over and regulate" its struggles?
3. Why does the EZLN pay so much attention to the Mexican national army?
4. How did President Nestor Kirchner restore the trust of Argentines for their national government? Why was this important?
5. Why did the Mexican government produce the *Guide for the Mexican Migrant?* What is the most important advice the pamphlet gives to illegal immigrants?

6. Of the sixteen demands in CONAIE's program, which do you think are most important? Which of the changes do you think the CONAIE can most likely achieve?

7. Do you think that the guerrillas in Colombia and Chiapas will ever lay down their arms?

8. What peaceful solutions are possible? Are other Latin American nations like Ecuador headed down the same road to guerrilla war?

9. Are you optimistic about the ability of Latin Americans to solve the profound problems that confront them in terms of poverty, social justice, and economic development?

10. Can you correlate the rate of inflation with military coups?

Order *Readings on Latin America and Its People, Volume 2* with

and receive a significant discount when the two titles are packaged together.

Please use **ISBN 0205717047** when placing your book order.

Please contact your Pearson representative for details or go to www.pearsonhighered.com for more information.